Teaching Primary
English

Education at SAGE

SAGE is a leading international publisher of journals, books, and electronic media for academic, educational, and professional markets.

Our education publishing includes:

- accessible and comprehensive texts for aspiring education professionals and practitioners looking to further their careers through continuing professional development

- inspirational advice and guidance for the classroom

- authoritative state of the art reference from the leading authors in the field

Find out more at: **www.sagepub.co.uk/education**

Teaching Primary English

Jackie Brien

⑤SAGE

Los Angeles | London | New Delhi
Singapore | Washington DC

First published 2012

SAGE Publications Ltd
1 Oliver's Yard
55 City Road
London EC1Y 1SP

SAGE Publications Inc.
2455 Teller Road
Thousand Oaks, California 91320

SAGE Publications India Pvt Ltd
B 1/I 1 Mohan Cooperative Industrial Area
Mathura Road
New Delhi 110 044

SAGE Publications Asia-Pacific Pte Ltd
3 Church Street
#10-04 Samsung Hub
Singapore 049483

Library of Congress Control Number: 2011927066

British Library Cataloguing in Publication data

A catalogue record for this book is available from the British Library

ISBN 978-0-85702-156-4
ISBN 978-0-85702-157-1(pbk)

Typeset by C&M Digitals (P) Ltd, Chennai, India
Printed by MPG Books Group, Bodmin, Cornwall
Printed on paper from sustainable resources

For all the children who have taught me, especially
Tom who has taught me most of all

CONTENTS

ACKNOWLEDGEMENTS

The extracts from *The Land of the Dragon King* by Gillian McClure on pages 71 and 72 are reproduced by kind permission of Frances Lincoln Publishers (*Land of the Dragon King*, Gillian McClure, 2008. © Reproduced by permission of Frances Lincoln Children's Books.) The extract from *Who's in the Loo?* by Jeanne Willis on page 53 is reproduced by kind permission of Andersen Press, Random House Publishers and the extract from *The Last Polar Bears* by Harry Horse on pages 190–191 is reproduced by kind permission of the Penguin Group (*The Last Polar Bears*, Puffin Books. © Harry Horse, 1993. Reproduced by permission of Penguin Books Ltd.)

I acknowledge, with immense gratitude, the generosity of Colette Ankers de Salis, Richard Bennett, Liz Chamberlain, Georgina Dawson, Prue Goodwin, Helen Holt, Pat Hughes, Sally Hughes, Professor Rhona Johnston, Professor Allan Owens, Barbara Pickford, Anne Plenderleith, David Reedy and Jane Weavers in sharing their expertise in the Expert reflections.

ABOUT THE AUTHOR

Jackie Brien worked for some years in East London, firstly as a primary teacher, then as a specialist teacher for children struggling with reading and finally as an advisory teacher for primary English. At the University of Chester she has worked with primary, early years and secondary student teachers as a Senior Lecturer, Co-ordinator of the Primary Postgraduate programme and, currently, as Leader of the English Team. She was recently seconded to work on Primary National Strategy for English materials for student teachers, being particularly interested in developing guided group work in speaking and listening. As well as the usual work of a University lecturer, Jackie is committed to encouraging writing in the community and is chairing the judging panel for the High Sherriff's Cheshire Prize for Literature in 2011.

PREFACE

Let's be realistic: no one comes to a book like this because they want an entertaining time. I imagine that you are a student teacher, probably near the beginning of your course and you've probably got an assignment due or a concern about school-based work. I hope this book will answer your immediate needs and give you some ideas for the future. Like all similar texts, this one has all the traditional information devices which allow you to find what you need efficiently and move on. As well as considering research, offering advice and explaining key ideas, I have included examples of children's language as these bring the subject to life far better than I can. The intention with all the types of text here is not to make the teaching of English seem artificially simple as this would do a magnificent subject a great disservice. My hope is that reading the book makes you think that, though teaching primary English is a bit more complicated than you realised, it is exciting, possible – and very well worth doing.

This book is being written at a difficult time for the teaching of English and literacy but, even as I type these words I can almost hear experienced teachers muttering, 'When isn't it a difficult time?' For the last few years the National Strategy and framework have shaped teachers' thinking and practice but we are now moving to a time after the strategies when policy is still uncertain and broad issues about the nature of the whole primary curriculum are being considered. You'll find that this book makes some references to the primary strategy. There are two reasons for this: firstly, change is gradual in schools so teachers will draw on strategy materials and approaches for some time. The second reason is that it is important not to discount what has gone before just because something new is coming. It is to be hoped that future work will build upon many of the excellent features of the strategy. I have focused on those things from the strategy which have improved standards and helped teachers and children to enjoy their work.

In times of change, it is essential that primary teachers are confident independent thinkers equipped with the skills and strategies to make informed decisions about what will work best for their classes. Even though, as someone starting a teacher education programme, having to make such decisions seems a long way in the future, the ability to do so is going to be based on the way you start thinking about the subject now. The approach of this book is to bring together interesting research, direct advice and examples of teachers' work but not to do the thinking for you! There are frequent invitations to pause, reflect, consider big issues or put yourself in the position of a teacher to decide what you would do. Each time you do so, you are taking a step forward to being ready to teach. Once the habit catches you, you'll find that you start to approach your reading, your observations and your reflections by asking yourself questions which start 'I wonder why . . .?' or 'What if . . .?' or thinking 'Yes, but … '. When you do this, you are taking an informed control of your own professional development.

I've included a lot of examples of student teachers working with children or reflecting on learning to teach English. These make points vividly and, I hope, give you a sense of how rewarding and how much fun teaching English can be. I am happy to admit that, wherever possible, I have chosen examples which are rude, funny or moving. People learn more from memorable encounters with text so I hope that these examples will amuse you, clarify points and stay in your mind. (It is also worth noting that whenever I write about 'a child' or 'a teacher' I use the pronoun 'she'. This is because 'he/she' is as tiresome to read as it is to write.)

Special features

 Expert reflections will give you a second perspective on the issues. They have all been written from the heart by eminent scholars, lecturers and practitioners to give insights into what really matters to them. These are the stars of this book and are well worth reading and thinking about (and citing in assignments).

 Chapter aims are included so you can tell if the chapter is likely to meet your needs.

 'Before' and 'after' boxes help you to see how your work as a primary teacher is part of children's learning from the earliest years to the secondary phase.

Key words and phrases start each chapter. You can use these as a quick way of deciding whether you are likely to find the information which you need.

 Activities are included so you can relate your reading directly to your work on placements. They will help you to focus on important aspects of teaching and learning.

 Things to think about and key questions are hints to the kind of interpretation you'll need for assignments. They are also stepping stones on the way to developing an informed professional philosophy about the subject.

 Points for discussion Of course I don't expect you to find a friend and engage in earnest conversation about these points. Have a discussion with yourself, as there are points which are capable of being seen from differing perspectives.

 Points for reflection These go further than your knowledge about the subject. They are things which may alter or upset the beliefs which you brought to teaching from your own experience. They will get you into ways of thinking which will be essential on your placements.

 Further reading is provided because this book gives you only a first taste of the big issues. When you need to look in greater detail, these sources will help.

Chapter summary at the end of every chapter.

CHAPTER 1

WHAT TEACHERS OF LITERACY KNOW AND DO

• attitudes • cognition • curriculum • imitation • innate • input • knowledge about language • language development • subject knowledge • processes

This chapter aims to:

- give a sense of the importance of literacy and English
- explore the responsibilities of the teacher of literacy
- provide insight into the ways in which children develop language
- identify what you'll need to learn
- give a sense of relief that you already know a great deal
- examine what happens in English lessons and why it happens

Teaching English is really important – that could really be the message of this whole book. Reading, writing, speaking and listening are central to the curriculum and permeate every aspect of the school day. They are wonderful accomplishments in themselves, bringing pleasure and power, but they are also essential carriers of every aspect of learning. This is a pretty strong case in itself but it is what happens in adult life to people with poor literacy that makes the work of the primary teacher so significant. The National Literacy Trust found recently that:

> 70% of pupils permanently excluded from school have difficulties in basic literacy skills. 25% of young offenders are said to have reading skills below those of the average seven-year-old. 60% of the prison population is said to have difficulties in basic literacy skills. (2008: 6)

Though these are horrifying statistics, it is also the everyday burden of low levels of literacy which impacts on the lives of many people. If you consider the number of times you use your reading and writing skills in a day it is easy to see what a burden it would be in our society to have problems in these key areas. Not being able to do things like using a television remote, sending a text message, finding an address would be a nuisance; being unable to read the instructions for taking a prescription or write well enough to fill in an application form could have enormous effects. Joan, a recently retired school dinner lady, described her feelings about her poor literacy levels like this:

> I nearly didn't go for the job because the thought of school still gives me the heebijeebies. All through my life I've been pretending – sore finger when there was writing to be done, forgot my reading glasses – I don't even have reading glasses. Then there's things I'd have loved to do – cooking from fancy recipes. I don't even like being in strange places on my own in case of getting lost ...

No one should go through life with this burden and, hopefully, things have moved forward so much that children who struggle with reading and writing are supported by sensitive, astute teachers.

If being literate is so important to adults then it is essential that primary teachers approach the teaching of literacy with flair, diligence and a determination that every child will be successful and will enjoy all the processes of learning. Enjoyment isn't window dressing for learning: it is essential for progress (DfES, 2003). If this simple knowledge that literacy really matters is constantly in mind, then everything else will fall in place and classrooms will be places where children thrive as language learners. The promise all teachers make is that we will do everything possible to ensure that no one leaves primary school frightened of speaking, reading or writing or unable to draw on language skills for work and pleasure as they move towards adult life.

 Expert reflection

Colette Ankers de Salis: The best teachers of literacy

Like all effective teachers, the best literacy teachers possess generic qualities that inspire and motivate children to want to learn. They have high expectations and believe in the young learners in front of them. They care. The best literacy teachers know that developing children's literacy skills is of fundamental importance. They know that there is an undisputed link between levels of literacy and life chances; that being literate unlocks all other areas of the school curriculum and enables people to function in the real world after school. It is thus the foundation for all learning and future opportunities.

The best literacy teachers are committed to nurturing a love of the written and spoken word; they know that it is alarmingly easy to turn children off reading and writing through mundane worksheets and purposeless exercises. So they plan engaging lessons with clear learning intentions and communicate effectively with the children so that they understand what they are learning and why.

The best teachers of literacy are interested in and understand *how* children learn to read and write and plan stimulating lessons that build on prior skills and knowledge. They recognise that explicit teaching of letters and sounds is important but that children need opportunities to apply their developing skills and knowledge, capitalising on children's interests to create such opportunities.

They are passionate about children's love of reading and enthusiasm for writing. They recognise and value children's early reading behaviours and emergent mark-making and seek to develop these skills further through stimulating and developmentally appropriate activities. These teachers understand that literacy skills depend on the development of language skills. They know writing effectively and reading for understanding are problematic in the absence of a wide vocabulary and an understanding of the grammar and richness of the English language. Thus they create a language-rich environment where things such as talk, discussion, songs and word-play are valued and embedded.

The best literacy teachers know much about how children learn to read and write yet recognise that they may not know everything. Thus they remain open to embracing new ideas and research findings through life-long learning.

(Colette Ankers de Salis is Senior Lecturer in Primary and Early Years Education, Liverpool John Moores University)

- What groups of children are most likely to struggle with literacy in the primary years? How can teachers ensure that they experience success?
- Is motivation the most important factor for learning literacy?
- Is difficulty with reading or writing more of a burden now than it was 50 years ago?
- Can you identify times in the school day when you won't be teaching literacy in some way?

What society has a right to expect of teachers of English

In 2007 the Teacher Development Agency considered the specific types of knowledge and understanding required by primary teachers (TDA, 2007). In their model the three main areas – subject knowledge *per se*, knowledge of teaching approaches and knowledge of children's development – interlink so

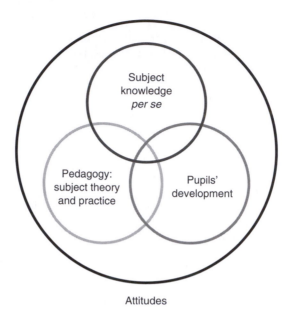

Figure 1.1 TDA model of subject knowledge needed by teachers. © Crown Copyright 2007. Reproduced with permission.

that when teachers are informed by all three, they work with confidence and competence. This is a good example of all the types of knowledge coming together as a student teacher makes decisions:

> My teacher wanted me to teach the children how to edit using a word processor. I was pleased because it is important for people to be able to use computers. This is how I researched and planned. First I read about children editing writing on the Strategy site and I talked to my English tutor. We decided that children were going to need to know how to delete, move sentences, change words and add words. Then I made sure I could do all this using the interactive whiteboard and the school laptops. Then I checked with my teacher what children had done with changing text and it was just changing fonts. Then I thought about whether the children would be ready to look so critically at their own work because that seemed very hard and I decided that it was better for them to edit something I wrote for them. My teacher thought it would be nice to do some shared editing before getting the children to do it on their own. (Kate, student teacher)

In the TDA model, the three intersecting circles of knowledge are shown inside a circle representing the teacher's attitudes to the subject and to the children as learners. The attitude of literacy teachers will influence every aspect of work. It is essential that teachers believe that all children can make progress in English and literacy, have a right to enjoy their learning and to have their needs met. We must also recognise that success in literacy will impact greatly on prosperity, achievement and probably happiness throughout life. Being a literacy teacher is a huge responsibility – one that we all must recognise and accept.

The subject knowledge of the curriculum

Teachers must (fairly obviously) know the material they have to teach in English lessons. The heart of this knowledge is stipulated in the National Curriculum; it is essential that children cover this in order to make the progress expected. The knowledge required to teach this should not be taxing for anyone on an Initial Teacher Training course as entry qualifications are far higher than this. However, not only must teachers be able to understand the material, they must also be able to make others understand it (Kyriacou, 1998). This is often quite demanding because we can be very effective users of our language without being fully aware of our own levels of understanding or the rules which are determining our choices (Fielding-Barnsley and Purdie, 2005) – being able to do something well doesn't necessarily mean that you can teach it effectively.

When we come to teaching something, our own language understanding can be strained because we have to explain things which have been instinctive or intuitive before. The conscious knowledge of the structures, rules and reasons of our language is now usually called 'knowledge about language' though some texts will refer to it as 'metalinguistic awareness'. It is this knowledge that we have to develop very strongly as teachers of English as it enables us to understand children's misconceptions and to help them to understand them too (Eyres, 2007). It also helps us with the 'why questions' about our language: being a great teacher requires confidence with the 'whys' of the curriculum as well as the 'whats' (the expected coverage) and the 'hows' (effective pedagogy).

Teachers also need to know how to translate their knowledge into terms which will be understandable to children. This will require careful thought about how to link the new concept to children's existing knowledge. It is also necessary to think about the technical terminology to be introduced and how it should be defined. One of the hardest things is to find examples which make the learning absolutely clear. For example, some people may choose to use metaphors to introduce new linguistic concepts, perhaps likening a complex sentence to a chocolate éclair! Wierzbicka (1996) explored the way in which we use figurative language to introduce new concepts. It can be an excellent way of making the concept clear but also leads to the question of when technical terminology has to be introduced. So it is sensible to explain that a complex sentence is like an éclair but less valuable to name it as one. It is debatable whether there is any value in teaching a transitional terminology which then has to be unpicked and replaced with the conventional words.

The material to be covered (the immediate subject knowledge) is simple to research. However, a teacher's knowledge of the curriculum has to be sufficiently secure to do other things (Ofsted, 2008). When asked an unexpected question or confronted with an unusual error, teachers must have the knowledge to respond immediately with accurate knowledge or have the confidence to say, 'I don't know but I'll find out for you'. Recently, one of our students was asked whether haikus ever used similes when written in Japanese. By admitting that she didn't know and later explaining how she'd found the answer, she did a great deal to enhance the child's knowledge of the subject, of research skills and of the value of independent thinking in the study of English.

Before a placement, your teacher will always let you know the English topics you will have to teach. When you know the topic, break it down into the key concepts which will become the learning objectives. For each one check that you:

- understand the concept at your own level
- know any rules or conventions
- know the key technical terminology
- can explain all these in ways which children would understand
- can identify some good examples
- can explain why it is worth learning

The teaching strategies of literacy lessons

As well as knowledge of the curriculum, literacy teachers need to know the most valuable ways of teaching the subject. When the 'literacy hour' was implemented in a very formal way, key teaching strategies were incorporated into the structure of the lesson. Though the timings are now much more relaxed it is probably still appropriate that, in every literacy or English lesson, children:

- work together as a whole class exploring ideas and developing knowledge
- work as a member of a group. This doesn't mean that they happen to sit near other children while working independently, but that the group of children work together on something which might be too daunting to do alone. Some of this time they will be led by the teacher, but at some times, equally importantly, they will be learning to make decisions and get out of difficulties by drawing independently on their own knowledge (Sainato et al., 1990)
- may also work on their own consolidating or applying the group or whole class learning
- may also increasingly, be offered by teachers one to one coaching and support for individuals. McKenna and Walpole (2004) have explored this in the context of the American primary system. It is also advocated by National Literacy Strategy (2009)

This list shows that the typical literacy lesson will involve a range of teaching strategies. The important thing is that they are a support not a straitjacket. They are all sensible things which, combined and blended thoughtfully, should ensure a range of appropriate teaching and learning activities. Teachers have to make decisions within this structure – and may sometimes choose to go outside it.

Within this structure of what children are likely to do, it is also sensible to list some key teaching activities:

1. Sharing the learning objective/outcome: you'll have to *translate* technical terms. You'll also need to explain how it links with previous learning and when it will be useful or appropriate.
2. Reactivating existing knowledge: you'll often start a lesson by *reminding* children of relevant knowledge which will act as the foundation for new learning. This requires reference to good *recording of information* in the past. You'll often *invent* a game for this part of the lesson. You may also take the opportunity to *coach* to address individual gaps in learning.
3. Shared work (speaking and listening, reading or writing): you'll *model* the effective use of the new skill or learning, often *commentating* on what you are doing by 'thinking aloud' the decisions you are making. You will *invite* contributions from the children, *listen* carefully to responses, *interpret* them, review them and respond encouragingly, *noting* successes and either *gently addressing* errors and misconceptions or *remembering* them for help later. You will also *instruct* directly, *explain* key concepts and ask question in ways which enhance knowledge and ensure full understanding. While doing this, you'll *assess* children's response through observing, and *evaluate* the effectiveness of your teaching.
4. Guided group work: you'll be using similar strategies to those in the shared work with the whole class. As the children have broadly similar needs, you'll be working with much more precision. You'll have to *create* a more relaxed (though still very productive) atmosphere so that all children have the confidence to contribute. In this part of the lesson you'll need to expect to *improvise* examples and explanations as your responses, instructions, examples and questions cannot always be predicted.
5. Independent work: This will be going on while you are teaching the group so your strategy in the lesson is going to be a benevolent overview. This is only going to be successful if the planning (see below) and working ethos are strong.
6. Plenary: With the whole class together again, you will *reiterate* the desired learning; *encourage reflection* on achievement; *assess* the learning against the objectives. Most importantly, you'll ensure that children finish the lesson with a knowledge of genuine success. Hopefully, you'll do the same for yourself – though your evaluations will identify things you could have done better, you will certainly have had some new achievements. Make a note of them and *praise yourself* too. If you don't identify what was good, you won't know it is worth doing again.

 Re-reading this list, my first thought was, 'Can anyone genuinely do all that?' Primary teachers do it all the time, much of it being so automatic that at the end of an excellent lesson the teacher might find it quite hard to explain what she had done. Make a list of the italicised verbs and check when you have successfully done each thing. As you gain experience, each of the teaching skills in this list becomes much easier.

Many new student teachers are surprised (or, more honestly 'horrified') by the amount of preparation and recording required for each lesson. Again, though the requirements won't lessen, your increased confidence and competence will soon make them much easier. Before every lesson you'll have to know:

- what you aim for the children to learn
- how you will know if they have learnt it
- whether there are any language barriers which make it hard for some children to make progress, and how you will overcome them
- what the children have previously learnt which is relevant to what you'll be teaching
- whether there are any children who will need support to bring them to a suitable starting point for the lesson
- whether any children are working to individual learning outcomes
- whether any children will need support with the language to be used in the lesson
- whether any children have already achieved the learning objectives and will therefore need different challenges
- the National Curriculum relevance of the intended learning
- the links to other curriculum areas
- the way the learning furthers the *Every Child Matters* agenda
- the ways in which children are most likely to learn the required material

In practical terms you also need to know what you, the children and any other adults supporting the lesson will do in all parts of the lesson. You'll need to locate and evaluate resources or possibly make your own. You'll need to think about where and when you'll be teaching, how the teaching area will be organised to maximise learning and how to make materials such as dictionaries, paper, websites, reference books, and stationery available so that children are encouraged to make independent decisions.

Your ITT provider will need evidence that you have made all the decisions needed and planned your lesson in good detail because the needs of children are always the first priority. Though the documentation may seem like a burden, it is a way of ensuring that you practise all the decision-making needed to prepare and teach excellent literacy lessons. Similarly, after every lesson, student teachers have to put on paper the things which experienced teachers of literacy often keep in their heads.

After every literacy lesson you will need to:

- think about how well you taught
- discuss achievements and areas of concern with any adults who worked with individuals or groups
- assess and record the achievements against the learning outcomes
- accumulate evidence in the form of written work, your notes, photographs (check the school's policy) etc.

- make note of any issues which need to be addressed in the next lesson
- consider your effectiveness in that lesson
- respond to all written work
- modify, if necessary, the planned work for the next lesson

Knowledge of children's language development

This is not the place for a detailed consideration of the different models of language acquisition. There are many excellent texts devoted to the issue if more depth is needed. It is important to have a view of how children have developed initial language because this will impact on the ways in which you expect them to continue to develop as language learners in your class. It is not something which is only important in the early years: language acquisition continues throughout childhood. The processes which spurred a baby into first attempts at communication will work to develop language further in the primary years. Our understanding of how children grow as language users should influence our teaching.

Models of language acquisition

Imitation seems the most obvious way in which children learn language. They learn to treat the linguistic sounds of their family language as different from other noises. They also learn to use the words which their families use. However, there are some things in young children's language patterns which can't have come from imitation of adults. For example, most children as they learn basic rules from others, over-generalise them. Children who have learnt that plurals are formed by adding 's' will speak about *sheeps* or *childrens*: this cannot be in imitation of adults.

This obvious weakness in the imitation model led to the development of ideas that children are born with an innate capacity to develop language given the right stimuli. The innate capacity would involve both the general principles of language learning and grammatical knowledge – an ability to form rules based on examples (Pinker, 1994). This approach explains why children develop speech so readily and rapidly but, doesn't fully account for children developing language very differently (Tomasello, 2003).

Cognition theories would argue that children process language in ways their thought development permits. In this model the language structures become linked to existing cognition. For example a child cannot use the language of comparison *Your dog is bigger than Daisy* until she has been given opportunity to make comparisons. The difficulty of this approach is that it is impossible to unravel the role of language in the development of concepts: a sort of chicken and egg argument. This problem is shown if the example above is put back into its original context.

Child:	Your dog is very, very, very, very big.
Me:	Her name's Polly. She's very big but she won't hurt your dog.
Child's mum:	Polly's much bigger than Daisydog. Daisy is big but Pollydog is much bigger, isn't she?
Child:	Your dog is biggerer than Daisy.
Me:	That's right. Polly's bigger than Daisy.

In this example, the mother and I are both automatically setting the context for language development and concept development so it is hard to know whether one preceded the other or if they arrived together. Another example could be the word *Schadenfreude* which means the lamentable delight we gain from the misfortune of our friends: it was only when I learnt the word that I recognised the concept.

Input can be seen in the example above. Both the mother and I worked to develop the child's language by repeating the desired word. Input theories became popular in the 1960s when linguistics became interested in the ways in which adults modify normal language when speaking to children. The characteristics of modified language are:

- repetition of ideas and phrases
- very short sentences
- restricted and repeated sentence structure, e.g. *who's a … where's the … that's a …*
- rising intonation at the end of speech to invite response
- paraphrasing or repeating when there is no response
- modification of words by shortening long words *banana/nana* or lengthening very short words *dog/doggy*
- there may also be an adult use of the child's pronunciation of a word *mooks/milk*
- in some languages the special version of the word may be a representation of a characteristic such as *woofwoof* or *poo*

Though this language adaptation was originally called 'motherese' because it was noted in maternal speech, it was soon noticed that its use extends beyond families; most adults speaking with babies and very young children seem to use some special language forms.

Hopefully, we have moved beyond the time of vehement adherence to any one model of language acquisition to gain a realisation that there is probably some value in each theory. Understanding is not yet complete but we can take a patchwork of ideas which give a satisfactory account of language development. This could be that humans are certainly predisposed to learn language but environmental factors impact on language development. Though children's language development cannot be in advance of concepts gained through experience, adult language modification enhances language learning (Hayes et al., 2001).

- What are the links between theories of language development and general learning theories?
- Do all children enter primary school with the same potential to develop as language learners?
- How should planning, teaching and assessing language take account of developmental issues?

Implications for the teacher

All teachers must be aware of the developmental achievements and needs of every child as a language user in order to know what needs to be taught next. 'Next steps' are mentioned frequently in governmental curriculum documents (e.g. DfES, 2006). Though this is usually valid as both language development and learning follow fairly predictable routes, we must also recognise that all children are different with differing approaches to learning and different strengths as learners. Perhaps it is better to see language development as a pebble thrown into a rocky pool. There will be ripples in every direction but where some will splash easily over rocks of difficulty, other rocks may be impossible to go over and the ripples will break to flow around the problem. The rocks are going to be different for every child but the wise teacher watches out for them.

The other implication for the teacher is that there is little point in having an excellent view of the child's language development unless this is a trigger for direct teaching. Perhaps the input model of language development is of particular value here; though children bring to us an eagerness to learn and ways of thinking which facilitate learning, it is the active, appropriate, deliberate intervention of the teacher which is the key to continuing progress. We cannot be people who set up environments in which language should thrive and make observations of how it progresses. Whatever age we are teaching, we need to be actively involved in furthering development through planned, informed action.

The models of language show the approaches to what a teacher needs to know, think and do when teaching literacy – which is all day, every day in school. If we accept that each of the theories nudges us a little closer to our understanding of children's learning of language, and we recognise that language development continues throughout the primary years, these seem to be the main implications for teachers.

As children are innately predisposed to learn language, the classroom must be organised and resourced to enable the active learning to be stimulating and relevant. The language-rich environment of the school must stimulate further learning of speaking and listening, reading and writing. The teacher's role is partially to enable, observe and enhance or modify opportunities as children progress. This often breaks down at KS2 as, in many ways, the classrooms of our Y6 children provide less rich opportunities for developing as speakers and listeners than they were given at nursery.

As children also learn from imitation, the teacher must be someone whose language merits imitation. For many student teachers this will require moving to a more formal language which, at first, seems very uncomfortable. This transformation of language gradually becomes as natural as putting on your work clothes when you get up but, for many people, the change is difficult.

As children learn language as part of cognitive development, the curriculum must be contextualised in ways which highlight the links between language learning and learning in all other areas. For example, it's important to decide when technical or subject specific terminology can be introduced successfully. This can also be considered from another perspective: children's lack of language skills can mask their understanding in other curriculum areas so the two aspects should be closely linked.

As children learn from adults more easily if language patterns are modified, teachers need to be careful about terminology, sentence structure, repetition, rephrasing and signals for response. In school, children have to learn to move gradually from the English of early childhood towards the English of broad, diverse communities and purposes. The pace of this transition needs to be considered carefully.

Standard English

Just as children move from the language of the home to the language of the community, so many student teachers find that they move from the language patterns of their own education to language appropriate for educating others. This is one student's recollection of an early experience in school.

> My mentor was sitting at the back when, looking at the children's worksheets, I said, 'You done that lovely'. I meant, 'You've done it lovely', so I realised it was wrong and I said it again. Then after the lesson my mentor said that even that was wrong! I should have said 'You've done it beautifully'. Or 'you've done lovely work'. She said 'lovely' isn't an adverb but I thought it must be because of ending in 'ly'. I wasn't happy about being picked up on it because it was just a little slip but when I told my mum she said she'd have been angry if I'd come home from school when I was young and I'd learnt something wrong from a teacher. I was very careful for all of that placement. That was in my first year. Now talking carefully seems easier. (*Laura, BEd student*)

Having read Laura's account it is worth considering whether you have any language patterns which need to be modified to ensure you give a good model for children. My own experience was even more embarrassing than Laura's. After listening to an explanation, my placement teacher commented, 'You're not very keen on consonants, are you?' My London accent changed very rapidly!

There's an expectation that teachers will use the structures of **Standard English** most of the time. This doesn't mean that **accent** will have to change because we can pronounce Standard English with any accent (though we have to ensure that our accent doesn't prevent children from understanding what we are saying). Teachers use structures which are most like reasonably formal written English as this ensures that children have excellent role models on which to base their own speech for formal occasions.

The previous paragraph may have made it seem that teachers use a uniform, rather bland language which distances them from the children. This is not the case at all: the most talented teachers have a wonderfully rich and interesting repertoire of phrases and words which they use to communicate effectively in all different aspects of teaching. They can hold attention and stimulate response through vivid choices of words. They may even, for particular effects, move away from Standard English but, when they do so, it is a conscious decision not a mistake. Here are some examples from Hazel (a very experienced teacher) of occasions, in one day, when she decided not to use Standard English.

> In literacy we were focusing on past tenses so I told Sid the Snake's *(puppet)* weekend news with non-standard verb forms for the children to correct. Maths … don't remember any there. Yes, I did! I didn't use sentences to respond when I wanted to ask probe questions. I started sentences and left them for Blue Table to finish because they needed that help to start them on their answers. After lunch, in the Tudor topic I made them laugh by using Elizabethan phrases to praise them –'thou hast warmed the cockles of my heart' was one. Nothing else – except when Niki fell over. I never mean to but I always find myself being very informal when children are upset. I suppose they want their mum and I try to be like mum for them.

The specific subject knowledge of literacy and English

Mallet (2005) makes a distinction between the content of English and literacy learning, and the processes associated with learning to be an accomplished user of our language. As teachers we need to be at ease with the content and confident about a range of successful ways of helping all children to learn. Just as, in primary school, we start every new topic with making sure the children are aware of what they already know, it is sensible to start your teacher education with the awareness that you probably already know nearly all of the content you'll have to teach. There will be technical issues, such as sentence structure, which you will need to learn in new ways and you'll have to learn some things which, like most other people, you've been skilfully avoiding for years – such as the way to use possessive apostrophes. Despite these, your knowledge is certainly good or you wouldn't have gained a place on an initial teacher training programme. Let's try to demonstrate that I'm right: read the section in italics and find some errors: *Primary teacher's must be proffessional at all times, their very important people in lives of children what they taught.* You can probably find six or seven errors which means that you already know a great deal. Teachers have to take this knowledge one step further to explain what is right and why this is so.

Most people would recognise that knowledge about punctuation structure and spelling are central to English but would place less emphasis on knowledge about literature. This is a great pity because, unless you know about a good range of books and other texts, it is difficult to find something which will move, inspire, intrigue or amuse a child. It is also very important that teachers read, and ideally write, for their own pleasure so that they can see the worlds of literature through a child's eye. This takes me back to the consideration of teachers' attitudes at the beginning of this chapter – if we can't show children that we enjoy reading it is going to be very hard to bring them to a love of books.

Ask some of the children in your placement class to recommend you books to read. Make a list of them and get reading. I hope there'll be something on the list which will make you step back in amazement at the brilliance of many books written for children. There will probably also be one book which you'll dislike intensely.

When you reflect on and can explain either reaction, you are well on the way to being able to choose texts for children and discuss them with knowledge and enthusiasm.

The knowledge needed to teach English probably seems daunting. It really isn't: it is very like the models of learning language. Most students who come into teacher education seem to have always wanted to teach – perhaps there is an innate predisposition to helping the inexperienced to gain insights we believe are important. We also have the cognitive ability to assimilate new knowledge and ways of working; the structures are in place for new learning. We also learn to teach through input. There will be plenty of people in your university and school-based studies who will model, explain and gently correct. Finally, there's imitation. Try to remember a teacher who inspired you and possibly may even be the reason why you decided that you'd like to teach. He or she was probably memorable because she made learning enjoyable, encouraged you to think more deeply, always seemed interested in your ideas, challenged you to take ideas further than you'd thought possible, and delighted in your successes. If you do the same, you too will be an inspiring teacher.

Look at this list of words and choose the five that you hope people would use about your first class after you have taught them for a year:

Able, ambitious, articulate, astute, assertive, calm, confident, considerate, competent, creative, critical, enthusiastic, diligent, excitable, imaginative, independent, insightful, motivated, resourceful, successful, talented, thoughtful, witty.

Now think how these qualities would be evident in their speaking, listening, reading and writing.

Finally consider whether you show them in your own literacy work and attitudes. If you don't, they won't.

Attitude to teaching and learning literacy and English

This is the heart of success. Everyone comes into primary teaching to make a difference to children's lives and to inspire them with a love of learning. We do this by believing that all children can make progress in all aspects of language learning. This isn't just about a drive to increase the skills of children but also includes all those things which can't be tested but are probably more important: the pleasures of picking exactly the right word, composing an original phrase, knowing that someone has been moved by the way in which you've expressed your ideas. In short, it is our attitude which equips children to use their language with confidence and flair.

This is Sarah's reflection on her learning while training to teach.

> When I began my studies in English I was amazed by how much I'd actually forgotten and hadn't practised since leaving school. Although I speak clearly and have good vocabulary, I needed support with punctuation, grammar and glossary of terms for English. I am a mature student and have spent a number of years raising a family at home. On reflection, I realise that during this time I have written very little on paper. I have done a fair amount of form-filling – my children's entry to school, applications for higher education, passport forms and the like. Rarely, if ever, have I during this time, sat down and written a letter or a piece of prose.
>
> During lectures, I have been taught how to plan for English lessons for different Key Stages. I recognise that to be a good teacher requires you to demonstrate and model the specific English for that lesson, whether it is skills of handwriting, structuring sentences, reading or spelling patterns. I also recognise that when I am teaching I am constantly working on language development – increasing the children's range and use of vocabulary. All these are important to the children's understanding of the correct use of English.
>
> When I am teaching, I am aware that my children will repeat the English that I use. I will teach them to express the way they feel about different things, encouraging descriptive words, and I will show them that combining these words can form sentences. My teaching will be very much about effective communication and providing the children with all the skills they will need in order to communicate effectively.
>
> Who knows how we will be communicating by the middle of this century, when the children I am about to teach will be adults? I am of the opinion that good English will always be important. Although our vocabulary is constantly evolving, the way we speak will, I believe, always say a lot about ourselves.

Chapter summary

- Literacy teaching and learning is important: really important!
- Children's language acquisition continues through the primary years
- We teach literacy one way or another throughout the school day
- Language development isn't always linear: we have to consider individual needs and strengths
- Teachers have to have excellent language knowledge so they can analyse and address errors
- Great teachers have purpose, knowledge, enthusiasm, sensitivity and a sense of fun

Further reading

Crystal, D. (2004) *Rediscover Grammar.* London: Longman.

Goodwin, P. (edn.) (2011) *Literate Classroom* (3rd edn). London: Routledge.

Medwell, J., Moore, G., Griffiths, V. and Wray, D. (2009) *Primary English: Knowledge and Understanding (Achieving QTS)* (4th edn). Exeter: Learning Matters.

Oates, J. and Grayson, A. (2004) *Cognitive and Language Development in Children* (2nd edn). Oxford: Wiley-Blackwell.

References

Department for Education and Schools (DfES) (2003) *Excellence and Enjoyment.* London: DfES.

Department for Education and Schools (DfES) (2006) *Primary National Strategy: Framework for Literacy and Mathematics.* Nottingham: DfES.

Eyres, I. (2007) *English for Primary and Early Years: Developing Subject Knowledge.* London: SAGE.

Fielding-Barnsley, R. and Purdie, N. (2005) Teachers' attitude to and knowledge of metalinguistics in the process of learning to read', *Asia-Pacific Journal of Teacher Education*, 33(1): 65–76.

Hayes, S., Barnes-Holmes, D. and Roche, B. (eds) (2001) *Relational Frame Theory: A Post-Skinnerian Account of Human Language and Cognition.* New York: Plenum.

Kyriacou, C. (1998) *Essential Teaching Skills.* Cheltenham: Nelson Thornes.

Mallett, M. (2005) *The Primary English Encyclopaedia.* London: Fulton.

McKenna, M. and Walpole, S. (2004) *The Literacy Coach's Handbook: A Guide to Research-Based Practice.* New York: Guilford.

National Literacy Strategy (2009) *Every Child a Reader e-newsletter* – [Online] Available at: http://nationalstrategies.standards.dcsf.gov.uk/node/182251 (accessed 2 August 2010).

National Literacy Trust (2008) *Offending and Literacy Behaviour.* London: National Literacy Trust.

Ofsted (2008) *Improving Primary Teachers' Subject Knowledge Across the Curriculum.* London: Ofsted.

Pinker, S. (1994) *The Language Instinct.* London: Penguin.

Sainato, D., Strain, P., Lefebvre, D. and Rapp, N.(1990) 'Effects of self-evaluation on the independent work skills of preschool children with disabilities', *Journal of Research into Exceptional Children*, 56(6): 540–549.

TDA (2007) *Developing Trainees' Subject Knowledge for Teaching.* London: Teacher Development Agency.

Tomasello, M. (2003) *Constructing a Language: A Usage-Based Theory of Language Acquisition.* Cambridge, MA: Harvard University Press.

Wierzbicka, A. (1996) *Semantics: Primes and Universals.* Oxford: Oxford University Press.

CHAPTER 2

SPEAKING AND LISTENING

 • dialogue • discussion • drama • explanation • grouping • links with reading
• links with writing • progress • questions • teaching roles

This chapter aims to:

- explore the value of a focus on speaking and listening in children's learning
- describe aspects of speaking and listening in the literacy or English curriculum
- examine the roles of the teacher in furthering children's speaking and listening
- consider the scope of speaking and listening across the curriculum
- suggest some valuable approaches to teaching in this area

Most children start their primary years as accomplished and eager speakers who have probably already developed an extensive vocabulary, possibly in more than one language. They are able to speak effectively for a number of purposes and can listen attentively, analysing not only a speaker's meaning but also the tone and purpose of the speech. As this is the case, teaching speaking and listening should be the easiest thing in the literacy curriculum and yet it is not. Ofsted, in its 2005 review of the English curriculum, found that:

Too little attention has been given to teaching the full National Curriculum programme of study for speaking and listening and the range of contexts provided for speaking and listening remains too limited. Emphasis on developing effective direct teaching approaches has led, at best, to good whole class discussion but, in too many classes, discussion is dominated by the teacher and pupils have only limited opportunities for productive speaking and listening. (2005: 1)

If children have few opportunities for 'productive' speaking and listening, we are missing a great opportunity to draw upon the strength in oral language which children bring with them into our classes. If 'productive' speaking and listening is not nurtured and celebrated, then 'unproductive' speaking is likely to break out in all sorts of undesired ways with teachers trying to achieve quiet and miss opportunities for the kinds of speaking and listening which can carry learning forward successfully. This chapter is going to look at speaking and listening both as the heart of the literacy curriculum for children and as the medium for most areas of learning.

Before the primary phase

Speaking and listening at home

Most of a child's oral language learning happens at home. Even before birth, embryos can distinguish between speech and other sound. Some studies suggest that embryos are particularly attuned to the mother's voice though Chamberlain (1997) points out that, as the mother's voice 'travels' through the body differently, it is unsurprising that it is heard differently. From birth children become more and more astute in identifying speech sounds so that their babbling soon uses the phonemes and intonations of the language which they will speak. Children's development depends then on the nature of the language used in the home. Ofsted has noted that teachers are concerned about the 'quality' of the language children learn at home and suggest that, due to the prevalence of background music and television, children's articulation and vocabulary are often poor when starting nursery (Ofsted, 2010). Teachers also note undesirable language traits such as swearing, interrupting and demanding too much attention. However, it is important to recognise that, though these traits are not desired in education, they may be very useful in adult life. The language valued and nurtured in the school is only a small part of the diverse language we all use.

Speaking and listening at EYFS

Colleagues in the **EYFS** have a very important role in bringing children forward from the language of the home to the language of the whole community. Children starting in nursery classes will often have a vocabulary focusing on the everyday interactions of the home. It is likely to include over 500 words (McAleer Hamaguchi, 1995). Their speech may be 'telegraphic' with some elements of the conventional sentence omitted as in *Look, mummy. Ellie doggy rolling* (she was in the park rolling in imitation of her dog). They may also have family words for familiar actions or objects and have very immature enunciation which, because the family understand it well, has not developed further. At EYFS the curriculum is centred on building on children's strengths as confident speakers while extending the range of situations in which language is used to include language for imagination, speculation, explanation and negotiation. They will also learn to understand the etiquette of speech including turn taking, listening carefully before responding to another person and judging when speaking is inappropriate. By the time most children start in primary school their vocabulary will be between 4,000 and 5,000 words (Bauer and Nation 1993). These will be combined in short but conventional sentences used for a broad range of purposes. In short, EYFS colleagues will have done an amazing job in equipping children with the language needed to thrive in primary school; we just need to ensure that this excellent start does not go to waste.

The speaking and listening curriculum in the primary school

Oral language has a strange place in the primary curriculum. In one way it is so huge and omnipresent that it becomes invisible: just the inevitable background to any activity. In another way it is a neglected area due to the easily made assumption that, if children are speaking or listening, they are learning to speak or listen. The chatter of most lively classrooms seems to suggest that the children are already excellent users of oral language so it requires little attention. This is a false assumption as the unplanned linguistic bustle of active learning, while reinforcing some existing language strengths, is not sufficiently focused to ensure progression.

Another issue for teachers is the ephemeral nature of the subject; it is transitory, elusive and very difficult to record or to 'test' objectively. Listening is particularly difficult to isolate and assess: I can only know whether the child is making progress in listening by her responses and these could be affected by other factors. This difficulty in assessment may have led to the decision not to include a standardised speaking and listening test in SATs but to rely on teacher assessments. This could have had an impact on the time devoted to speaking and listening in school as it might be seen to have a lower status.

Speaking, listening and active learning

The Primary National Strategy grouped the full range of speaking and listening activities which should be occurring in every classroom. These are:

- Speaking (appropriately, confidently and fluently in different ways for different audiences and in different situations)

- Listening and responding (confidently and courteously in appropriate ways for different audiences and in different situations, showing the internalisation of what has been said)
- Group discussion and interaction (all the activities in which children explore and develop ideas together)
- Drama (ranging from **role play**, problem solving in role through to performance)

All normal classroom speaking and listening activities seem to fall into these categories and some, such as discussing in role, seem to fit into them all. All these activities could happen in any curriculum area, which may be one of the reasons why the Ofsted report cited above found weaknesses in all aspects of speaking and listening across all key stages. There may be too much repetition of teacher-led speaking and listening activities for the children to make significant progress. Myhill and Fisher (2005) concluded that far too much of the talk in the classroom is controlled by the teacher. For example in what is termed a 'discussion' the teacher poses a question, chooses a child to answer, speaks about that answer and then moves on to question another child. The rest of the class are probably pulling the elastic out of their socks, daydreaming or doing much worse things. The teacher is doing about two thirds of the speaking and is controlling all the development of the subject by acting as a gatekeeper for desired and undesired responses. There is little scope in this sort of activity for children's abilities as speakers and listeners to be extended (there is usually precious little point in listening) and their thinking is restricted to wondering what will please the teacher and not what they are learning about the topic.

 Expert reflection

Professor Allan Owens: Doing stories together in drama

Before story was written it was spoken and performed. The roots of Western European Drama stretch back to Greek Theatre, but the use of drama in storytelling goes way beyond this to the earliest civilisations. The image of our ancestors gathered round the fire not only listening to, but watching each other tell the stories of their daily struggles and nightly dreams, hopes and fears is powerful for me.

Contemporary drama education practice lies in part in this tradition of oral, participative, community-based storytelling. The ancient circle has remained part of the practice. Not a fire at the centre but an open inviting space. Rather than the shaman it is the teacher who invites participants to gather, listen, watch and 'do stories' together in drama in order to make sense of their lives in society.

'Doing' stories in drama is about much more than simply performing them for others to watch. It is about stepping into the world of story. A key way to do this is to ask questions of the story that you yourself do not know the answer to. For example, in the Japanese tale 'Momo Taro' a very old and kind woman cuts open a peach early one morning to find a baby inside and believes the gods have sent the child to her. 'What on earth would the other villagers think, feel, say and do when she wakes them up to tell her story?'

In taking on the roles of sleepy-eyed villagers the participants can quiz, question, support and challenge the old woman played by the teacher-in-role. The drama quickly opens up the metaphorical possibilities of the story for learning. We step into other people's shoes to see how they think and feel and whilst having much fun simultaneously ask the hard questions to see the situation from multiple perspectives, for example, 'Who is responsible for bringing up a child in society?'

The 'is like' and 'is not like' of metaphor allows participants to make connections through role between the closely observed reality of the drama and the largely unobserved realities of their daily lives. This is the unique dimension that drama can bring to story.

(Allan Owens is Professor of Drama Education and National Teaching Fellow in the Faculty of Education and Children's Services & the Faculty of Arts and Media, University of Chester)

It could be that speaking and listening is tightly controlled in many classrooms because teachers are concerned about management (Waugh and Jolliffe, 2008). As you can no more stop children interacting than you can stop water seeping out of a paper bag, it is far wiser to harness the vast energy of children's speech as the way of powering the whole curriculum. Oral language is children's great strength; good teaching always starts with identifying, consolidating and drawing on existing knowledge and capabilities so in order to do justice to any curriculum area the teacher has got to overcome any reluctance to permit the glorious cacophony of children's active learning.

The teacher as model of speaking and listening

One of the most startling rites of passage for most primary teachers is when they first overhear children playing schools. What is said in the classroom will be echoed in the playground; every linguistic whim or nuance is copied for the reason that the teacher does a lot of talking and is a very important role model in children's lives. This places a demand on us to offer a model of speaking and listening which is appropriate for children to adopt. This is not so much about the modification of an accent to make speech accessible or being very careful about sentence structure as it is about offering a more general model of desirable oral language use. Qualities which you would want children to note and learn from would include:

- Active listening – so children learn the roles of the listener in supporting, encouraging and learning from a speaker
- Clarity of expression – so that spoken sentences convey the meaning clearly and appropriately
- Observation – so children see the teacher's use of non-verbal feedback to modify speech
- Breadth of vocabulary – so children encounter new words and phrases in spoken language and learn to reach meanings for words through the clarity of the context
- Variety – so children learn that we all use a range of speech patterns in different situations and are able to choose between them
- Vividness – so children learn that well-chosen words can bring a subject to life
- Courtesy – so that children learn the social conventions of language, such as following on from a speaker rather than interrupting, from the model which you give at all times
- Confidence – if we want children to become confident about speaking in a range of situations we need to show confidence ourselves
- Vulnerability – so children are aware that through speaking and listening to each other we formulate, extend, or consolidate our ideas. It is through an acceptance of vulnerability that speakers grow in confidence

This is a simple list of the things that are modelled by the teacher's speech. Other aspects may well be important depending on the class. The model offered by the teacher must be progressive so that it takes children smoothly forward into the next stages of their own development. It is worth listening to experienced teachers talking with classes of different ages; they adjust their vocabulary, sentence length and structure and duration of speech automatically. Student teachers often have to do this consciously.

How can teachers work sensitively with children whose home **dialect** and register differ greatly from those demanded in the education system?

Use the list above to make a tally chart for the different purposes for a teacher speaking in a single complete session. Then, using the same chart, see if it varies in different lessons or with different teachers. You could also use this tally chart to note whether you are developing a full range of language use. Ask your mentor or a peer to keep a tally of the way you use language when teaching.

Oral language teaching skills

Asking questions

As well as consistently offering a model of how adults use language effectively, teachers have some specific approaches which are worth considering. The most obvious 'teacher specific' language form is probably questioning. It is usual to categorise questions as 'open' or 'closed', with open questions being those where you are not seeking a specific answer and closed being those where you ask the question to find out whether the child has gained a particular simple piece of knowledge. Open questions are often considered to be more desirable because they demand more thought to answer. However, the context of the lesson will determine the type of question asked. For example, in a phonics lesson I would probably ask more 'closed' questions than I would if I was working with children to create a poem.

There are also degrees of openness – questions could seek children to use inference, interpretation, analysis, appreciation, evaluation or empathy to reach an answer. These are a very rough hierarchy of questions demanding individual responses drawn from the text, other sources, their beliefs, opinions and preferences. The more children bring to their response the more they will usually gain from responding. In this, the skill of the teacher as listener is all important; if you ask open questions you need to delight in the range of answers you are likely to be given. Some teachers (and please don't become one of them) confuse children by appearing to ask open questions when they have a single desired response already in mind. This is an extreme example but one which makes the point well.

Teacher: [*finishing telling a story in assembly*] so in Hell there were ten foot long chopsticks and everyone was starving. In Heaven there were ten foot long chopsticks and everyone was feeding each other. So what does this tell us?

Ozzy: Eat with your fingers?

Teacher: [*slightly furious*] It tells us to help each other.

It is also worth noting that Ozzy, knowing that he is pushing his luck, phrases his response as a question as this allows him to distance himself from the answer.

Perhaps another of the skills of teachers' oral language should be a willingness to answer questions. Forming a question often takes more thought than responding (particularly in situations where you might want to use closed questions to assess learning). If the situation is turned round and children pose the questions, they may learn more. In this example a teacher is using a glove puppet (Wilf the forgetful wolf) at the end of a phonics lesson.

Teacher: Shall we check on what Wilf's learnt today? Remember, we were hoping he'd learn about vowel digraphs. Laura, you ask him.

Laura: [*holding up a card with the word 'sheep' on it*] Wilf, what does this say?

Teacher/Wilf: BAAAAAAAAAAA!

[*Much laughter*]

Laura: Silly wolf! That's what sheep say. What does the word say?

Teacher/Wilf: Sh-e-e-p.

Laura: Good! Can you say the sounds?

Teacher/Wilf: Sh-e-e-p.
Laura: No! Sh-ee-p. The middle ones stay together -ee
Teacher/Wilf: Sh-ee-p.

Here the child has demonstrated a much greater depth of knowledge by asking questions (and analysing answers) than would have been possible if she had simply responded to a conventional question. She identifies, analyses and addresses the problem with ease. This example leads to the uncomfortable issue of whether teachers may, by closely controlling the activities, inadvertently restrict children's opportunities to develop oral language.

Explanation

Explanation must be the heart of teaching. Knowledge is transferred through observation and language with the nature of the activity being dependent on what is being taught and to whom. Clear, careful explanation often seems very difficult but is essential if children are to learn effectively. Book et al. in an influential study in the 1980s found that children who were given explicit explanations of what to do and why it was important made significantly more progress and developed greater understanding (Book et al., 1985). Andrews (1997) concluded that teachers' knowledge was very significant in effective explanation. This seems fairly obvious: it is difficult to explain something you don't know but the research went further, considering what sort of knowledge was needed to explain clearly. Necessary knowledge could be summarised as:

- Adult level knowledge
- Knowledge of the children's closest secure understanding
- Knowledge of how to segment and order explanations
- Knowledge of the language best suited to conveying the information

Here is a student teacher's first attempt to explain compound words to her peers during an activity on explanation:

Lucy: There are three kinds of words, simple, compound and complex. Simple words have got one morpheme and compound words have two or it can be more than two. So 'fish' and 'cake' are simple words but 'fishcake' is compound.

This is Lucy's second attempt after guidance from her peers:

Lucy: Who knows what a compound is when it's chemistry?
Jenny: Two chemicals making a new chemical?
Lucy: Yes. It's the same with words. Imagine I've just invented a new food and it is fish mashed up and made into cake shapes. I'd need a name for my new invention so I might look at it and say, 'It's made out of fish but it looks like a cake. So I'll call it a fishcake.' I've compounded the words together

to make a new one – like a scientist compounds together two chemicals to make a new one. What's a compound word, Jenny?

Jenny: Two words put together to make a new one?

Though Lucy's first definition shows that she understands the material and knows the technical terminology, her second explanation is much more effective because she bases it on what her peers already know. She then makes the analogy clear through creating a story which she asks them to imagine (engaging them actively in the example). Having set the context of the need for compound words, she gives a definition. Then she returns to the secure existing knowledge and links the new knowledge to it again. Finally she asks her listener to demonstrate the new knowledge. Though it isn't always necessary to go through all the stages, Lucy's second example could work well as a template for structuring explanations in the classroom.

Listen to teachers explaining new concepts in different subjects. Consider:

- how they link new learning to children's existing knowledge
- how they use examples
- how they contextualise the new learning in life beyond school
- whether they use metaphors and/or similes
- how they ensure understanding

Responding to children

Both questions and explanations can be formal parts of a planned lesson or may be given in response to children's speech. The way in which teachers respond to children will have a great impact on their language development. A child who is encouraged by an interested teacher who is listening attentively and makes it clear she'd like to hear more is likely to make far better progress than one who is not. It can be very difficult when teaching a large class to give as much time to responding as every child would like so it is important to ensure that every response is constructive. The 2003 National Strategies document *Speaking, Listening, Learning: Working with Children in Key Stages 1 and 2* offers some very helpful guidance for constructive teacher response. This includes:

- Supporting children to extend their responses by additional questions and prompts
- Giving children time to respond (not moving on too quickly to another child)
- Varying the type of response so that you do not always question, evaluate or repeat what the child has said. You could offer a contrary opinion, ask for clarification, offer another example or invite a further comment
- Leading forward from a wrong answer by asking the child to explain what she was thinking and then unravel the misconception
- When appropriate, responding without assessing or evaluating

The guidance also points out that it is inadvisable to accept incomplete and limited responses. In this case, your demand for more careful response shows your confidence in the child as a speaker. It also suggests that children cannot be expected to respond as you wish if you haven't demonstrated the terminology and language structures necessary. Your response should always be based on your evaluation of the effectiveness of your own teaching. This is also related to the issue of giving time to allow children to formulate what they want to say; if they do not do so, you need to consider whether your response or your teaching is inhibiting them.

Should teachers speak more or listen more than the children? As your response can have a great impact on children, it is very important to set classroom ways of talking which ensure that you are not put in the position where you cannot give a supportive response. Children find it quite hard to understand that they are a member of a large and busy class where you cannot give them all the attention that they'd like. A great deal of inappropriate behaviour comes from children finding it is the only way to gain the teacher's attention, so ensuring you establish a routine in which ample time is devoted to children talking and you responding, may be an important step in cutting down the inappropriate speech at inappropriate times.

Direct instruction

We are oddly reluctant to instruct children directly. It is a cultural quirk that we prefer to phrase instructions as statements or questions. 'Who's talking?' means 'stop talking' and 'I'd like you all to line up now', means 'Move now preferably without too much fuss'. Though children are usually adept at translating these masked managerial instructions and responding appropriately, the language of instruction within lessons can cause problems if it is ambiguous. Though literacy lessons are evolving from a rigid structure, every good lesson will include a range of teaching and learning modes which will be signalled by the use of instructions. For example, during shared work there will be instructions to look, listen, decide, discuss with a partner and offer ideas. If these are ambiguous, children may miss opportunities for active participation in the activities which form the foundation for the subsequent learning.

Dialogic teaching

Professor Robin Alexander has been working on advancing the teaching of speaking and listening. Dialogic teaching (Alexander, 2008) seeks to move forward from the prevalent question and answer interchanges where the child is often expected to guess what the teacher is thinking. Dialogic teaching involves the development of new understanding together through analysing, sharing ideas about and reflecting on what is being said. This involves both children and the teacher, though as children become confident, the teacher is able to stand back. Here's an example of Year 6 children engaged in a discussion about the moral of the text *Death in a Nut* (Maddern and Hess, 2005), which is about the consequences of imprisoning Old Man Death.

> *Dan*: It's hard but maybe … I think it's saying that there has to be death because …
>
> *Josh*: The chicken's got to be killed so people can eat.
>
> *Ben*: No, there's vegetarians.
>
> *Josh*: Carrots then. They can't chop up the carrots. The carrots can't die. It's all death. Carrots have to die and get eaten.
>
> *Ben*: Yes. I get that but the story doesn't work if … this is hard … if nothing can die there's no food. But if there's no food people would starve to death but death has been destroyed.
>
> *Josh*: And if death is destroyed you would starve to death but not be dead.
>
> *Ben*: So there'd have to be something that isn't life or death.
>
> *Dan*: Living death.
>
> *Ben*: Everyone'd be the living dead. Like zombies! Zombies! [*He gets up and staggers round the table*]
>
> *Dan*: That's the moral then: there can't be life without death – like I said.
>
> *Ben*: [*as if dictating*] So the moral is 'Death is necessary for life. Life lives off death'. Done. Agreed?
>
> [*Others make assenting gestures*]
>
> *Ben*: Agreed! Done.

This is far from the normal run of classroom discussions. The boys are managing their work without teacher intervention, keeping to the task and taking it seriously. (The only time one of them is tempted to deviate into zombies, another brings him back on task.) Everyone's ideas are taken seriously and each contribution reflects upon and follows on from the previous speaker. This is not competitive, persuasive argument but a mutual creation of something that the children would be unlikely to manage individually.

Oral work of this quality can't be achieved unless the teacher has worked hard to teach children ways of creating constructive dialogues. This may have included:

- A focus on learning through oral language across the whole curriculum
- Speaking being seen as having as high a status and as much rigour as writing
- Activities being planned which require depth of thought and extended speech
- An ethos where uncertainty is seen as constructive and is met with patience and support (as in the example above where no one interrupts when Ben stumbles, pauses and then reformulates his ideas aloud)
- There has been an expectation of children forming their speech carefully to be coherent and comprehensible
- There has been an expectation that children listen to each other and respond to what has been said

Additionally, teachers have to make sure that planned activities stimulate children; this requires knowing the curriculum, the children's attainment and interests very well. Perhaps the hardest thing is to draw back from the dialogue. At first children will require the scaffolding of teacher support and guidance but perhaps the scaffolding poles should be made of ice so they will gradually melt away to allow independence.

Dialogic teaching has great implications for all aspects of teaching literacy because it brings thinking and learning to the centre of the purposes of oral language. This goes a long way towards clarifying why oral language is such an important foundation for reading, writing and the whole curriculum. Carefully structured teaching of this kind gives children access to the ways of thinking which ensure progress in every aspect of learning. It makes high demands of the teacher as well as the children. For example, the day after the discussion about *Death in a Nut*, Ben asked whether doctors should always keep people alive. The teacher, very bravely, allowed time for the discussion and offered his opinion when asked for it. This took the class into difficult, uncomfortable places. Maybe those are the places where real learning happens.

 Why is discussion valued so highly as a tool for learning?

Speaking and listening as subjects

At the beginning of this chapter I suggested some of the reasons why speaking and listening have a lower status than is merited in many classrooms: because they are omnipresent they can get overlooked. Moving away from their role as facilitators of all other learning, it is important to make the case that these are crucial skills in their own right which need to be taught as carefully and enthusiastically as any other subject. We need to teach the skills of speaking and listening because they are important – not just as useful vehicles for other learning.

If we believe that children learn by being encouraged to move with support into areas which are new and challenging, we are posed with particular problems with our planning for oral activities. Children are already probably good communicators in everyday school circumstances, so to extend their learning we need to focus on adventurous, innovative work. I'm including some examples from student teachers to show what can be done. In each of these cases, the student teacher has grabbed hold of an unexpected opportunity to enhance the children's spoken language.

Listening

My Y1 class were working on the RSPCA and my tutor had just adopted a very badly treated dog. We arranged for her to bring it into school and the children all prepared questions. We warned them that the dog was very scared so they'd have to be very quiet. The session lasted an hour and no one spoke above a whisper for all that time and I know that they really listened because they remembered everything.

Speaking

J was very shy but he loved the Vampirate books. The author was doing a talk at the university and I asked one of the lecturers if he could go. She said of course and would he like to do the introduction? I thought he'd be much too scared but he wrote a brilliant intro at home and he did it! He was very good and I was so proud. I think this had a big impact on J. Not just in his speaking but in the way he thinks about himself.

Group discussion

An old lady was going to come into school to talk about being an evacuee so I set the children in groups discussing what we should do to make sure that her visit was enjoyable. It was the best language activity I did because it seemed real and important. I think they liked it that I had let them make the important decisions. One group even decided that old ladies like to drink from nice china cups and saucers so one of the girls brought in her family's best china. When I did my reflection I thought the activity was good because it was a discussion that was going to be acted on. If we take children's ideas seriously then they see the point in working hard.

Drama

My teacher wanted me to do an assessment of the children's understanding of the terminology of the grammar work we'd been doing. I decided to do it by getting them in groups and everyone in the group explaining something to the others and asking questions and recording it on the DigiBlus. Then I thought that if I had to do that I'd be scared so I let all the children choose a character and explain their bit of grammar to three other characters. This took the pressure off them and made it a fun thing to do. It was a bit strange to hear Simon Cowell explaining how to use suffixes to Rio Ferdinand, The Stig and Jack Sparrow. What I learnt from this is how powerful it is to be able to be someone else because if you go wrong it isn't your fault.

Look at the lesson ideas described above and think about how you could:

* adapt the idea for a different age group
* take the key elements of the work and apply them to a different activity
* decide what children had achieved and learnt

Speaking and listening as starting points of reading and writing

In all but exceptional situations, children need good spoken language before they can move on to becoming successful readers and writers. Children need a wide and varied vocabulary which includes many types of words. They also need to know that we use language in different ways in different situations, and to be able to select the word which is the best match to the desired meaning in a particular context. As well as a broad vocabulary children need to have been taught to understand the structure of sentences so that they can use this knowledge to make sense of their reading and to make their writing intelligible. These relationships seem pretty straightforward but the knowledge about language needed by a child to add reading and writing to their repertoire of language modes is certainly not simple.

In their evidence to the Cambridge Review (Alexander, 2009) the United Kingdom Literacy Association made the point that it is unhelpful to think that 'speaking and listening' lead to 'reading and writing'. They assert that listening has strong links to reading because both involve receiving, processing and making sense of the ideas of another person. Similarly, speaking has strong links to writing because both involve transferring ideas to another person through **composition** using words, phrases or sentences. This certainly seems to be a very helpful way of subdividing the area because it makes the links much clearer.

Kress (2003) shows that it is important not to think that, for example, the knowledge required by the speaker is the same as the knowledge of the writer because each medium has its own characteristics and makes particular demands on the child. Writing is much more than speech translated into symbols on the page.

Some of the key differences between listening and reading are:

- Speakers usually use intonation and pace to enhance meaning. Reading involves drawing similar cues from punctuation
- Speakers usually check that the listener understands them. A book does not do this
- Speakers adapt their language to meet the specific needs of the listener. Authors write for a specific but quite wide population
- Speech is usually generated by and between two active participants. Even someone who is listening to a formal speech will give information which influences the speaker. The reader does not create text with the writer
- It is possible to question a speaker if you don't understand – you can't ask an author to rephrase the complicated parts
- Listening involves the immediate capture and processing of transitory messages. A book is permanent so you can read at your own pace
- Writers and readers may be far apart in time. (For example, a wooden 'postcard' found at Hadrian's Wall was a request from a Roman soldier for his wife to send warm vests! He couldn't have imagined that people would read it hundreds of years later.) Speakers and listeners work together at the same time so they are able to ensure together that meaning is clear

The list above only needs a little modification to show the main differences between speaking and writing.

These differences mean that the typical 'say what you want and I'll write it for you' approaches to early writing can engender misconceptions about a simple relationship between speaking and writing. These two examples show approaches by Teaching Assistants working with beginner writers.

| Cora (TA): | What's this about? [*looking at child's picture*] |
| Courteney: | It's all the furniture. Going into the lorry for us moving. And that's my bed and that's my boxes. |

[*Cora writes 'All the furniture went into the lorry'.*]

| Cora: | Can you read this for me? |
| Courteney: | [*not looking at the writing*] It's about moving day. |

Later, Cora attended a staff development session on writing. This example shows a very skilful approach to drafting:

| Cora: | What shall we write about this picture? |
| Niall: | [*at dictating speed*] I got a Woody and a Buzz Lightyear. |

[*Cora writes 'I got a Woody and a Buzz Lightyear'.*]

| Cora: | [*reads*] I got a Woody and a Buzz Lightyear. Can you check that I wrote the words you wanted? |
| Niall: | [*moving his finger under each grapheme in turn*] I got a Woody and a Buzz Lightyear. That's right! |

Though this sort of work will have been undertaken before the primary years, it is important that the same approaches to the relationship between speaking and writing are consolidated and extended in every shared or guided writing session in the primary years. The speech leads into the writing but the changes the writer needs to consider have to be made clear. When we take the burden of the secretarial parts of writing from children, we need to ensure that they are led to making the authorial decisions including editing for desired meaning. If this is taught:

- first through the teacher's modelling
- then as shared work
- then as **guided work** focusing on explaining specific elements
- then as supported individual work
- then as planned independent work,

children will have the knowledge and skills to make informed decisions without prompting or support. They move to becoming everyday, accepted ways of thinking which are tools for future work.

Moving on as speakers and writers

As children progress as speakers and writers, transference of knowledge becomes two-way. One of the teachers involved in the excellent *Talk for Writing* (DCSF, 2009: 2) project noted that:

Bridging the gap between quality talk and quality writing is always challenging. With my Year 1 class I often wondered why, after providing lots of opportunities for speaking and listening, writing outcomes didn't reflect the varied and interesting vocabulary used in their talk. The question for me was, 'Can children modify their writing more effectively if they hear it and keep making changes until the talk for writing becomes the writing?'

The project found that as well as carefully focused talk supporting writing and enhancing quality, the close linking between the language modes also enhanced children's spoken language. Vocabulary, sentence structures and language conventions learnt from reading become part of the spoken language in appropriate situations – such as debate, explanation, reporting or persuasion. In each of these formal situations, successful oral language follows the conventions of the written form. New **genres** are often explored through reading, assimilated through speech and finally adopted in writing. The oral work in this process is essential for children to stretch and challenge their language skills without the pressures imposed by the written form. The model of gradual withdrawal of teacher support shown above is still valuable though children move much more quickly through the stages and many are able to transfer ways of thinking to tackle new genres or to skip a couple of stages in the process. By the last couple of primary years the boundaries between 'learning about language to learn to read' and 'reading to learn more about language' should begin to be broken down. For the accomplished, maturing learner, all the links are in place and speaking informs reading which informs speaking which informs learning which informs reading ... and so on, with every new activity strengthening the knowledge brought to subsequent work. It can be very impressive indeed.

Oral language across the curriculum

I'm going to start by stating something absurdly obvious – you simply can't teach without using language. This means that in every lesson, children will be using, consolidating, practising or extending their speaking and listening skills; in a real way every lesson is a language lesson. If we believe (and we certainly must) that every lesson should be a good one then, regardless of whether it occurs in literacy or history, the language modelled for the children and the language they are expected to learn to use must be appropriate and relevant.

The usual model, certainly the one advocated in the Primary National Strategy, was that children's language development is led from dedicated literacy lessons. However, if this is the only time in the day when the focus is on the quality and range of language used then the impact on children's learning is likely to be limited. The fact that there is oral language in a lesson doesn't mean that it is necessarily of good quality. The National Secondary Strategy background paper (2007) notes that there is still too little focus on the range and quality of speaking and listening across the curriculum. They have identified that there is a predominance of teacher-led discussion; though this is often excellent because teachers use questions very well, it is still often little more than a disguised tool for assessment where a minority of pupils participate with simple, brief responses.

Though the example above comes from the secondary sector, it seems to be valid in primary classrooms too. 'Discussion' is planned in many lessons but it has usually as little relationship to true discussion as processed cheese slices have to Stilton. If I were having a discussion with someone I would certainly not ask them a question, half-listen to their answer, tell them if I liked it and then move on to someone else. That isn't a discussion – it is being downright rude and, just as it has no place in adult interaction, so it has no validity in the classroom. If teachers want every child to have a chance to share ideas, then the most satisfactory way to do this is to stop dominating the work and allow children to interact with their peers. If the task is well-planned and interesting they will not wander from it so teacher involvement isn't necessary for managerial purposes. Nor is it needed for assessment; feedback to the whole class yields the information needed to track progress.

If discussion is a major element of cross-curricular language use, it must be good discussion which reinforces the skills, structures and procedures taught in literacy lessons. However, it is important that speaking and listening does not come to mean just discussion. Every type of speaking and listening activity should be reinforced, consolidated and extended across every curriculum subject. Opportunities for drama are lurking in every curriculum area: I recently observed a splendid science lesson on sustainable lifestyles in which children took on the roles of banana farm workers, supermarket owners, shoppers, doctors and parents in order to discuss the most ethical sourcing of food. One of the most moving lessons I have ever seen was when a group of children re-enacted some of the events during the outbreak of the plague in Eyam. There can be very little which isn't made more important, memorable and personal by the use of drama.

It would be easy to make the same case for sustained speaking and for listening to a range of speakers and for different purposes. The important thing is that the demand made is in keeping with what children are learning in literacy. If, for example, the activity is designed to extend the children's knowledge then it is often wise to transfer the subject matter to the literacy planning. All the non-fiction units in the PNS were left deliberately content-free so that they could be linked closely to relevant work drawn in from any appropriate subject area. Hopefully, we do not generate 'artificial' material simply for the purpose of teaching a language skill. We draw in subject matter to contextualise the learning and make it relevant. It is probable that about a third of literacy lessons in every school year are given across to activities which teach both language knowledge and content from another subject as a medium for learning. As the curriculum evolves, this is likely to become a central element of thematic planning. What will remain important is that both children and their teachers know what is being learnt and how it is valuable.

 What could you do to create an excellent classroom environment for oral language development?

Danger areas

Changing opinions

Some danger areas have been considered above in terms of teaching. There are other aspects which need careful thought when planning speaking and listening activities. The first is the difficult line between debate and indoctrination. In choosing subjects which are of interest to children we are likely to get into areas where beliefs are not shared by all participants. The classroom ethos must ensure that children are at ease with the expression of minority views because they know that every contribution will be treated courteously. Problems can be overcome by work in role as this distances the child from the opinion being presented.

It is often necessary to step back from discussions on controversial areas, particularly if you have a strong opinion. Status as a teacher is going to give your view a great importance to the children and it is never part of the literacy teacher's role to impose opinions. Good oral language lessons frequently conclude with the view that the issue was rather more complicated than first imagined and that most perspectives have some validity.

Shy children

This is a difficult one. A child has every right to be shy and therefore to prefer to avoid the hurly burly of a full-blooded discussion or debate. However, we are aware that being unable or unwilling to speak confidently in a range of circumstances is going to be a serious problem in adult life. One way of reconciling the need to equip children with important skills while recognising their right to their preferences is to agree individual targets with the child. These may be kept secret from other children and need to start with such small steps that there is no feeling of threat. Good starting points are:

- any work with puppets or masks
- paired work where the other child feeds back to the class
- specific role in a group discussion (perhaps note taker)
- performance poetry as a member of a group
- directing other children to perform

It is very easy for the shy child who prefers to participate as a listener to slip into non-participation which prevents learning.

Class personality

In every class there is a complex network of friendships and dominance which can impact significantly on the success of teaching of speaking and listening. This can get to the extreme where discussion is viewed as a competition which must always be 'won' by a particular group. In other classes certain children expect the most important parts in any drama activity. Anything of this sort prevents progress for the majority of the children and therefore has to be sorted out swiftly. It could be worth trying a radical movement from the speaking and listening activities with which the class is familiar so that established patterns are broken. Random grouping can also be successful as it breaks down the traditional power structures among the children.

 What has the greatest influence on children's development as speakers – home, school, peers or media?

 After the primary phase (KS3)

For many students, the focus shifts firmly to teaching to learn at KS3. They will be expected to engage in formal and informal activities where the focus is on reflection, analysis, evaluation and arguing a case. They will be expected to create subject specific vocabularies and use appropriate phrasing to suit the genre being utilised. The secondary strategy emphasises the need for the full repertoire of desired genres and structures to be taught in language lessons as well as being utilised across the whole curriculum.

All students are likely to have a drama curriculum which extends the range of genres and the nature of participation. They will also be prepared for GCSE English which includes speaking and listening activities.

 ## Chapter summary

- Speaking and listening are the basis of nearly all successful learning in the primary years
- Oral language needs to be taught as consciously and carefully as every other aspect of the English curriculum
- Teachers have a great influence on children's speaking and listening but so do home, peers and media
- Teachers need to work sensitively with children whose home dialect and register differ greatly from those demanded in the education system
- Teachers have to be great listeners as well as good speakers

Further reading

Browne, A. (2009) *Developing Language and Literacy 3–8* (3rd edn). London: SAGE.
Cremin, T. (2009) *Teaching English Creatively.* Abingdon: Routledge.
Grugeon, E., Hubbard, L., Smith, C. and Dawes, L. (2006) *Teaching Speaking and Listening in the Primary School* (3rd edn). London: Fulton.
Wyse, D. and Jones, R. (2008) *Teaching English, Language and Literacy* (2nd edn). Abingdon: Routledge.

References

Alexander, R.J. (2008) *Towards Dialogic Teaching: Rethinking Classroom Talk* (4th edn). York: Dialogos.

Alexander, R.J. (ed.) (2009) *Children, their World, their Education: Final Report of the Cambridge Primary Review*. London: Routledge.

Andrews S.J. (1997) 'Metalinguistic awareness and teacher explanation', *Language Awareness*, 6: 147–161.

Bauer, L. and Nation, P. (1993) 'Word families', *International Journal of Lexicography*, 6(4): 253–279.

Book, C., Duffy, G., Rochler, L., Meloth, M. and Varvus, L. (1985) 'A study of the relationship between teacher explanation and student metacognitive awareness during reading instruction', *Communication Education*, 34(1): 29–36.

Chamberlain, D. (1997) *The Foetal Senses: A Classical View.* The Association for Prenatal and Perinatal Psychology and Health [Online]. Available at: http://www.birthpsychology.com/lifebefore/fetalsense.html (accessed 2 August 2010).

Department for Children, Schools and Families (DCSF) (2009) *Talk for Writing*. London: DCSF.

Department for Education and Schools (DfES) (2003) *Speaking, Listening, Learning: Working with Children in Key Stages 1 & 2*. Nottingham: DfES.

Kress, G. (2003) *Literacy in the New Media Age*. London: Routledge.

Maddern, E. and Hess, P. (2005) *Death in a Nut*. London: Frances Lincoln Children's Books.

McAleer Hamaguchi, P. (1995) *Childhood Speech, Language, and Listening Problems: What Every Parent Should Know.* New York: John Wiley & Sons.

Myhill, D. and Fisher, R. (2005) *Informing Practice in English: A Review of Recent Research in Literacy and the Teaching of English*. London: Ofsted.

National Secondary Strategy (2007) *Teaching Speaking and Listening.* Background and Context Paper [Online]. Available at: www.standards.dfes.gov.uk/.../speakingandlistening/.../sl_background_context.pdf (accessed 13 August 2010).

Ofsted (2005) *English 2000–2005: A Review of Inspection Evidence* (HMI 2351). London: Ofsted.

Ofsted (2010) *Reading by Six: How the Best Schools Do It* (100197). London: Ofsted.

Waugh, D. and Jolliffe, W. (2008) *English 3–11: A Guide for Teachers.* Abingdon: Routledge.

CHAPTER 3

READING FOR UNDERSTANDING

• adult reading • checking strategy • comprehension • decoding • guided reading • independence • miscue • modelling strategies • shared reading • understanding • word recognition

This chapter aims to:

- show the complexities of the reading process
- explain how decoding and language comprehension work together to enable readers to understand text
- show how different types of text require different approaches
- consider the types of understanding needed by readers
- describe key teaching strategies

It is odd that the teaching of reading arouses such passion in so many people. Perhaps the sheer complexity of the reading process is why much current debate centres on the beginnings of reading: the doorways into the understanding of text. Each possible route into reading will certainly ensure that the new reader gains essential insights into reading and makes a start on the long process of learning to read. However, our aim as teachers is always to guide children towards the ease with reading experienced by the competent, confident adult and due to the complexity of the task, no single approach will, on its own, take the child beyond the early stages.

Before the primary phase

Fortunate children will be surrounded by texts from babyhood. People read to them and share their enjoyment of the written word. They may own books and choose between them, having favourites which are reread. From these experiences they will learn about the permanence of text and the range of ways of getting information from the text. They will also learn about the usefulness of reading from observing adults. Much of this reading may be information based.

In EYFS interactions become a daily encounter in which children are encouraged to participate through discussion, prediction and reflection. Gradually they will be taught to isolate individual words and to recognise them in differing contexts. Their decoding skills will begin through systematic teaching and play activities. Alongside this, they will be given many opportunities to choose to develop reading-like behaviours. Reading and writing will be closely linked so that children are aware of the importance of written language.

The UK is committed to starting the teaching of reading when children are very young. Other countries start formal instruction much later. What are the strengths of each approach?

How adults read

Reading is one of those peculiar abilities which, once mastered, are very difficult to break down into their ports. For most people it is probably better to regard the process of reading one the more magnificent mysteries of life. But, as a student teacher, you will need have a good understanding of how adults read so you can guide young readers successfilly. I recently asked new student teachers which of these three statements best described the reading process.

You start at the top of the page on the left, decode each word, memorise it and then move on to the next.

You read a couple of words then scan the sentence for the important ones. You fill in the rest from your own understanding of the subject and the style.

You decode the first syllable of each word and then make a guess about what it probably is.

Most student teachers thought that the first statement was nearest the truth and they certainly have a point. Reading does involve the **decoding** of words but it also involves a great deal more. Depending on the nature of what is being read and the purposes of the reading, adult readers do all the things described.

Silani et al. (2005) undertook a study involving MRI scans of adults when reading, showing that some aspects of reading require the activation of eight brain areas. Interestingly, the reading activity which required the fewest brain areas was the decoding of strings of letters which the participants had been told were non-words, probably because the reader knew there was no need to attempt to understand the text. This research shows that the recognition and pronunciation of groups of letters is only the first of the many things which the reader does while trying to make sense of a text. For example, you probably corrected the errors in the first lines of the paragraph above without being conscious that you were doing so, using context, register and **syntax**. Look at these examples of two student teachers reading the same phrase to gain an idea of what we tend to do when we come against something we cannot easily understand:

Student A: '... the giraffe ate the shoots of the ack -ack -a -see -a tree'
Tutor: How did you decide what kind of tree it is?
Student A: I sounded it out. I've never heard of it.
Student B: '... the giraffe ate the shoots of the ... [*pause*] a case ear tree'
Tutor: How did you decide what kind of tree it is?
Student B: We've got an acacia at home but it is nothing like that – more a bush, but I can't think of any tree that could have that spelling except 'acacia'.

Student A has offered a pronunciation based on **synthetic phonics** as the only system she can rely on. She has not been able to check whether this pronunciation is valid because she expects the word to be completely unknown. The pause in Student B's reading is significant. She has also found the word daunting but has referred to her knowledge of syntax to realise that the position of the word narrows the possible word types. She then checks her decoding against her knowledge of trees and reaches a pronunciation for 'acacia' (a word she has heard), over-ruling other phonically regular possibilities.

This example shows one of the most important aspects of adult reading: we check what we are reading by drawing on all sorts of other knowledge. The more we know about the world and the more we know about how language works, the easier it is for us to avoid mistakes in reading. We combine decoding with predicting and checking (Sereno et al., 2006) so fast that it is only when there is a confrontation with the unknown, that we become aware of what has become a smooth, semi-automatic activity.

One of the turning points in our view of the reading process happened in 1967 when Goodman described it as 'a psycholinguistic guessing game'. By 'guessing' Goodman did not mean anything simple, random or trivial. It is very informed guessing that occurs, more like the deductions of Sherlock Holmes where details are noted, interpreted and brought together, than like picking lottery numbers. The purposes of the 'game' can be very serious indeed so the processes have to be accurate and rigorously controlled by the reader.

  Expert reflection

David Reedy: Becoming a reader – more than reading words

Throughout the last few years the teaching of reading has been high on the political and policy agendas. Almost universally pronouncements are from a deficit viewpoint. The recent Education White Paper, published in November 2010, states that the coalition government, in schools in England, intends to:

> Ensure that there is support available to every school for the teaching of systematic synthetic phonics, as the best method of teaching reading. (DfE, 2010)

Thus, at a stroke, becoming a reader is reduced to learning how to decode words using phonics. This is a highly reductionist and dangerous definition. We know that phonics is an essential part of cracking the alphabetic code of English but nowhere near sufficient to the development of well rounded readers. (It is not even sufficient for word reading as many common words are not phonically regular, for example *come, was, the.*)

Really successful primary schools do not simply teach decoding skills:

- They have a broad and rich reading curriculum and have a balance of phonics, whole word and meaning based approaches to teach children to read.
- They are clear that the purpose of reading is to make sense of what is read not simply to say the words.
- They promote engagement and enjoyment. Engagement is increasingly seen by researchers as central to progress in reading. Children who are motivated want to read more and more, and get better and better at it.
- They are knowledgeable about high quality reading resources and have many of them, organised in a welcoming school and class library.
- They introduce all children to a wide range of children's literature and explore ways in which reading literature can broaden the experience of life and give a sense of what is possible.

As teachers we must address all these areas if we are to encourage our children to grow as readers.

(David Reedy is President of United Kingdom Literacy Association (UKLA) and Principal Adviser, Primary-London Borough of Barking and Dagenham)

Reading for and with understanding

Understanding cannot be separated from reading; it isn't an extra. It's the sole purpose of the activity and, without it, reading is nothing more than making noises in response to squiggles. This means that understanding must be at the heart of reading even from the earliest days when a child gains pleasure and understanding from listening to text. Understanding is also related to reading in another important way: readers need to bring their understanding to the text. This is far more than understanding of how letters and sounds link together, though this is certainly important. To read we need to bring our understanding of the world to our interpretation of the text. Because we all bring different things to a text, the combination of existing knowledge and the knowledge from the reading gives us each something slightly different.

Here's a good example from three children and Louise (BEd student) working together on adding a verse to *The Highwayman* by Alfred Noyes. (As in so many of the best lessons, the discussion moves away from Louise's careful plan.)

Louise: I wondered about this. The poem goes straight from Tim's jealousy to the soldiers coming. He doesn't tell us what Tim did. Why do you think that is?

Lily: Grassed him up to the redcoats so he could get Bess.

Tara: In his dreams!

Lily: But he doesn't know he's rank. He like thinks she'll be all over him if he can get the Highwayman gone. He wouldn't use the words in the poem about himself, would he? He'd say, "Where the handsome ostler listened … "

Louise: This is great. But why isn't all this in the poem?

Rachel: Because it's obvious.

Louise: Anyone else?

Lily: And … And if it was there I'd go 'yaaaawwwwnnn'. He's left it out to make you feel good about understanding without it …

Rachel: Like the verse he didn't have to write.

Louise wisely decided against her planned activity and went on to exploring the poet's words and the details added in the mind. I've included this example because it shows both the knowledge of the world and the knowledge of literature that the children are bringing to their understanding.

Our understanding of text happens at many levels depending on:

- experience of reading
- life experiences, knowledge and attitudes
- nature and complexity of the text
- purpose of the text
- purpose of the reading

What we gain from texts depends on who we are, what we are reading and why we are reading it. Understanding is not just a part of reading: it is its purpose, and its power.

How young readers understand texts

Every text lays down a range of cues which lead the reader to the author's meanings. The genre of the text determines the sort of information available and how overtly it is made clear to the reader. So, for example, the illustrator of a picture book for young children will probably choose to give pictorial representations of key narrative points. She may also choose colours and style to evoke a particular atmosphere and will make very sure that nothing in the illustration contradicts the information given in the words. However, a picture book for more experienced readers (such as the astounding *The Arrival* by Shaun Tan) will use the illustration to encourage the reader to interact deeply with the text, speculating about meanings and interacting with what the author gives to create a unique interpretation of a complex text.

The child who is fortunate to be immersed in a world of high quality texts shared with an enthusiastic adult is ideally situated to learn to draw meaning from text based on:

- The *semantic information* – the text is likely to remain true to the genre and the subject indicated by the cover or title (Vera the Violet Fairy is unlikely to be abducted by MI5 agents; a book on dinosaurs isn't the best place to look for information on assembling flatpack furniture)
- The information given by the *sentence or_____structure.* Understanding of the way language works teaches the reader that only certain types of words will fit into specific places in the structure. The structure leads the reader to the category of the unknown word
- The information given by the *structure and layout* of the book itself
- *Punctuation* is immensely helpful to the reader

If you look back to the second bullet point you'll see that a word has been omitted. When you read this part, you may have done one of two things: either decided that you couldn't be bothered with playing daft games or quickly worked out the word and moved on. If you skipped the word, that's fine as one of the aspects of understanding a text is knowing what you can safely not bother with. This depends on why you are reading and the type of text being read. If you decided to work out the missing word you'll have used several sorts of knowledge:

- Syntactic knowledge will have told you that the word has got to be a noun
- Semantic knowledge will have told you that it has to be reasonably close in meaning to the word 'sentence'
- Your knowledge of structure will have told you that each dash probably indicates a letter

This information will probably have led you to be confident that the word is either 'clause' or 'phrase'. The fact you couldn't reach a definite answer is the responsibility of the writer not you the reader. It's worth thinking about two closely related things:

Were you aware that you used these approaches when reading?

Do you remember being taught these skills?

Each of these cueing systems beckons the reader towards understanding. Taken this way, a child's interaction with books adds to the understanding that meaning can be drawn from a silent page. Whether by being read to, playing at reading (reading-like behaviour) or moving into shared or independent reading the child is being given experiences which focus on meaning. These experiences must be purposeful and enjoyable as it is just as easy for a child to come to an understanding that the text is boring and reading inexplicable as it is to come to understand that books are wonderful and reading one of the great pleasures of life.

Expert reflection

Prue Goodwin: Narrative and knowing

Stories have been told to enchant, entertain and educate people since time began. Stories are absorbing, thought-provoking and satisfying; in fact, narrative is such a pleasurable part of our everyday lives that we are unaware of what an important role it plays in learning. Not just in childhood; narrative helps us all to learn, understand and remember what we need to know.

Many stories were originally told as warnings or lessons about life. From folk and fairy tales, among other things, we learn:

- not to talk to wolves when walking to grandmother's cottage through the wood
- to use brainpower to outwit physical strength if confronted by a troll
- that true love will conquer all

Some stories have special names that signal their didactic intention – parable, allegory, fable – but others are just tales that provide 'messages' about how the world works. Many of the strongest beliefs we have about being human are learned by children via simple tales about families or friendship – caring, sharing and helping each other. Engaging in the imagined lives of story characters enables even very young children to consider realities of life and to recognise its binary nature (good and bad, rich and poor, brave and cowardly). Stories reinforce concepts such as empathy, fortitude, compassion and kindness – attributes which may prompt us to aspire to be the best that we can.

(Continued)

(Continued)

No matter what age our children are, we should never worry that telling, reading or watching a story is a waste of time. An ever-increasing knowledge of stories is one of the most effective things we can give children to support them as they learn both in the formality of school and the hurly-burly of their daily lives. Narrative is an essential part of being human and stories link us all to the whole of humanity, across time and across the globe.

(Prue Goodwin is the former president of UKLA and Lecturer at the University of Reading. She is now a Freelance Lecturer in Literacy and Children's Books)

Questioning for understanding

Far too often 'comprehension' seems to refer to a set of formal exercises given by a teacher to determine how much a reader has understood from a text. The traditional model of comprehension is that it can be divided into a neat model in which there are several levels of complexity (derived from Barrett's taxonomy). These are:

- Literal comprehension – being able to understand the text
- Inferential comprehension – being able to understand the implications of the text
- Evaluative comprehension – being able to understand what may be around and beyond the text
- Appreciative comprehension – being able to understand the qualities of the text

Many of the questions set by teachers are related to literal comprehension. The problem with this relates back to the activity above: readers can often use a system of cues to locate the answers without really understanding the text.

Pungle had a tuppish, dark-croosk bisser called Bishbonk.

You'll be able to answer these 'literal level' questions without having any idea at all what the sentence means:

What did Pungle have?

What sort of animal was Bishbonk?

What colour was the bisser?

Who had a bisser?

Literal questions simply skim the surface of a text; there are occasions when this is exactly what the reader needs to do, particularly in instructional texts to find the material which needs to be read in greater detail. However their value with fiction is very limited and can be detrimental. If children are consistently set questions of this type, they are encouraged to believe that this is the only level of understanding. They may well become surface skimmers rather than being prepared to dive through the levels of understanding offered by every great book. This can also happen when schools set 'reading challenges' when children have to read a certain number of books in order to gain a certificate. Very fast reading is very often superficial.

 Perhaps we all develop as teachers by the sudden, startling incidents which turn our preconceptions upside down. This is a snatch of conversation which happened on my first day as a specialist teacher working with children who were struggling with reading. Leon had brought his class reading book with him.

> *Me*:   What's this book about?
> *Leon*: I don't ****ing know. It's my ****ing reading book.

This was one of the most important moments for me in my teaching career.

- What does this suggest about Leon's view of reading?
- How would you approach helping him to read?

Reading fiction for understanding

Gamble and Yates (2008) challenge the view that reading just involves moving the desired message from the writer's mind to the reader's through the medium of the text. They see the reader as having a far more active and individual role where the understanding may be derived from experience, beliefs, attitudes and knowledge in response to the text. This suggests that any text may be capable of yielding a whole range of understandings to readers and that an individual's understanding of a text may change if it is read a second time. For a teacher this means that there will have to be an acceptance that children may have different equally valid responses to a text.

The focus on comprehension in fiction should be at inferential, evaluative and appreciative levels as the mutual exploration of ideas will give children models of how to interact with a text when reading independently. There is also a place for exploring unusual vocabulary together and discussing the effectiveness of features such as unusual phrasing, imagery and evocation of emotions. This knowledge helps with both reading and writing.

Understanding too much, too young?

Children need freedom to choose texts which appeal to them or they will find reading to be a dull chore. However, you may have to exert some level of censorship over children's reading. A typical example of this is the CHERUB books by Robert Muchamore. (*It must be emphasised that the publishers make it clear that the books are unsuitable for younger readers.*) These are gripping adventure stories which take the hero from the age of 11 to 17. Typically children read the first of these at about the age of ten and few adults would have much problem with the occasional mention of urine and the hero's interest in the size of breasts. However, by the final book, the hero has all the interests of the average 17-year-old. The 10-year-old reader is likely to read the first book, love it, finish it in a week and want the next. He could be ready to read the final book in a couple of months not the six years that have passed in the hero's life. Should the teacher prevent the reading of the first book because later books may not be suitable? The answer will be a balancing of the knowledge about the child, the school policy, the view of the parents and the teacher's own degree of caution. It does mean that you will have to have read every book in your classroom and be certain that they are appropriate.

Teachers may, rightly, be very cautious about access to material which could be inappropriate. The problem with caution is that it may lead to the selection of bland, safe texts which in turn could decrease the motivation of the children. This is particularly the case with boys' reading. Safford et al. (2004) identified the type of texts being offered to boys as one of the factors in their reluctance to read. Since boys tend to enjoy more adventurous, gritty fiction, it may be that their needs are not being met by the selection of texts chosen for discussion and study. One way to resolve this may be to embrace a much wider range of genres (as recommended by the renewed Primary Framework), including electronic sources and graphic novels. We need a balance of texts to become balanced readers.

    Expert reflection

Pat Hughes: Reading and history

The Roman God Janus symbolises the importance of history. The god is two faced, one looking forward the other looking backwards. Janus represents a very human need to be able to look and evaluate the past as well as looking forward. As individuals we all learn from the past: some more effectively than others. Part of our role as primary educators is to ensure that we help children to do this as well.

Many of the non-fiction texts used in schools have a historical flavour even if they are not directly historical. This includes the picture books which have historical illustrations such as great children's classics like *Peepo* (Ahlberg and Ahlberg, 1983) and the *The Baby's Catalogue* (Ahlberg and Ahlberg, 1990). Pat Hutchins's *Rosie's Walk* (2001) requires a fairly in-depth understanding of farming in the past. There is a wealth of historical fiction used at KS1 and 2, and a surprising number of children's computer and handheld games, which are greatly enriched if those playing with them can link in with the historical narrative.

Historical content challenges the reader to make sense of context which is often heavily dependent on 'understanding chronology, exploring change and continuity over time and understanding why and where things happened' (QCDA, 2010). Unless teachers recognise this, there are difficulties in reading comprehension which can be challenging for even the confident reader and writer.

Neate (2008) takes an in-depth approach looking at the linguistic features of subject related texts. Sometimes these are specialist to the subject areas, e.g. 'dolly peg'. More often they are commonly used words which have different subject specialist connections. 'Change' in science has a very different meaning from 'change' in history, PE or in mathematics. Primary teachers need both historical context knowledge and linguistic understandings of subject texts, in order for children to have some chance of being able to understand where they and others are in time – and place.

Pat Hughes is Senior Lecturer in History, Faculty of Education, Liverpool Hope University

Reading non-fiction for understanding

Lewis and Wray (1997) undertook a very influential study on non-fiction. One of the key messages was that the reading from non-fiction texts (paper or electronic) needs to be taught with care or children will approach them as story. Though biography and recount are often structured as traditional narrative, most texts are not. They require the reader to:

- Frame questions before reading
- Know how to locate the necessary information as quickly as possible
- Know how to distinguish between fact, opinion and persuasion
- Know how to discover the authority of the writer

All these skills need to be taught through shared and guided reading or children can get very frustrated with knowing that all the information is out there but they can't find it or use it. This is an account of James's work with a group of gifted readers in science:

One of them wanted to know how many eggs a frog laid and what proportion survived to the next year so I sent him to the school library to find a relevant book. He came back very angry that he couldn't see a book on frogspawn. He was a talented reader but he didn't know how to use a library. I showed the group about how the library system worked – going from animals to reptiles and amphibians to finding frogs and then frogspawn in the books using the table of contents and index. The sad thing was that after all this work we didn't get the answer so we had to use the internet to find an expert and emailed him. (It's less than 2%.)

Once information has been located children may still struggle with non-fiction because the text may be very dense; it may include a number of unfamiliar words or those used in ways specific to the subject and it may use structures which are unknown. For example, a colleague came across a child who had just read 'Only one bear lives south of the equator' and felt very sorry because it would be lonely.

When text has been understood at a literal level, children need to bring their existing understanding of the subject to it. For example, *Bananas are red* is accessible literally but everything you know suggests it is wrong so you reject the information. You might, however, wonder whether there might be a smidgeon of unexpected truth in the statement and a quick internet search will lead you to discover the Cuban Red banana. This notion of checking with self or other sources is central to understanding in non-fiction.

Talk to a child who has a particular interest in a subject out of school. It could be Dr Who, dinosaurs or anything, it doesn't matter. In your conversation discover how the child finds out more about this subject. Make a note of:

- Listening to experts
- Asking questions
- Reading books for children
- Reading other sources
- Using electronic sources

Listen for the enthusiasm the child brings to the subject and the pleasure she gains from research. Consider how this enhances your insights into non-fiction reading.

Teaching reading: the initial stages

The recognition of the complexity of adult reading underpins all informed approaches to teaching children. However, there have been many different responses to the issue of the most appropriate forms of teaching. One is to say that as skilled reading requires the synthesis of skills beyond the scope of the novice reader, the best approach is to work closely with an adult who will take over those parts of the process which the child cannot yet manage independently. Another approach is to limit the texts to be read to those which demand only the skills being taught. A third approach is to focus the initial teaching on one key skill such as **grapheme/phoneme** correspondence as an access point into reading. Though adults read by drawing together and interweaving several strands of knowledge, we cannot expect a young child to do the same, so it is appropriate to focus on the best starter points while knowing there is much more to be taught.

There are many possible routes into the beginnings of reading. The one advocated at present, synthetic phonics, is very sensible because English has a written code which is based on each of the 26 alphabet letters indicating a single or small range of linguistic sounds. Children who master the phoneme–grapheme correspondences will be able to pronounce the majority of words. This will certainly offer a toehold on reading. However, as shown above, competent reading involves a repeating cycle of attempting, checking, assimilating and moving forward. To do this successfully, readers need to use different strategies to check the reading if the chosen strategy has yielded an implausible reading. Repeated use of the same strategy is unlikely to solve the problem. In Chapter 4 there is a more detailed consideration of the teaching of phonics.

If children only learn a single approach to reading they are underequipped to check the reading. This leads to dependence on experts to tell whether they are right or wrong rather than dependence on the text and their own knowledge of syntax, the way texts work and the world. Perhaps the popular concern should move on from focusing on the best way of enabling children to make their first steps as readers: phonics works well for most motivated beginners. It is the next step which is so important: developing systems for checking the decoding of the word through assessing the attempt in the context of a growing understanding of the text.

- How much is our view of the best way to teach reading determined by whether we perceive children as receivers of adult knowledge or investigators of the world around them?
- Adults use a complex range of strategies to read. Should beginners be taught all these strategies or should they start with a single approach?

Bringing the approaches to early reading together

Rose (2006) advocated a sophisticated resolution of the central problem that adults read in complex ways and young children aren't equipped to handle the whole process at first. So how should reading instruction balance these two facts? The model is based on Gough and Tunmer's work (1986) which split reading into two main requirements: decoding through phonic and visual methods and processing language to gain understanding.

Figure 3.1 shows four possible outcomes for a child's reading of a text. These depend on the ability to decode and the language comprehension. The model works best if it is considered as a way of describing the way understanding is drawn from a specific piece of text.

Read these four sentences and decide which quartile best indicates your reading comprehension for each of them. Ask yourself whether you could read the sentence out loud with confidence and whether you could explain what it means.

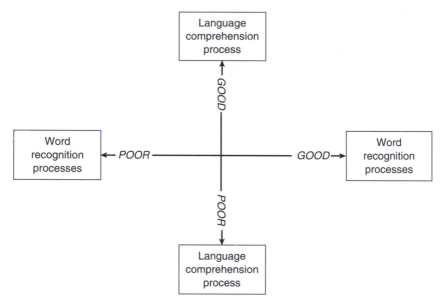

Figure 3.1 The simple view of reading (Rose, 2006). © Crown Copyright 2006. Reproduced with permission.

1 Twas brillig, and the slithy toves did gyre and gimble in the wabe.
2 In one of the stories in this anthology a water buffalo is resident at the end of a girl's street.
3 The cryostat using a Plaistow/Cholmondley[3]/LZe model was indicted as non-lyophilic.
4 Ozothamnus rosmarinofolius requires full sun and well-drained soil.

Each of these texts places different demands in terms of decoding and comprehension. Unfamiliar genres, vocabularies and subject matter challenge us all our lives. Whatever the text, this view of reading describes the interplay between decoding and checking understanding which ensures true comprehension.

The current view of reading suggests that children will only begin to make sense of text when they have enough aural and oral language experience to recognise the structures, tones, purposes and vocabulary which they will need to draw upon as they begin to read. Many families and EYFS stage settings provide children with a wonderful start on reading by encouraging a love of language and a deep desire to find out about the world. The toddler whose favourite word is 'why' will make a smooth transition from pestering adults to interrogating texts. The child who loves to play with the patterns of language in rhymes, jokes and songs is going to find it easy to use the patterns of word structure to 'make the black marks speak' (H. Dombey in Cremin et al., 2009: 43). The child who can do both is set to start on formal instruction in reading.

Teacher as motivator

Learning to read is difficult and takes a long time. It is the teacher's responsibility to ensure every encounter with text is fulfilling. Morgan et al. (2008) have found that children who experience early failures in reading are less motivated to read and will spend less time reading. This seems fairly obvious but has huge consequences for our teaching of reading. Firstly, it shows that young children can reflect on performance and are aware of their progress as readers. Secondly this may have implications for ability grouping as it could be a factor in children's poor motivation. The third thing to consider from this research is the impact of poor motivation on voluntary reading. No one is going to master reading solely from the time spent in formal instruction. The newly taught skills and approaches need to be practised and enjoyed frequently to consolidate them and to lead to progress. Once motivation is lost it is very difficult to recover, so a downward slide easily begins; the unmotivated child becomes less and less able to achieve.

A reading ethos

The following things may help engender children's motivation:

- frequent opportunity to choose to read
- texts relating to children's interests with some materials selected by the children
- an attractive area of the room devoted solely to reading
- new books and other publications displayed and available to read
- approach to reading which recognises the power of electronic sources
- thematic approaches
- variety and changes in what is offered

However, a reading ethos is about much more than great provision and the hope that children will ingest a love of reading. Children also need a teacher who:

- makes her own love of reading evident
- devotes time to conversations about books, listens to opinions and is prepared to offer her own without imposing them
- has read the books which the children are reading
- is prepared to choose materials and methods to suit the individual and the text
- notes and praises all steps towards independence
- addresses problems immediately and subtly
- knows that reading is vitally important
- believes all children can make progress
- takes responsibility for ensuring they do so

Teaching reading to a whole class

This is often called shared reading. It should be a time for teaching what will be the next steps in independent reading for most of the class and the next but one step for some. This means that what is taught in these sessions will vary enormously, based on analysis of patterns of recent achievement. It should always involve:

- the exploration of a text which is too slightly complex for most of the children to handle independently
- the demonstration of strategies which you would like children to start to use, talking through your decision-making as you approach the text
- modelling of things you want children to try when reading in groups or individually
- participation – would you want to sit on a hard floor with nothing active to do for 15 minutes? Children need the opportunity to engage with the text through activities which both draw them in and challenge them
- interaction – partner work is excellent as it enables children to develop their ideas with confidence
- a focus on meaning
- the posing of open questions and an acceptance of unexpected answers
- developing activities which make children work on, in, around and through the text to gain understanding

Working with a group

Most teachers devote 15 or 20 minutes a day to working on reading, writing or oral language with a group of children of similar ability. This usually means that every child in the class gains one session of closely focused work tailored to her individual needs once a week. Kutnick et al. (2008) studied group working in primary schools and found that children were often only nominally part of a group. They were frequently working on individual tasks and were reliant on the teacher rather than their peers. Children often sit very close to other children but are not allowed to talk to them. This is a poor model as it doesn't allow children to support and challenge each other.

Another issue worth considering is why the children are grouped together and whether the grouping is for the teacher's convenience or the children's needs. It is far better to form temporary groups for reading (probably for a week to three weeks at most) based on analysis of previous attainment and identification of specific needs. This also acknowledges that children do not have a single, identifiable ability in English but a mishmash of strengths, gaps, enthusiasms and knowledge which are best addressed in different ways.

These are factors which may influence your grouping for a specific teaching focus:

- children who are in the same quartile of the Simple View of Reading at that level of difficulty for the genre being studied
- children who will support each other by respecting ideas and opinions
- children who have similar approaches to reading

Hallam et al. (2004) also considered the generic issues of the purposes of grouping and worked with ideas of the purpose and planned activities determining the nature of the group. One aspect which seems clear is that a group, however it is formed, should not be a huddle of individuals working independently while supervised by a teacher. The best of group or guided reading involves the teacher as expert leading a group of children in working on the next step which would be too difficult for them to attain individually or without support.

Here's a good example of a student teacher (Pippa) working with a group of children in Year 1 who all tend to over-rely on language comprehension. Her target is to teach them to use their phonic knowledge as a checking device. She has chosen to use a highly illustrated book, *Who's in the Loo?* (Willis and Reynolds, 2006) as a transition to texts which will offer fewer cues, as well as being a book which should certainly engage the group.

Pippa: Let's turn over now. What's on this page?

Claudette: A tiger doing a … [*laughter from the whole group*] tinkle.

Pippa: That's certainly what the picture's telling us! Now let's look at the words. Who can find me the first word we should check?

Mark: Here. This one. t-i-g. Tigger

Pippa: Do you remember what we learnt about **split digraphs?**

Jon: Not 'tigger' – 'tiger'. Saying the letter name?

Pippa: Yes. Do you all remember? You had a really good example this morning in phonics, Mark. 'The man had a mane!' Remember?

Dion: And 'a pin in a pine'

Pippa: That's it. That's great. We've had a good chance to use our new learning. Claudette, could you remember that for the plenary? Let's go on to another word to check. What does the word tell us? Everyone look closely. Word, Jon, not the picture.

Jon: T … tiddle

Pippa: Read the whole word to make sure.

Claudette: [*laughs*] … have to check the whole word because it could be 'tinkle.'

[*Whole group, including student teacher, laughs*]

Jon: It's 'd-d' so it's 'tiddle'.

Pippa: Great. Could you all please read that page in your heads checking all the words as you go?

(*Extract from Who's in the Loo? by Jeanne Willis reproduced with permission of Andersen Press*)

This example shows the teacher supplementing existing strengths through an emphasis on necessary new learning. The teacher's knowledge scaffolds the children's learning as they move through group work to individual attempts.

 This book has certainly engaged children's interest and yielded very constructive responses. Would you feel happy working with a text which includes similar words?

Working with an individual

Individual work was for many years one of the cornerstones of reading instruction. Certainly, a great deal of time was spent on 'hearing children read' which might not have been wholly constructive: the idea of 'hearing' rather than teaching rather indicates the weaknesses of the approach. There may be times when individual work is the most effective teaching method. These may be:

- when a child has been absent for a crucial piece of teaching
- if a child has not achieved the objectives in a group session
- when a child is reluctant to take an active role in a group session
- when a child tends to dominate group work
- when a child's logical next step in reading is unique
- when you are flummoxed about how best to enable progress
- when you need a more detailed picture of the child as a reader
- when children are unlikely to choose to read on their own
- when closely monitored practice is needed to ensure new learning is embedded

Very often, individual work is assigned to a teaching assistant or classroom volunteer. Look at this list and decide in which of these contexts you would be confident in asking such a colleague to teach the child. Decide what sort of briefing you'd need to give.

Vellutino and Scanlon (2003) make a strong case for the value of individual tuition to prevent children falling behind or remaining behind. It is easy to see occasions when a little individual help will prevent the development of low self esteem, low motivation and low achievement. However, individual work should not just be offered to children who struggle: every child will benefit from high quality tailored work with an astute teacher.

There is no perfect formula for constructive individual work but there are two basics which will certainly help: you have to give it enough time to be valuable, never less than five minutes, and you must give the child with whom you are working your complete attention. A session is likely to have these elements:

- Identification of the teaching and learning focus – this has to be specific and attainable
- Preliminary talk about the text to help the child to focus

- Coaching while listening (balanced with encouraging independence)
- Praise and articulation of achievement with the child
- Identification of a context in which the new skills and knowledge will be used

When working with a child, your response and your encouragement will make a great difference. This is highly skilled, intense work because you make split second assessments, analyses and coaching decisions. To do this effectively, you need to identify what is being achieved and reinforce it while addressing what is going wrong. Far too often teachers, in a proper zeal for progress, focus on errors but all learners also need achievements noted and praised. This enhances confidence and highlights successful strategies. It is probably best not to interrupt the flow of reading to praise but to wait for a natural break in the text. You might choose to praise:

- Word recognition: *I was so pleased you managed to read 'orange'. I heard you pause and then you managed it. How did you work it out?*
- Expression: *I loved the way you made your voice go deep and slow for the troll. It made it really scary. What made you decide that's how the troll should speak?*
- Use of punctuation: *I thought the way you paused for the commas was really good because it made it much easier for me to understand. Did it help you too?*
- Self-correction: *I got worried when you forgot to read 'after'. Then you went back to it and put it in and made it right. When did you realise you'd left it out?*

Each one of these examples pinpoints the success and poses a question designed to enhance the reader's conscious awareness of useful strategies. Informed praise is not an extra: it is a primary teaching strategy.

You will also need to be able to analyse and respond appropriately to errors. Teachers still draw on Goodman's work on **miscue analysis** (1969) which saw text as offering cues to which the reader responds. When the child misuses a cue it is called a miscue. The main things which can go wrong when reading are shown in Table 3.1.

The hardest teaching skill when working with an inexperienced reader is keeping your mouth shut. If something goes wrong and you immediately offer help or guidance, you are taking over the responsibility for analysis and making the child dependent on you, reinforcing feelings of inadequacy. Francis (1999) showed the importance of self-correction in children's development as readers. Children need time to realise the problem and self-correct as this ensures that they process the text and monitor their accuracy in reading. (I find it useful to recite a limerick in my head when a miscue occurs; if it hasn't been corrected by the time I've finished, then it is safe to conclude the child needs help. This delay also gives time to consider the child, the text, the recent teaching and the recent pattern of attainment as all these factors will help you to decide the best way forward.)

Table 3.1   The main kinds of miscues children show when reading

Miscue	Explanation, example and suggestion for helping. The correct sentence is: *Tizzy was a lurcher puppy*
Omission	The reader misses out a word or phrase *Tizzy was a puppy* At a logical breaking point, tell the child you are going to reread the sentence as she read it and you want her to find the word which got missed out. (Sometimes words are omitted simply because the child is rushing forward in the story. Other children move swiftly over a problematic word in the hope you aren't listening properly and won't notice). The coaching will have broken the flow of meaning so, if you want the child to read more, you will have to reread enough to her to re-establish the context.
Substitution	The reader substitutes a real word (take note of whether it is similar in structure or meaning) *Tizzy was a lunch puppy* The substitution is similar in structure so your intervention needs to focus on checking for meaning. Pose a question which focuses on the unlikelihood of the reading. Then praise the amount of decoding which was correct and identify the graphemes which need further work. *Tizzy was a lovely puppy* This substitution fits the context well so you need to encourage the reader to check by using decoding skills. She has looked at the first letter and then made an intelligent prediction so you need to decode all through the word. If the word is likely to be a new addition to the child's vocabulary you must define it.
Refusal	The reader makes no attempt *Tizzy was a …* It is usually best to work together on decoding the word. Then use sentence structure and knowledge of the subject to reach a meaning. The coaching in both prime approach and checking strategies will give greater confidence for the future.
Mispronunciation	The reader's decoding does not give a real word *Tizzy was a loocher puppy* At a logical breaking point, tell the child you are going to reread the sentence as she read it and you want her to find the word which seems a bit strange. In this example the correct word is probably unknown so you need to focus on phonic skills to reach a good pronunciation. *Tizzy was a lurcher poppery* Tell the child that the word is one she knows and that she's done well because she's got the right beginning. Then ask her to predict from her vocabulary and language comprehension and check by decoding the whole word (it must be the whole word because the child has probably got into the habit of making wild guesses after the first letter).
Addition	The reader adds something to the text! *Tizzy was a little lurcher puppy* This miscue needs sensitive handling as it is a sign of a child who is engaging thoroughly with the text. If the error occurs in fiction it is best to take the approach that the writer probably thought about including the added words but decided against it. Then discuss the advantages of each version. Additions in non-fiction texts need to focus on the importance of learning from the text and bringing existing knowledge of the subject to the text.

Miscue	Explanation, example and suggestion for helping. The correct sentence is: *Tizzy was a lurcher puppy*
Reversal	The reader approaches a word or phrase from the right rather than the left *Tizzy saw a lurcher puppy*
	Reversals are a specific form of substitution and need to be approached in similar ways. Many new readers reverse occasionally but if reversals are very frequent, it's sensible to make careful notes to establish a pattern, as this may need referral.
Omission of punctuation	The reader ignores the instruction given by the punctuation marks This error shows that the child is so fixed on getting the words right that she is losing sight of the meaning. Work on the passage together using the punctuation to convey the meaning.
Inappropriate pause	A pause is either in the wrong place or is too long. *Tizzy was a … lurcher puppy* In this example, the pause shows that the child needed time to decode the daunting word. This needs informed praise followed by you quietly rereading the sentence so that it is fixed as a unit in her memory, giving the information needed to move forward in the reading.

The class reader

Many students recall the pleasure of the teacher reading to them every day. This practice has seemed to have fallen away now as we frequently read to children as part of the shared work within lessons. This isn't the same as the time when children were allowed to enter into the book world solely for the pleasure it could offer: no comprehension activities, no analysis of authorial devices, no discussion of characterisation or structure – just a wonderful wallow in another world. A recent survey (Ward, 2009) confirmed that whole book reading was uncommon but found most head teachers felt that a return to it would be beneficial. It is the way that many children are introduced to the pleasures of books and gives a real reason for persevering with the arduous work of learning to read. Last Christmas, my 95-year-old father was delighted to be given a copy of *Black Bartlemy's Treasure* by Jeffery Farnol, a book he remembered being read to him when he was ten. I can't think of any better evidence for the value of drawing children into the world of books by reading to them. If reading to children can still have an impact 85 years later, it has to be worth doing.

 Talk about the books you remember loving as a child, particularly the ones read to you at home or school. What made them special? Do they give you any ideas about choosing books to read to the class? Read one book which a friend loved but is new to you.

After the primary phase (KS3)

Though most children will have developed well as readers at primary school, they will not, at 11, be equipped with all the skills and knowledge needed to handle the secondary curriculum. Colleagues teaching at KS3 will therefore prioritise:

- Reading for understanding across a range of genres
- Reading as a research tool
- Evaluating text
- Appreciating the author's intentions
- Responding to texts
- Handling demanding genres
- Developing stamina as an independent reader

Teachers will ensure that the texts provided are of the correct technical difficulty for the readership but will also participate directly in teaching reading skills related to a specific subject – reading as a scientist or reading as part of drama for example.

Chapter summary

- Reading is a complex process in which decoding and understanding work together
- Understanding, in its many forms, is the purpose of reading
- Teachers need to model both how to read and why to read every day
- Children will make little progress unless they enjoy reading and find it purposeful and rewarding
- Teachers undertake a wide range of activities to teach reading

Further reading

Gamble, N. and Yates, S. (2008) *Exploring Children's Literature* (2nd edn). London: SAGE.
Goodwin, P. (ed.) (2011) *The Literate Classroom* (3rd edn). Abingdon: Fulton.
Rose, J. (2006) *The Independent Review of Early Reading*. London: DCSF.
Wyse, D. and Jones, R. (2008) *Teaching English Language and Literacy* (2nd edn). Abingdon: Routledge.

References

Ahlberg, J. and Ahlberg, A. (1983) *Peepo*. London: Puffin.
Ahlberg, J. and Ahlberg, A. (1990) *The Baby's Catalogue*. London: Puffin.
Cremin, T., Mottram, M., Collins, F., Powell, S. and Safford, K. (2009) 'Teachers as readers: building communities of readers', *Literacy*, 43(1): 11–19.

Department for Education (DfE) (2010) *The Importance of Teaching: The Schools White Paper* 2010. London: TSO.

Francis, N. (1999) 'Self-correction patterns and metalinguistic awareness: a proposed typology for studying text-processing strategies of proficient readers', *Journal of Research in Reading*, 22(3): 304–310.

Gamble, N. and Yates, S. (2008) *Exploring Children's Literature* (2nd edn). London: SAGE.

Goodman, K. (1967) 'Reading: a psycholinguistic guess game', *Journal of the Reading Specialist* (May): 126–135.

Goodman, K. (1969) 'Analysis of oral reading miscues', *Reading Research Quarterly*, 5(1): 9–30.

Gough, P. and Tunmer, W. (1986) 'Decoding, reading, and reading disability', *Remedial and Special Education*, 7(1): 6–10.

Hallam, S., Ireson, S. and Davies, J. (2004) 'Primary pupils' experiences of different types of grouping in school', *British Educational Research Journal*, 30(4): 515–533.

Hutchins, P. (2001) *Rosie's Walk*. London: Red Fox.

Kutnick P., Ota, C. and Bernondini, L. (2008) 'Improving the effects of groupwork with young children, attainment attitudes and behaviour', *Learning and Instruction*, 18(1): 83–95.

Lewis, M. and Wray, D. (1997) *Extending Literacy: Children Reading and Writing Non-fiction*. London: Routledge.

Morgan, P.L., Fuchs, D., Compton, D.L., Cordray, D.S and Fuchs, L.S. (2008) 'Does early reading failure decrease children's reading motivation?', *Journal of Learning Disability*, 41(5): 387–404.

Neate, B. (2008) *Finding Out about Finding Out: A Practical Guide to Children's Information Books*. Winchester: Neate Publishing.

QCDA (2010) *The National Curriculum*. Coventry: QCDA.

Rose, J. (2006) *Independent Review of the Teaching of Early Reading*. London: DfES.

Safford, K., O'Sullivan, O. and Barrs, M. (2004) *Boys on the Margin: Promoting Boys' Literacy and Learning at Key Stage 2*. London: Centre for Literacy in Primary Education.

Sereno, S., O'Donnell, P. and Rayner, K. (2006) 'Eye movements and lexical ambiguity resolution: investigating the subordinate bias effect', *Journal of Experimental Psychology: Human Perception and Performance*, 32(2): 335–350.

Silani, G., Frith, U., Demonet, J.-F., Fazio, F., Perani, D., Price, C., Frith, C.D. and Paulesu, E. (2005) 'Brain abnormalities underlying altered activation in dyslexia: a voxel based morphometry study', *Brain*, 128(10): 2453–2461.

Vellutino, F. and Scanlon, D. (2003) 'Emergent literacy skills, early instruction and individual differences as determinants of difficulties in learning to read: the case for early intervention'. In S. Neumann and D. Dickinson (eds), *Handbook of Early Literacy Research*. New York: Guilford.

Ward, H. (2009) 'Primary teachers shun whole-book reading in class', *Times Educational Supplement*, 4 September.

Willis, J. and Reynolds, A. (2006) *Who's in the Loo?* London: Andersen.

CHAPTER 4

TEACHING PHONICS FOR READING AND WRITING

• analytical • decoding • discrete teaching encoding • grapheme • *The Independent Review of Early Reading* • Letters and Sounds • phoneme • Sir Jim Rose • syllable • synthetic • systematic phonics teaching

This chapter aims to:

- give an understanding of the current view of the place of phonics in early reading and writing
- consider why the subject has caused such controversy
- provide a baseline knowledge of the influential research in this area
- give definitions of the new terminology you'll need to understand
- explore ideas about recommended approaches to planning, teaching and assessing progress

The subject of phonics merits a chapter to itself because it is one of the first really difficult subject issues you'll need to address in your training to teach. As a primary teacher, you'll either be overtly teaching phonics at KS1 or consistently drawing on, reinforcing and contextualising the learning at KS2. The government has placed great faith in systematic synthetic phonics as a means to improve standards in early reading and spelling and schools have made significant changes to approaches to teaching. The way in which you teach phonics won't be the same as the way you were taught so it is important to grasp what is expected of you as a teacher and why the changes have been made.

The independent review of early reading

In 2006 the Department for Education and Skills published the *Independent Review of the Teaching of Early Reading*. Written by Sir Jim Rose (you'll often find it called the Rose Review), it recommended that 'high quality phonic work should be taught as the prime approach in learning to decode (to read) and encode (to write/spell) print' (Rose, 2006: 70). It would be easy to misinterpret this statement as meaning that good phonics teaching leads to good reading and writing but this is certainly not what the review recommends. It shows clearly that formal phonics work must be preceded by the development of speaking and listening. Phonics must also be set in the context of a 'broad and rich' language curriculum. So, Rose certainly didn't say that phonics was the sole method of learning to read or even that it was the first priority for teachers. The review suggests that phonics is the best way to begin formal reading instruction with most five-year-old children.

There are several issues to untangle from the previous paragraph. The first is that it would be easy to assume that before the Independent Review there was little teaching of phonics. This certainly wasn't so; because the English writing system is based on the symbols representing linguistic noises (unlike some systems where the symbols represent meanings) learners have always needed to be taught the complex relationships between letters and sounds. There were several programmes for teaching phonics available, with **Jolly Phonics** in particular being used a great deal. So you could argue that Rose was validating the way most teachers were thinking and that the changes advocated weren't very large.

The second thing which merits a bit of extra thought is the meaning of 'prime' in the quotation above. It is an interesting choice of word which could be interpreted to mean 'first', 'best', 'chief' or 'main'. The context set by Rose certainly suggests that speaking and listening work comes first – not formal phonics teaching. Early years specialists such as Browne (2009) certainly maintain that introduction to formal phonic work before the prerequisite ease with oral and aural language is secure could be detrimental to children's development. The interpretation of 'prime' to mean 'chief' is also clearly wrong as Rose is emphatic about the necessity for contextualising phonics so that children learn both to love the written word and to understand how meaning is drawn from text.

This leaves 'best' and 'main' as the most likely meanings; the recommendations of the Independent Review suggest that the intended interpretation is somewhere between the two when referring to the skills of reading. Phonics is seen as the best method for easing children into reading and the main method so that they are first taught the strategies which are most likely to offer success. Rose certainly recommends that formal teaching of the skills of decoding text should focus on the correspondence between phonemes and graphemes and the best strategies for blending these to reach a probable pronunciation for the word on the page.

It is worth dispelling a few prevalent myths about the *Independent Review of Early Reading*. Rose does not say that children should be taught to read through a formal programme of discrete phonics teaching at KS1. He does recommend, however, that short daily lessons of high quality phonic teaching should be a part of the formal teaching of reading. Nor does Rose state the programme that needs to be followed, though he shows clearly that it should be based initially on the systematic teaching of skills and knowledge of synthetic phonics. Though the review suggests that it is in the best interests of learners to be completely at ease with the phonics system and adept at using it in both reading and spelling by the end of Key Stage 1, Rose doesn't suggest that it is wise to start formal teaching too soon. His first recommendation is that speaking and listening need to be in place first. They are the giant shoulders upon which all literacy stands.

The research background

The Government's commissioning of the Independent Review came out of a context of increasing, though not always strongly evidence-based, concern about the standards of children's reading. This, and the publication of influential research which advocated the efficacy of synthetic phonics in enhancing reading standards, led to the remit of the Independent Review including 'what best practice should be expected in the teaching of early reading and synthetic phonics' (Rose, 2006: 7). It is important to be aware that the inclusion of synthetic phonics was a given at the outset of the fact-finding and research for the review. The intention was to identify how phonics could be taught effectively.

So, the parameters were set before the review was undertaken. They derived from a growing research focus on the value of phonics in early reading. As in all changes of this kind, it is hard to identify a single source; there was a gradual move back to the systematic teaching of phonics shown in the publication of phonically based reading schemes such as *Bangers and Mash* (1976) and *New Way* (1989) as well as support materials like *Letterland* (1985). This movement away from the 'look and say' and 'whole language' approaches shows that the growing research interest was influencing teachers and publishers.

This was not the first use of phonics in teaching reading. There was a focus in early twentieth century education on **sub-lexical** features (units smaller than the word); this was very much concerned with breaking words into **syllables**. (You will often see hyphens separating the syllables in very old children's books.)

The next important focus on phonics was in the 1960s when there was a recognition that English, due to its splendid inconsistencies, presents particular problems to the inexperienced reader. This led to educationalists changing the language structure in 'reading books' to make the decoding more logical, modifying the language so that phonic strategies would always be successful. The Initial Teaching Alphabet which offered a unique grapheme (written symbol) for each phoneme (linguistic sound) had a long period of popularity (Downing, 1964). Another system used different colours to distinguish nuances of pronunciation, rather disregarding the proportion of boys who have some degree of colour blindness.

Inevitably, teaching methods which modified the task so children learnt to read a 'beginners' language gradually faded away when teachers realised that the transition to reading and writing conventional English was difficult for many children. Systems that taught that reading could be mastered with a single stratagem failed to equip children with the range of approaches demanded by the real language.

Interest in phonics resumed in the 1980s. In British studies, Bradley and Bryant (1983) were very significant as they reported a strong link between children's ability to recognise rhyme and their development as competent readers. It was almost the educational equivalent of splitting the atom – the word wasn't the smallest useful unit for the beginning reader. If children could understand what went on inside the word, they would have greater insights into the ways in which the 'sub-atomic' building blocks link and combine to create language. This approach was extended in the work of Goswami and Bryant (1990) which divided monosyllabic words (or each syllable in longer words) into the onset and rime, with the rime being the **vowel** and any **consonants** which follow it and the onset being any consonants which come before the vowel. Again, this research found that focus on units smaller than the word was greatly beneficial to readers because it led them to strategies for decoding the unfamiliar. It formalised naturally occurring linguistic play and drew upon it to develop reading skills and strategies.

The long history of playground chants, rhymes, riddles and tongue-twisters shows us that children enjoy playing with words. This play usually focuses on sound patterns as in this example overheard while on playground duty:

Wayne: There once was this boy called Lee
            Who done a wee in his tea
Lee: There once was this boy called Wayne
            And he done the same

While this isn't the sort of evidence we usually collect for assessment purposes, it shows the spontaneous use of some very sophisticated language analysis! These six-year-old children were using their phonic knowledge for the sheer fun to be derived from the language: I hadn't the heart to tell them off. There is another point to including this example: the language children bring to school and use to enhance their phonic knowledge may not be desirable. There is a real issue for teachers who believe in an inclusive, individualised education. Whose existing knowledge do we cherish and celebrate and whose do we discard? It is all English; it is all a basis for further learning.

Though the research mentioned above had encouraged us to teach about the structures within words, the focus was on splitting the syllable into onset and rime, then deriving knowledge about groups of letters and their corresponding sounds which then could be applied to other contexts. For example if children knew 'chip', the onset 'ch' could then be used to help decode words such as *ch*ocolate, *ch*ildren, *ch*oose etc. The rime 'ip' helps with all words with 'ip' endings. Essentially, children had to analyse groups of known words to discover the common linguistic elements and could then identify these to approach unknown words with similar patterns. This approach became known as **analytic phonics**.

The alternative approach to this analytical method has become known as **synthetic phonics**. It involves children being taught the 44 phonemes of English and the graphemes most likely to represent them. To pronounce a word, children identify the graphemes, pronounce each and then blend them together. They decode the word by consideration of each phoneme in sequence. When children use the same knowledge to spell, they isolate each phoneme in the spoken word, choose the most likely grapheme and then write these sequentially.

    Expert reflection

Professor Rhona Johnston: Phonics and the teaching of reading

I knew nothing about phonics as a child – I was born and educated in England and phonics had gone out of fashion by the time I started school. My first experience of phonics was when I was on a teacher training course in Scotland. One of my classmates showed me some materials that she made for her class, which showed how adding an 'e' to words like 'tub' and 'cub' changed the pronunciation. I was astounded! As a teacher I found the phonics approach to be very effective. As a lecturer in a psychology department I was fortunate enough to meet Joyce Watson, who was a lecturer in a college of education. We embarked on studies of the effectiveness of phonics teaching, which culminated in the Clackmannanshire study. In our research we found that the synthetic phonics approach was much better than the analytic phonics approach that was used in Scotland and England. In the synthetic phonics method, children are taught to sound and blend letter sounds in unfamiliar words right at the start of teaching. For example, after a few lessons where the children learnt the sounds for the letters 's', 'a', 't', and 'p', they read words such as 'tap', 'pat', 'sat', 'as', 'at' and 'sap' for themselves via sounding and blending. They also learnt to

> segment spoken words like these for spelling. This led to the children reading very well indeed. At the end of the 7th year of school, the children in our study read words 3.5 years ahead of what was expected for their age. Their reading comprehension and their spelling was also significantly better than expected. Both boys and girls did very well, but the boys had better word reading and spelling! There were also very low levels of underachievement, even though nearly half of the children came from schools in areas of deprivation.
>
> *(Professor Rhona Johnston, Department of Psychology, University of Hull)*

This approach has been very influential recently, mostly due to a large research study undertaken by Johnston and Watson (2005). This project followed a decade of earlier research in several settings and drew on the work of other researchers such as Turner (1990).

Wyse and Goswami (2008) are among the researchers who question whether the accumulated evidence of the value of synthetic approaches merits the claims made for it. Though Rose acknowledged 'uncertainties' (2006: 4) in the research findings he advocated synthetic approaches as being 'the best and most direct route' (2006: 4) into early reading. Johnston and Watson's research informed the recommendations of *The Independent Review of the Teaching of Early Reading* (Rose, 2006) and the model of hierarchical teaching of *Letters and Sounds* (DfES, 2007).

 What have you been taught about how young children learn? How well does this fit the models of teaching phonics?

It would be very tempting to leave the research here. As a student teacher coming to an understanding of early reading, you may think, 'The decisions have been made; now tell me how to do it.' However, your role is to make the current framework of expectations for teaching work as well as possible for every individual child. To do this, you need to know both the strengths of phonics so that you can teach with knowledge, confidence and enthusiasm, and any potential areas of difficulty. There has been a great deal of controversy about the value of synthetic phonics teaching; understanding the concerns will enable you to ensure that the children you teach enjoy reading and make good progress.

The agreed strengths of the phonics approach are that, as English has an alphabetic system, it is important that readers are taught the probable relationships between letters and sounds. Grugeon et al. (2007), in their excellent overview of the research, identify the compelling wealth of evidence that systematic phonics teaching plays an important role in early reading. It is also important for spelling, as Davies (2000) suggests; even if phonic strategies will not always lead to an accurate spelling of every word thay ar likelee too mayk yore ide ears com pree hence ibell too yor reeder.

Another important strength is that phonics teaches strategies which help children gain some independence as a reader very quickly. For example, if a teacher spends a week teaching the words *up, down, fun, go, ball, the,* the children will know six words. If the same time is spent teaching *s, a,t, p, i, n* children can use this knowledge to attempt to read or spell about 30 words (one of my groups of students found 40 words but they weren't all English, useful or suitable for five-year-olds). This independence gives an opportunity to use the learning throughout the school day and in the home. Frequent successful encounters with print build competence and motivation; good phonics teaching offers these.

The concerns about phonics teaching are not therefore about whether it has a place in the early teaching of reading. They are much more about what type of phonics, what else is needed, and when phonics should be introduced. One issue about using a solely synthetic approach to early reading (which is *not* advocated by Rose) is that there is little focus on deriving meaning from text. For example these two blocks of graphemes would be equally easy to 'read':

Fred saw a kitten and a guppy

Grut oot e fidder erp e fotty

If children are taught to believe that reading means making the correct noises in response to the stimulus of the graphemes, they are unlikely to find it purposeful or enjoyable. Equally importantly perhaps, they will not bring their knowledge of the world, of how language is put together, or their vocabulary to the text. This means that they will have little way of checking whether they have read something correctly or not. If reading is the process of gaining meaning from a text, decoding the symbols is an essential step, not the end of the journey.

The second criticism is that decoding, for the inexperienced reader, is very slow. The reader has to identify the first grapheme, recall the most likely phoneme correspondence, store it in the memory, return to the text, identify the next grapheme, recall the most likely phoneme correspondence, store it, return to the text ... etc all through the word. Then she has to store that word in her memory before going on to the next one and going through the whole recognition and decoding process again. Experienced readers have to decode words too but we do it so quickly that there is less problem about gradually building an understanding of the writer's meanings through augmenting our stored knowledge with each new word.

As suggested by Harrison (2004) it is also worth considering when we use synthetic phonics as a first stratagem and when a checking device. In the *Fred* example above, you probably predicted the final word as 'puppy' but then checked, using graphemic knowledge, to recognise that the text was playing spiteful tricks on you. You used a combination of approaches to reach an accurate reading. This leads to one of the most pertinent issues relating to synthetic phonics. If we are fairly sure that adults use several strategies to gain meaning from text, we need to consider whether teachers should work with only one of the strategies. All readers need to have ways of checking whether they are right. Haylock (2010) shows, in the context of maths teaching, that children need to move to a different stratagem to check their work effectively. The same is true for reading. If we teach only one way, we give no way of confirming that the right reading decisions have been made.

The most basic concern about programmes based on synthetic phonics is the implied model of the child as a learner. In this system we start all children with something they could not be expected to know and then progress as swiftly as possible along a linear programme. This model assumes that all children learn in the same way and that what they may have previously discovered about reading from home and environment isn't of much relevance. This seems to be very much in contrast to the best practices of early education where we celebrate the diversity of learners and base our teaching on what they already understand. We could argue that, if this is our belief about the rest of the curriculum, there is no reason for reading to be different. Children bring rich and varied experiences to all their learning, and continue to do so throughout their formal education. In reading, as in all education, this should be our starting point.

Recently, when mentoring a student teacher during a reception phonics lesson, a girl was working with miniature beanbags with the letters *s a t p i n* on them. She selected *s i t,* pronounced each corresponding phoneme, blended them perfectly and then remarked cheerfully, 'When you've learnt me "h" I can make a swear word.' From a very little formal instruction in phonics, she had worked out the way the system would work, including the consonant **digraph**.

What does this incident imply about teachers' role in determining the pace and sequence of phonic knowledge taught through Letters and Sounds?

Before the primary phase

Starting with phonic work in EYFS

Success as a primary teacher is based on the hard work undertaken by EYFS colleagues, families and the children themselves. A great deal of learning about language will have happened before the children reach Key Stage 1 with most children reaching the stage of recognising simple grapheme/phoneme correspondences by the end of the reception year. However, it is important to keep in mind that children develop in different ways and in different time scales, and a summer born child simply hasn't had nearly as much time to learn about language as an autumn born classmate. The great skill of EYFS teachers is matching the learning to the child so that a confident eagerness to learn is acquired through consistent success.

(Continued)

(Continued)

You can be sure that during the Early Years Foundation Stage all children will have been taught to:

- distinguish linguistic sound from other noises by listening carefully (important because children live in a sound-rich world and have to be able to focus attentively on speech before they can begin to work with words and sounds)
- divide blocks of speech into separate words (in normal speech there are seldom gaps between words. We can't teach about words until we have taught children to break down phrases)
- group words by sound patterns, identifying rhyme and alliteration (this is a significant landmark achievement as children have to be able to group by a new criterion, previously they have built their knowledge of words around meaning)
- break words into syllables (this needs to be based on a rich provision of rhymes, jingles, songs and games)
- break down words into their phonemes by careful listening (when children can do this they are probably ready for systematic teaching of phonemes and graphemes)

This section is no more than a quick overview for student teachers on primary programmes. Further reading is suggested at the end of this chapter. It is also essential that every primary teacher has time to watch a really good EYFS colleague at work on early literacy. It's always impressive.

Teaching phonics at Key Stage 1

Sometimes when you teach, an answer to a question shows you just how much you had been assuming. Recently, one hour into a session with student teachers on discrete phonics, a sudden awareness of the mystified looks on a couple of faces made me ask what was puzzling them. One student replied, 'If I've got to teach it discreetly, wouldn't it be better not to have separate lessons? I mean, won't they notice that it's phonics?' At this point I realised that I had blithely been using terminology which was confusing the students. 'Discrete' means separate: an easy way of not getting the two words confused is to remember that when it means 'separate' the two 'e's are separated by the 't'.

All Key Stage 1 classes should have a short discrete phonics lesson every day. This is likely to be taken directly from or based on **Letters and Sounds** which gives a clear hierarchical programme with a recommended pace which enables children to have cracked the phonics code and be using it independently and easily for both reading and spelling by the time they start Key Stage 2. Some schools will use sources such Jolly Phonics or Big Cat Phonics to give ideas for activities and to provide materials. Increasingly schools are basing phonics teaching on schemes such as **Read, Write Inc.** which offer a comprehensive coverage of early phonics.

Daily lessons are important because they enable teachers to build on what has just been taught before children forget it. The lessons are short because of the intensity of the work which is undertaken. Another advantage is that, in a short session, it is easy to keep the focus on one clear, simple objective involving new learning. This should ensure a sense of achievement: every lesson the children are promised a new, useful piece of knowledge, and if the lesson is well-planned, skilfully taught and engaging, children will make good progress.

Table 4.1   Planning for a typical discrete phonics session at KS1

	Approximate time	What you do	Why?
Revisit and Review	3 minutes	Remind children of what they learnt and enjoyed in the previous lesson. Ask them how they used this in the rest of the day. Praise them for remembering to use the new knowledge. Involve children in a very quick familiar game to revise the material covered on the previous day.	Children forget easily so knowledge has to be re-enforced. If you start with something which children have done before, you set an ethos of achievement for the whole lesson.
Teach	5 minutes	Explain what you are going to learn and why it is useful. Model the new learning, being very careful about terminology and clear pronunciation. It is often helpful to narrate your thought processes as you make decisions. Play a fully participative, multi-sensory game or work on an activity. As you are teaching, observe carefully and note children who are struggling.	Modelling the new learning will give the children confidence. They must be fully involved so that they learn actively (avoid turn taking around the class). Observe carefully so you will know where to make best use of your time.
Practise	3 minutes	With partners, ask the children to play a different game using exactly the same words or graphemes, or work together on a simple activity. You might also add in some material covered very recently. Use this time to guide anyone who had problems in the previous part of the lesson.	This is step towards independence. Children need to make decisions rather than follow direct instruction in order to grasp the new knowledge.
Apply	5 minutes	Model how the taught phoneme–grapheme correspondence can be used for encoding. In pairs play a writing game or work on a simple activity.	The children need to be aware that reading and writing are closely linked and that knowledge can be valuably transferred between the language modes.

Table 4.1 shows the normal organisation of a phonics lesson at KS1. The timings are very approximate and will vary day by day. This is the usual model but you may find it valuable to add another very short element which is best described as a 'trailer'. Finish the lesson by pointing out the opportunities there will be that day to make use of the new knowledge. Children could also be asked to think about opportunities to use the knowledge at home.

(In the plenary of a lesson on 'digraphs which are double letters')

Teacher:	... and at home? When might you read 'll' at home?
Molly:	Bedroom. On my door. My nan got me a sign with my name on. So I am going to read it. I've got a 'll' in the middle of Molly and I can read it and go in my bedroom.
Aleysha:	I've been to your house two times and I know where your bedroom is without reading!
Teacher:	When will you use 'll', Aleysha?
Aleysha:	My mum needed the Yellow Pages and we all looked and looked and I read 'yellow' and I found it.
Molly:	I don't need to read a 'll' to find it. It's big and yellow.

I rather like this example as it shows that the children can draw on phonic knowledge but also bring a shrewd understanding of the world to the solving of problems. When teaching phonics, the significance of what children already know should never be under-estimated.

There is a strength in the unvarying model of the discrete phonics lesson given above. Many children thrive on the security of a routine, particularly one which gives a new success every day. The consistent approaches to discrete phonics lessons could, without excellent teaching, also be a weakness as it is very easy to allow something so routine to become repetitive and dull. The teaching of new grapheme–phoneme correspondences could very easily be simply a matter of recognition and blending and the practise element just trying to write some words which include the focus grapheme. It takes skill to give new engaging contexts to the learning so that children both enjoy the novelty and appreciate the security. Here's an example of a student teacher getting the balance just right:

We were doing a topic on Water in my Year 1 class. The week before I had played phonic fishing by making fish with the week's graphemes on them. This week I wanted to move on to children blending adjacent consonants. I made a washing machine out of a box and got lots of different pairs of old socks. In each pair of socks I put two graphemes which can be blended. We started by making washing machine noises.: sw sw sw sw for the water going in, then fl fl fl for the washing flopping round, then sp sp sp sp for the very fast spinning and finally dr dr dr dr for the water draining away. We invented movements for each part of the cycle.

Then we took out all the socks and the children had to match them together, pronounce the phonemes and then blend them together. Some of the children didn't understand that most pairs of letters could only be blended in one pattern, e.g. CL was possible but LC wasn't so it was a good chance to teach it. Then they practised with a partner. They had to take one sock from a pair and guess the grapheme that there would be in the other one. To apply this each pair got two new socks, chose one of the adjacent consonant patterns and wrote two words to put in the socks. The next day we started our lesson by playing 'guess my pair'; we read the word in one sock and guessed what would be in the other. Later in the week we made a washing machine dance using the movements we had invented. *(Clare)*

Using the model of the discrete phonics lesson above, write a lesson plan for the learning and activities described here. Remember to start with an objective (or learning outcome) drawn from Letters and Sounds. Clare notes a misconception – think about how you would ensure you identified and addressed this.

Building on phonics at Key Stage 2

In Key Stage 2 the focus moves from 'learning to read to reading to learn' (Rose, 2006) but that certainly does not mean that children at the age of eight have gained the full range of reading skills which will carry them through adult life. As other reading strategies develop, children need to consolidate phonic knowledge for two main purposes: as an approach to unfamiliar words, and as a checking device to balance other strategies.

Phonic knowledge remains vital as a means of approaching new words even for fluent readers as, if a pronunciation can be drawn from the written word, children can then search their vocabularies created from aurally acquired knowledge to gain a meaning. Here is a fairly typical example from an eight year old boy reading a passage from *The Land of the Dragon King* by Gillian McClure (2008):

Liam: The people were [*Liam pauses then pronounces each syllable of the next word separately*] utt-er-ly utterly [*Liam pauses again, then breaks the next word into syllables*] miss-er-able, oh it's 'miserable' the young people were utterly miserable.
Teacher: Could you put that sentence into your own words?
Liam: Very sad?

(Extract from Land of the Dragon King by Gillian McClure reproduced with permission of Frances Lincoln Publishers)

Liam's phonic knowledge is enough to give him an accurate reading of 'utterly' but, unsurprisingly, doesn't take him to a correct pronunciation of 'miserable.' But here, his knowledge is still of immense value as it takes him close enough for him to find the nearest plausible pronunciation in his vocabulary and to correct his initial attempt. Even when approaching an irregular word, phonic knowledge will give enough information to access the reader's other knowledge (except in the cases of completely bizarre words such as 'yacht' whose very eccentricity usually amuses children so much that they learn them with enthusiasm).

Later in the same guided reading session Liam used his phonic knowledge as a checking device.

Liam: [*reads*] Then the magpies began their long flight up ... With wing overflapping wing and tail overflapping tail. [*He stops and looks again at 'overflapping'*] No there's no 'f'. Overlapping?

Teacher: That's right. Look at the picture. Can you see all the wings and tails over each other? They are overlapping. But 'overflapping' would be a lovely word, just right to describe a flock of birds flying together. Maybe you could remember it for when we rewrite this story in a different setting.

(Extract from The Land of the Dragon King by Gillian McClure reproduced by permission of Andersen Press)

In this example, Liam draws on his knowledge of birds to make an excellent prediction. However, when he looks carefully at the written word he recognises that his attempt must be wrong and corrects to what he realises the word must be even though he does not know it. Here the reading has enhanced the child's vocabulary.

In both these examples, the teacher is demonstrating the admirable skill of keeping her mouth shut. She gives time for Liam to recognise and rectify the error independently before offering support and encouragement. By doing this, the child is encouraged to draw on his knowledge to make independent decisions which enable him to draw meaning from text. His phonic strategies are gradually becoming embedded in his thinking so that he synthesises information from a range of sources to reach accurate readings.

Phonics for spelling at KS1

At Key Stage 1 children's spelling should reflect the gradual growth of phonic knowledge. The earliest attempts will show much more confidence with consonants than vowels because they are much easier to distinguish and easier to predict. Much early spelling will also reflect the child's accent. By the start of Key Stage 1 spelling should be horizontal and should represent the major sounds in the word from left to right. As children are taught through careful shared and guided work, and given opportunities for both independent writing and playing with words, there will be a parallel development of **encoding** and **decoding** skills using phonic strategies.

However, just as in spoken language development, there may be evidence of children learning and over-applying rules. Both these common Key Stage 1 mis-spellings – *gril* for *girl* and *whent* for *went* – are evidence of rule application drawn from reading. In *gril* the child has reasoned that the word certainly needs both sounds and as *gri* is quite common and *gir* infrequent, the first option is worth a try. The teaching stratagem here would be to pronounce the word slowly emphasising the individual sounds so that the child recognised the order of sounds rather than playing the odds with the letter combinations. *Whent* requires a different approach, praise for recognising the common pattern and an admission that *went* is one of the few words which are easier than you expect.

Though, as in the examples above, there is a danger of children seeing the common written patterns of graphemes within words when reading and then over-applying them, the rule creation more frequently creates accurate spellings. (The difficulty is that it is very much easier to analyse an error to understand what has gone wrong than it is to derive evidence of knowledge from an accurate spelling.) Rose (2006) drawing again on the Clackmannanshire evidence is confident that early phonic spelling is a mirror image of early phonic reading. This is very different from the traditional methods used in schools first advocated by Peters (1985). These, for example, linked the component letters of digraphs through kinaesthetic methods such as frequent practising of flowing hand movements creating a joined handwriting style. In discrete phonics lessons it is valuable to incorporate these methods into the segmenting of words for spelling. Children are taught to split the spoken word into phonemes, decide the graphemes to use and then write them with consistent movement. This happens in virtually every discrete phonics lesson.

Phonics for spelling at KS2

Most children will start Key Stage 2 using phonics as a first stratagem for encoding unfamiliar words. This should have given them an adventurous approach to vocabulary choice so that they will attempt words which they cannot yet spell conventionally. If reading involves comprehending the ideas of others, then spelling involves making your ideas comprehensible to others, as in this sample of Year 3 writing (a retelling of the Three Little Pigs).

> Captin Piglick said 'Singkrongiz your wodges and keep dow men. The woollfell soon be here' [*Synchronise your watches and keep down, men. The wolf'll soon be here.*]
>
> 'Yes sir'
>
> 'Here he comes. Downt pannick men. His armied veehickle wownt nock down this house.' [*Don't panic men. His armoured vehicle won't knock down this house.*]

Though this extract shows that the child's spelling is not yet conventional, he can convey his meaning with flair. His phonic knowledge has freed him to draw on a broad and rich vocabulary which engages the reader. All the wrong spellings are excellent phonic representations (when asked about 'wodges' it became clear that the writer had taken the phrase from an American movie and this was how he recalled the pronunciation; he thought it was some obscure equipment and was amazed when told that the soldiers were synchronising watches).

At this stage every teacher has to think very carefully about response: too much emphasis on accuracy at first draft may inhibit writers and even make them restrict their vocabulary to words which they know they can spell accurately. However, children also need to be taught that comprehensibility is no longer enough. If a piece of writing is to be published for a genuine audience, it needs to adopt conventional spellings. Importantly children have to recognise the importance society places on accuracy in spelling so need to move forward to a stage where phonics remains a useful strategy for writing a word quickly to convey the intended meaning which can then be corrected by drawing on other strategies (see Chapter 9).

At Key Stage 2 many children become anxious about spelling because they are flummoxed by the complexity of the system (Bell, 2004). Again phonics can be a great help. One of the problems comes from our perception that there are a great number of words which we cannot spell when, actually, this isn't the case at all. There are really a great number of words which have a problem area but the rest is accessible to phonic methods. Most adults can spell most of every word. The problem areas are usually to do with our peculiar vowel system or partial understanding of rules. This is a typical example from a colleague:

> In the session, I asked the students who couldn't spell 'professional'. Most agreed that they couldn't so we broke the word down. I asked who could spell 'pro' – everyone could. Everyone could spell 'ess' 'ion' and 'al' using analogies or phonics. We then agreed that the only problem was whether it needed a single or double f. From being a difficult word we had cut the problem down to being manageable. Then we thought again about knowledge of how syllables work and realised that there was no need for the syllable to start with a double letter.

It is easy to assume that, because phonic knowledge won't give complete mastery of the English spelling system, it is of little use with irregular words. This leads to teaching methods which make the task of learning unnecessarily difficult: there would, for example, be no advantage to using a look-cover-write-check method with 'professional' when we can work out most of the word phonically and only have to recall the tricky bit in the middle. Phonic approaches will get the word almost right; when combined with other approaches, accuracy can be attained. With spelling as with reading, children do not grow out of phonics but, through good teaching, learn to draw on them along with other strategies to ensure a confident accuracy with a complex task.

After the primary phase (KS3)

The Key Stage 3 strategy advocates the teaching of phonics in two different ways:

- For students who reached age expected standards in KS2, phonics teaching is embedded within each unit, with particular emphasis on spelling for overt teaching.
- Students who are still struggling with reading and or writing, are given additional help with phonics in separate lessons. There are also short coaching interventions for some children, often in the summer before starting secondary school.

The focus at KS3 is ensuring that students have the literacy skills to access the full curriculum and make progress. The strategy emphasises that students are still learning to read while reading to learn; new subject-specific terminology, for example, will place new challenges on existing phonics learning so phonics teaching is a responsibility for teachers of all subjects.

The successful aspects of Key Stage 2 phonics teaching are carried through to secondary school through teacher modelling demonstration and individual **target setting**.

Phonics across the curriculum

Children will not learn to use phonics as a central part of approaches to reading or spelling if they see 'phonics' as an isolated lesson which happens every day or something which gets mentioned now and then in literacy lessons. There has to be an expectation that phonic skills will be used across the whole curriculum. Whenever children need to read or write, they have the opportunity to draw on what they have been taught. However, there is a real danger of the reinforcement of phonic skills swamping the curriculum and turning every lesson into 'phonics in a different frock'. To avoid this, the planning for the curriculum objectives must always be the first priority; the opportunities to consolidate phonic knowledge are a bonus, but a bonus which can be planned.

These ideas should help to reconcile the need to ensure that children have every opportunity to see that phonic skills are useful with the rightful primacy of the subject being taught:

- at Key Stage 1, derive the example words for discrete phonics lessons from the topics to be taught across the curriculum. For example, if working on a topic of plants at the same time as vowel digraphs root, shoot, seed, soil and bean would be valuable words to choose
- make the links overt by linking forward to lessons when the words will be used or back to the time when the phonic knowledge was taught

- if working on spelling in any subject, work on one word only in your whole class work but ask children to make a note of any others which use taught patterns
- similarly, focus on decoding only one word in any shared reading work for another subject
- ask the children to report on the ways they have used phonic knowledge across the curriculum in the review part of the next phonics lesson
- use displays to remind children of the usefulness of the material, gradually adding words as they are read or written
- praise all independent use of phonic knowledge in any curriculum subject
- when assessing, identify words which the child should have been able to encode but ensure that you make written comments against the stated subject objectives: if someone has written an excellent report for science, it is grossly unfair to comment only on the spelling
- remember that difficulties with reading or writing can mask attainment and understanding in other subjects. If too much emphasis is put on the reinforcement of phonics, children may become less enthusiastic about subjects which they previously enjoyed and may not achieve their full potential

Phonics in the study of languages other than English

Many schools will choose to study one or more modern European language, usually starting at Y3 when the phonic knowledge and understanding for English is secure. The more children learn about other languages the easier it becomes for them to understand and describe the way in which the phonic system of English works. The sounds of the language, the rhythms and rhymes may differ but the similarities are vast. Children's phonic knowledge of English is intensified by experiencing different phonic patterns. Most MFL teaching will start with a focus on listening and then speaking with reading and writing coming a little later. This is an excellent opportunity to allow children to realise their English knowledge more openly as they compare the way another system works.

In learning a modern European language they will realise that the phoneme–grapheme correspondences are rather different even though the same basic alphabet is used. Children will also learn, if studying a modern European language, that most have devised more logical approaches to vowel phonemes and graphemes. This seems to help children acknowledge the difficulties of the English system, recognising that their spelling problems are largely because the system is just too complicated to be handled easily.

Some schools may take the opportunity to teach a phonically based language which uses a different set of alphabet symbols. This would give excellent opportunities to reflect on the known phoneme–grapheme correspondences of English and to make overt the processes of recognition and blending which many children, by Y3, will be using effortlessly. If a school has the opportunity to teach a logographic language, children will appreciate that the relationships between sounds, symbols and meanings can be approached very differently. Whatever the language that children learn, the opportunity to stand back from English and view it in the light of new perspectives will always strengthen existing knowledge.

Chapter summary

- Phonic knowledge and understanding is essential for reading and spelling
- Phonics teaching must be fast-paced, systematic and engaging
- The teacher must be able to model the sounds of English and use the technical terminology accurately
- Systematic, discrete phonics teaching occurs throughout Key Stage 1
- At Key Stage 2 teachers build on knowledge and apply it across the curriculum, with particular emphasis on spelling
- In the early years children are taught the beginnings of phonics
- It is essential that children are encouraged to use their phonic knowledge in every curriculum area
- Learning a new language will enhance phonic understanding for English

Further reading

Browne, A. (2009) *Developing Language and Literacy 3–8* (3rd edn). London: SAGE.
Johnston, R. and Watson, J. (2007) *Teaching Synthetic Phonics*. Exeter: Learning Matters.
Lewis, M. and Ellis, S. (eds) (2006) *Phonics: Practice, Research and Policy*. London: SAGE.
Nicholson, T. (2005) *Phonics Handbook*. Oxford: Wiley-Blackwell.

References

Bell, M. (2004) *Understanding English Spelling*. Cambridge: Pegasus Elliot Mackenzie.
Bradley, L. and Bryant, P. (1983) 'Categorising sounds and learning to read – a casual connection', *Nature*, 301: 419–421.
Browne, A. (2009) *Developing Language and Literacy 3–8* (3rd edn). London: SAGE.
Davies, A. (2000) 'The Phoneme Test: should all teachers pass it?', *Dyslexia Review*, 11(4): 9–12.
DfES (2007) *Letters and Sounds: Principles and Practice of High Quality Phonics*. London: DfES.

Downing, J. (1964) *The ITA Reading Experiment*. London: Evans.

Goswami, U. and Bryant, P. (1990) *Phonological Skills and Learning to Read (Essays in Developmental Psychology)*. London: Psychology Press.

Grugeon, E., Cremin, T. and Dembey, H. (2007) 'Literacy in the Early Years'. In T. Cremin and H. Dombey (eds), *Handbook of Primary English in Initial Teacher Education*. Leicester: UKLA/NATE.

Harrison, C. (2004) *Understanding Reading Development*. London: SAGE.

Haylock, D. (2010) *Mathematics Explained for Primary Teachers* (4th edn). London: SAGE.

Johnston, R.S. and Watson, J. (2005) *The Effects of Synthetic Phonics Teaching on Reading and Spelling Attainment: A Seven Year Longitudinal Study*. Scottish Executive Education Department. [Online] Available at: http://www.scotland.gov.uk/Publications/2005/02/20688/52449

McClure, G. (2008) *The Land of the Dragon King*. London: Frances Lincoln Books.

Peters, M. (1985) *Spelling: Caught or Taught?* London: Routledge and Kegan Paul.

Rose, J. (2006) *Independent Review of the Teaching of Early Reading*. London: Department for Education and Skills.

Turner, M. (1990) *Sponsored Reading Failure*. Worlingham: IPSET Education Unit.

Wyse, D. and Goswami, U. (2008) 'Synthetic phonics and the teaching of reading', *British Educational Research Journal*, 34(6): 691–710.

CHAPTER 5

LEARNING AND TEACHING WRITING: THE KNOWLEDGE AND PROCESSES OF COMPOSING TEXT

• audience • composition • development • enjoyment • genre
• independence • model • motivation • product • process • purpose
• reader • response

This chapter aims to:

- describe what writers do
- demonstrate the roles of the teacher throughout the writing process
- consider why some children find writing so difficult and unrewarding
- describe the main genres of writing expected in the primary school
- suggest constructive ways of responding to children's writing
- ensure that you feel motivated and excited about teaching writing

Writing is difficult. As you are reading this chapter, it is fairly likely that you have an assignment due; if that's the case you probably empathise with the view that writing isn't easy. In many ways the problems encountered when writing an assignment at university are an indication of the problems of virtually every kind of writing. Some of them are:

- it makes you feel vulnerable
- a lot depends on getting it right
- your reader isn't there so you don't get an immediate response
- people might judge you, not just your text
- it requires a great number of skills and many kinds of knowledge

If skilled, successful adults feel like that, it is unsurprising that young children often find writing very hard indeed. Yet one piece of research from the 1970s which had a huge influence on classroom practice showed something unexpected which certainly could be relevant in our teaching. Graves (1994) talked to and observed four- and five-year-old children in their first days of school. The majority told him that the purpose of school was to learn to read but all believed they could write and, when given an opportunity, produced attempts at writing. This initially seems very surprising; if we had to rank the language modes by difficulty, most of us would rate writing as being the hardest – yet little children confidently make marks which they believe convey their meaning. The solution may be that young children aren't yet aware of the magnitude of the task ahead of them. Even when the complexities of spelling and syntax are mastered, huge difficulties remain. Writers have to have something worth communicating and understand the most effective ways to convey meaning to an audience. Throughout our professional lives, particularly as teachers, the questions remain: Do I know enough to write? Will people understand what I'm trying to say? These are the important issues of writing and will be the focus of this chapter.

Martello's (1999) research indicated that school entrants not only believed that they could write but could produce at least one recognisable word. The emergent writing movement was informed by much early work on what children already knew about writing. It encouraged early attempts at written communication while modelling more advanced writing skills for children to imitate. It is a great pity that our primary education system does not continue to emphasise the fun and freedom of writing. It seems all too often to focus on the aspects of writing which children find very difficult, particularly spelling and handwriting, while discarding the confidence and knowledge which children are able to bring to the first steps of becoming a writer.

 ## Before the primary phase

In the home, most children will have seen adults writing for real purposes (emails, texts, lists, cards, notes, letters) and for real, specific people. They'll also have seen the ways people respond to writing and will have probably discovered that it is important for conveying information and enhancing relationships.

In EYFS children are given opportunities to experiment with mark making. They will frequently be involved in shared writing activities which introduce them to processes and will be given insights into a broad range of text types. They will be taught that linguistic sounds differ from other noises and can be represented by symbols. They will learn to recognise letters and to ascribe a corresponding sound to them.

Children as writers

Early voluntary writing is undertaken with panache. Here Molly is explaining what to write in a birthday card.

> *Molly*: This is for my nana. And it says 'I love you from Molly'. You see the crosses? They're kisses. When you make a card you have to kiss it and you put a cross shape on it for every time that you kiss it and that's how the person that it's for knows that you love them and you kissed the card. Didn't you know that?

Molly (aged four) has got the basic idea of writing: it has a communicative purpose, a real audience and a special code which lets the recipient know what you are thinking. What's more, she wants to do it because she knows that her card will bring pleasure to someone she cares about. We need to celebrate early enthusiasm, nurture it and help children grow into writers with something to say, a knowledge their work will appreciated, and the necessary skills to convey their ideas successfully.

Grainger (2005: 88) recommends that teachers offer children 'engaging invitations' to write while teaching them about how text works and how writers work to create text. She suggests that teachers need to participate fully with children throughout the writing process showing that we find writing useful and enjoyable. For children like Molly, this involves building on the knowledge they have gained about writing at home. For other children, teachers give a first taste of the power and pleasure of text. The powerfulness of text can certainly be one of the 'engaging invitations' for young writers as it gives them the opportunity to convey their beliefs, opinions and imaginings to audiences far beyond their families, schools and communities. The power of text is so strong that there was controversy in the nineteenth century about whether poor children should be taught to write (Collingwood and Collingwood, 1990) which led to riots.

It could be that both the current experience of young learners and the historical data offer ideas about criteria which make writing important to children:

- They have to have something important they want to write about rather than something they have been told to write
- They have to know that someone is going to read their work for its intended purpose (not to assess it or criticise it)

- They understand the form of writing which best matches their purpose
- The writing activity is not going to outlast their stamina as writers
- They have time to think and plan
- They have a right to make decisions
- They can seek help from others

Expert reflection

Liz Chamberlain: Take one question and then one more

'What do you need if you are going to do some writing?' If you ask Reception children this question they'll tell you that they can use paint, or sand, some glitter, or even alphabet beads to do their writing with. These children are all at the mark making stage of writing but they already see themselves as writers. If you ask Year 4 children what's required, they'll tell you that you need a pen or a pencil, some paper and more often than not a rubber. But for one boy, all you need is 'a pen and an idea'.

Having an idea seems like a very good place to start because without having something to say and someone to say it to, writing remains a task rather than a unique opportunity to explore a thought, to expand an idea or the chance to be creative. When we talk with children about writing, they can sometimes think that we mean the type of writing that leads to an end product or an enterprise that results in an engagement with the skills of punctuation, spelling and handwriting.

This can often lead to children seeing a type of writing that happens at school, which differs to the wide range of writing activities they engage with outside of school. We need to help children move away from a narrow view of writing defined only by the transcriptional or secretarial skills and move towards a shared understanding of writing as a process of capturing ideas, drafting, refining and ultimately finding an audience for those ideas.

When one child was asked 'What does your teacher need to know about you and writing?' he responded, 'Even though I'm not very good at it, I still really enjoy it'. Asking questions can be a very good starting point in knowing about the young writers you have in your class.

(Liz Chamberlain is a Senior Lecturer in curriculum English, University of Winchester and was Strategic Consultant for 'Everybody Writes')

Motivating children to write

If you turn the list of criteria above into negatives, you get a fair description of some of the reasons why writing seems so unattractive to many children. There is extensive research across the English writing world into the reasons why children are underachieving as writers, much of which clusters the factors into three very broad areas: the nature of the writing being demanded; the ways in which we teach and assess; and issues to do with ways in which children get the words onto paper or into the computer (National Commission for Writing, 2003). Though much of the current British research focuses on boys' under-achievement in writing, it could be that the factors which lead boys to dislike writing also influence girls, but they are less likely to make their feelings obvious in their performance (Bruce, 2002).

UKLA's (2006) research also grouped the issues about motivation around what children are expected to write and how writing is taught and assessed. The issue of motivation being related to perception of competence was also explored by Bearne and Warrington (2003) who identified the following things as being important. Though their focus was specifically on boys, everything in this list is appropriate for all young writers.

- Engage children in talk before writing
- Demonstrate the writing to be undertaken (with a commentary which makes the decision-making obvious) in shared, guided and paired work
- Broaden the view of what counts as text (to include visual and multi-media work)
- Consolidate writing of new genres across the whole curriculum systematically
- Focus first on compositional aspects in any writing (the focus on presentation and spelling come in once the ideas are captured and developed)
- Give enough time for writing to be sustained and completed (this can't be rushed. We all need time to think, experiment, plan, draft and polish our texts)

Select a lesson which you have already taught and try to modify it to incorporate all the bullet point ideas above. Identify those which need consideration in medium term planning and in other curriculum areas.

I would add one thing to this list: never ask children to write something which you haven't tried to write yourself. If you find it hard to motivate yourself to write, it is certain children will too. Here's an example from Laura's reflection (*second year BEd*).

> We were doing diaries and I got the children to do another diary entry for Anne Frank's diary. It was horrific. None of them got more than about four lines written. I told my mentor and she sat me down with a sheet of paper and told me to do the same task. I couldn't do it. I think part of it was because I didn't know enough to write it and another part was that it felt disrespectful to make a fiction out of something like that when it had really happened. So next lesson I talked to the class about how I'd felt when I tried to do the writing and I asked them to write a reaction diary (I did one too) – just about what reading the Anne Frank diary made them think and feel. This was much better.

Expert reflection

Georgina Dawson: Talk for writing – The Mantle of the Expert

To enhance children's writing, I believe that teachers need to develop contexts for learning that are purposeful, authentic and meaningful, exploring the language and meaning through a drama convention called Mantle of the Expert, invented by Dorothy Heathcote in the 1980s. This involves children being themselves, but thinking, discussing and making decisions as if they are responsible for things that happen within the adult world.

I like to challenge children, so one of my favourite scenarios, usually carried out with Year 5 or 6 classes, is based on marine conservation. I start by explaining MoE and then go into role as Head of International Conservation Services in order to inform the children that they will need to complete new Curriculum Vitae pro-forma as their originals have been mislaid. Children then have to think quickly and record what knowledge and skills they will need, sharing and comparing ideas.

The children then find out that a previously unrecorded stingray has been found dead and is to be sent to our base; they will need to undertake an examination of it in order to determine the cause of death. Before our 'stingray' arrives, children have opportunities to find out about stingrays through a short PowerPoint of pictures and some information strips. Once it does arrive, a group take on the autopsy under the guidance of their 'colleagues'. As the work develops, children's knowledge and understanding grows, as does their ability to present their findings, because they are truly their findings.

Although the example above progressed very much as I intended, children often take on so much control that the emphasis shifts. Working with a group of gifted Year 4 and 5 children writers for a whole week on story writing, we became a 'Charitable publishers', taking over from the missing owner. All children signed a contract to complete a story of at least 500 words which they honoured, but, in addition, they investigated the missing owner, 'found' letters from him and some went on a space voyage to Zog, where they encountered, recorded and classified the creatures they found.

MoE is not just for older children. I worked with F2 who had been researching penguins. Everyone put their coats on and went on a journey to stop the penguins walking the wrong way, slipping on the ice and falling in snow-holes on our journey. The maps of their journey then produced were complex and children were able to explain their journeys in detail.

The impact of this approach on children's learning is well documented. The opportunities they have for talking, doing and taking responsibility enable them to develop their thinking and acquire and use more sophisticated vocabulary, all of which feeds into their writing.

(Georgina Dawson is an educational consultant specialising in working with whole school policy on enhancing writing through talk)

The writing process

One of the points above was about extending the time taken on a single piece of text so that children have the opportunity to write in ways similar to adult writers. When adults need to write something important whatever the form, we tend to do these things:

- identify the task
- give ourselves time to think
- research the subject
- talk about it
- refer to successful models of similar writing to research the form
- consider the needs of the audience and the way we hope the writing will be perceived
- create a plan
- draft the writing
- share the draft
- make changes to the content
- check for accuracy and make changes
- if writing by hand, produce a final copy
- get the writing to the intended audience
- (immediately regret making the writing public as the many ways in which it could have been better become apparent)
- receive feedback

For most writers this takes a long time and also involves a great deal of movement, deferral activity and what, if we were ten, would probably be described as sulking. If the process is demanding for adult writers, it is even more so for children but, if you look at this model of the writing process, you will see that some of the stages we find so necessary are denied to children. The thinking and talking are essential to the process but are seldom recognised as such in school. When children wander around, ostensibly gathering equipment or seeking help or permission to go to the toilet, they are often seeking the time to think about their writing.

Even young children can undertake all the parts of the writing process listed above if they are supported and, even more importantly, the writing merits this considerable effort. Children are asked to do a great deal of writing which seems hurried, trivial and without a real purpose; it is unsurprising that they find the editing processes particularly unrewarding in these circumstances (Woodward, nd).

The teaching of writing should be focused on leading children towards adopting adult models of the writing process. This is not simple, as young children and inexperienced writers need a great deal of support while more experienced young writers need to have more opportunities to work independently. When moving to a new form of writing or considering the needs of a new audience, even experienced children will need a great deal of teacher support.

A basic model of teacher support is shown in Table 5.1.

The movement to independence needs to be monitored carefully. If children are expected to undertake too much of the writing process before they are ready, there will be failure and despondency. In this context, writing frames (see Lewis and Wray, 1998) are valuable in bridging the gap between teacher guided and fully independent work. However, overly prolonged support on any genre leads to over-dependency where children are reluctant to make decisions about work (e.g. ESTYN, 2006).

This section has focused on the processes used by all readers, and the models of support which lead children to being able to undertake work independently. These two elements are closely interwoven in a classic 'apprenticeship model' where a novice is taught through example so that the exemplification becomes internalised. When the knowledge is internalised the writer stands alone *on that specific genre*. Each new form of writing will require the same approach, though knowledge about editing and considering the audience needs will be transferred. Each revisiting of the process, while reminding the children of the ways of working, will move forward more swiftly.

Table 5.1 The teaching roles for different parts of the writing process

Stage of the process	Teaching activity	Why this is valuable
Identifying the task	Teacher talks about why this is worth writing and what she hopes to achieve.	Sets a context of importance which then offers ways of thinking for children to use to recognise the value of other writing tasks.
Thinking time	Teacher muses aloud about initial ideas and feelings about the writing.	Shows children the kinds of thinking writers undertake.
Researching the subject	Depending on the genre, the teacher shows how information is gathered or reminds herself about the features and success criteria for fiction writing in terms of audience response. This usually combines shared and modelled reading.	Involves the child with the writing by activating existing knowledge and providing the information needed to complete the work successfully.
Talking prior to writing	The teacher shares plans for the writing while incorporating children's ideas and answering their questions and responding to their ideas.	Talking acts as a rehearsal for writing, consolidates ideas and acts as an oral form of editing, saving time and effort by screening out poor ideas. It should also engender excitement about the writing.
Research the form of the writing	The teacher and class together identify the text organisation, vocabulary and language features of the type of writing. This is often undertaken as shared or guided reading.	Researching the form allows the children to generate a model of what the writing should be like. This enables the creation of success criteria.

Table 5.1   (Continued)

Stage of the process	Teaching activity	Why this is valuable
Consider the audience	The teacher and class formulate ideas about what the intended reader will already know and what she intends to gain from the text. Together they reach decisions about vocabulary and the formality of the writing.	Considering the audience helps writers to make choices between possible words and structures. By imagining the response, they are beginning to find ways of evaluating the effectiveness of their writing.
Create a plan	The teacher shares the writing of the plan with the children showing that different forms of writing need different planning structures. She then checks with the children that the plan takes account of all the decisions reached in the previous phases.	Planning helps children to feel secure when writing and to pace their work effectively. The mutual development of a plan then gives children a template for subsequent independent planning in the same genre.
Draft the writing	Depending on the class and the nature of the text, the teacher will focus on demonstration, shared writing or some combination of these with some group or individual writing as well. The focus will be on getting the ideas onto paper effectively rather than on secretarial aspects. During all this work the teacher will offer a commentary which clarifies decision-making.	Teacher modelling is particularly valuable in showing the children the decisions made during writing. The commentary offered by the teacher then becomes the model for the decisions children need to take as independent writers.
Share the draft	The teacher offers children the opportunity to read and comment on. the draft, making suggestions or identifying bits which need more work. They may be asked to imagine they are the intended readers and respond with their likely reactions.	This work is essential before children can begin to edit. It is a pause in the writing. process which teaches the skills of evaluation. When children are confident about responding to other people's work, they will be ready to reflect upon their own in the same terms.
Make changes to the content	The teacher and class together work to add to, delete, change or move parts of the texts. All the time they refer back to the intended purpose, structure and audience as the basis for changes. This work should be undertaken electronically (usually linking the IWB to the word processor) but may also be done physically by cutting and pasting.	Adult writers are never satisfied with the first draft so children need to learn the skills of making work better for its purpose. By working on editing a shared text before working independently, they gain skill with the four basic editing processes.
Ensure accuracy	(This always comes after editing for content as there's no point correcting material which you might decide to delete.) The teacher brings subject knowledge expertise to identification of any errors which the children cannot identify. Spelling strategies can be consolidated and punctuation checked to increase clarity.	Many children see editing solely as correcting accuracy and dislike it intensely. They need to see that accuracy is a matter of courtesy to the readers and a way of ensuring that the purpose of the writing is achieved.

(Continued)

Table 5.1 (Continued)

Stage of the process	Teaching activity	Why this is valuable
Produce a final copy	If word-processing, the editing and final draft flow together well but the teacher will work with children to choose appropriate font, layout and other textual features. In handwritten work, the teacher focuses on clarity and the needs of the reader.	Again children need to focus on the intended audience when they make decisions about the presentation of the work. By learning that there are choices to be made, children take control of the presentation, recognising the different forms appropriate for different circumstances.
Publish the writing	The way in which the work is published will depend on the decisions about the audience form and purpose. The teacher takes the responsibility of ensuring that the work reaches the intended audience.	It is essential that children recognise that writing is for real reasons and for real people. This is a far more powerful motivation than focusing on attractive genres or ways of working.
Reflect on the writing	The teacher and children together evaluate their writing, what went well, what made them proud and what they have learnt from it.	This shared evaluation enables children to focus on positive aspects, raising their confidence. The shared target setting gives control of their own progress as writers.
Receive feedback	This completes the activity. The teacher needs to encourage the audience to respond to the writing in ways which the children will find helpful. This is not in any way linked to marking. It could be through the readers doing what you had hoped, or expressing appreciation of the writing.	This again focuses on the writing being real. Children learn the power of text by being made aware that their writing was successful in its purposes.

Processes of writing development in individuals

It is also possible to consider the writing process in another way: the processes of moving from being a non-writer to a skilled writer. Many adults would regard writing as one of the truest examples of lifelong learning as every new challenge seems to zoom us back into the vulnerabilities and uncertainties of the beginner. This is important to consider in any developmental model: there isn't really an end point to the development and the stages along the way are linked to the familiarity of what we are being asked to do.

A developmental model informed the PNS which used a hierarchy of difficulty of genre and work associated with it. In this model, the demand of the curriculum leads the child's development. The strategy subdivides writing into different elements, acknowledging that not all may develop in parallel. Researchers into writing development such as Farr (1999) suggest that writing is a complex interaction of different developments so the process of learning to write requires children to progress in several ways.

Children's developmental processes in writing encompass the compositional aspects:

- Subject – from familiar to speculative
- Viewpoint – from personal to impersonal
- Audience – from known to unknown
- Genre – from those based in oral language to those only found in specialist texts
- Register – from informal to formal
- Vocabulary – from general to genre specific
- Sentence structure – simple to complex

There are also models of development of the **secretarial aspects** of writing:

- Spelling – from single letter icons to accuracy
- Handwriting – from mark making to cursive
- Syntax – from single word to complex sentences
- Punctuation – from no use to accurate use of all common symbols

When these different approaches are put together it can be seen that teachers have to make decisions which help children advance in their individual skills and understanding across a range of aspects of writing, advance in independence in producing texts and advance in what they have the skills, knowledge and stamina to research, plan and write.

Composing text across the curriculum

The previous sections suggested that writing development is both complex and demanding. Like most other learning, advances in writing need to be consolidated through repetition and practice. Equally importantly, unless children find their growing expertise as writers useful, they will find it difficult to remain motivated. For these reasons writing needs to be nurtured in all curriculum areas, though care must be taken to ensure that it doesn't overwhelm the lesson or take focus from the main learning objective. In the current model of the curriculum, non-fiction genres are taught through the topics children are studying. So for example, persuasive writing could well be linked to a topic on rainforests. Wray (2006) shows how the act of writing can enhance learning as well as being a way of producing evidence of learning. This distinction is important as it indicates that writing in any subject must be appropriate to the children's stages of writing development and must be integral to the learning in the subject.

What we ask children to write

The National Curriculum in 1989 gave broad guidelines about what children should be taught to write in each primary key stage but it was with the introduction of the National Literacy Strategy (1998) that there was a framework of what was to be taught each term. Though the renewed Framework reduced this and added more opportunities to build on previous learning, the writing curriculum is still product-led with the focus very often being on preparing children for formal assessment in Year 6. Wyse and Jones (2001) criticised the focus on products rather than writing processes as a step back from what had been learnt about how children best develop as writers. However as one of the criticisms of the time before the strategies was of the limited range of writing undertaken by children (HMI, 1980), it could be that the strategies have over-compensated in terms of range of writing. There has to be a balance between process focused creative decision-making and model-led product focused writing.

The things which need to be considered in selecting types of writing are:

- Cognitive development so that children are not asked to write things which they aren't ready to understand (e.g. young children can seldom manage balanced discussion).
- Knowledge of the form. We never ask children to write in genres which they don't know well.
- The skills and knowledge. Children need to recognise the distinctive features before they can use them.
- The need for children to experiment and make informed decisions. Children aren't always going to produce what is expected; sometimes what they write will break out of normal genre constrictions with spectacular success. When this happens we need to celebrate what has been achieved not criticise writing for being unexpected.

Forms of writing in primary education

Table 5.2 (see next page) is based on the excellent NLS *Grammar for Writing* materials. It shows some of the main types of writing expected, the expectations of the reader and the distinctive features. I've subdivided them into aspects of the form and the language structures used.

This table is to be considered, like the Pirate Code in *Pirates of the Caribbean*, 'more what you'd call "guidelines" than actual rules'. Confident, experienced writers sometimes decide to move outside them to make writing vivid and original.

A simple view of writing?

Gough and Tunmer's (1986) view of reading which is, at present, the prevalent model for teaching and assessment in our schools, suggests that the skills of reading can be grouped into two main categories: language comprehension and decoding skills which come together to enable reading comprehension. It may be helpful to consider writing in a similar way.

Table 5.2 A selection of writing genres taught in primary schools

Type of writing	Reader expects …	Main structural features	Distinctive language use
Retelling of story	– to be able to predict events and language structures	A narrative structured round a complication and its resolution.	Some repeated structures. Use of alliteration/rhyme, onomatopoeia
Adaption of a story	– to be surprised at some points	A distinctive authorial voice. Some 'play' with setting, characterisation or complication.	Teeters on parody by exaggerating features. Often written in first person.
Original story	– to be drawn into an exciting place	Balance of description and narration. Well formed characters. Resolution in keeping with theme and sub-genre.	Vocabulary chosen to enhance effects. Chronological connectives. Direct speech.
Poem	– to enjoy rhythms and patterns – to go beyond the literal	Intensifies forms of any genre through use of language, scansion, layout. Has an emotional as well as an intellectual appeal. Expresses ideas beyond the humdrum.	Words and phrases selected for sound and rhythm as well as meaning.
Play script	– to have instructions for performance	Conventional layout of speech and directions. Characterisation shown through action.	May use non-standard phrasing to distinguish characters. Stage directions use abbreviated sentences.
Recount (autobiography)	– to be told truth from a known perspective	always first person. Moves logically through events. May offer opinion. Inclu des all necessary information but doesn't give tedious detail.	Chronological connectives. Careful use of pronouns. Often uses compound sentences (because it is accessible to inexperienced writers)
Report	– to read diagrams, charts, sub-headings, captions etc.	Present tense, non-chronological, moves from general to specific, offers evidence not opinion	Uses causal connectives. May uses phrases or single words in captions etc. Defines technical language.
Instructions	– the purpose to be clear – the steps to be logical – all necessary information	Second person. Present tense. Presented in chronological order. Often includes diagrams, bullet pointed lists.	Imperative verb forms. May not use complete sentences. Few adjectives or adverbs. Some logical connectives.
Persuasion	– to identify author's opinion – to be given evidence	Simple present tense. Includes an opening statement of the assertion (may be in the title) uses evidence and opinion.	logical connectives. Mixes complex sentences for information with pithy slogans for impact. Emotive use of adjectives.
Discussion	– a balanced perspective – evidence and conclusion	Unobtrusive authorial control. Third person. Material divided into paragraphs. No bullet points or diagrams. Points presented in order of importance. Sometimes uses sub-headings.	Complex sentences linked by logical connectives. Few adjectives or adverbs.

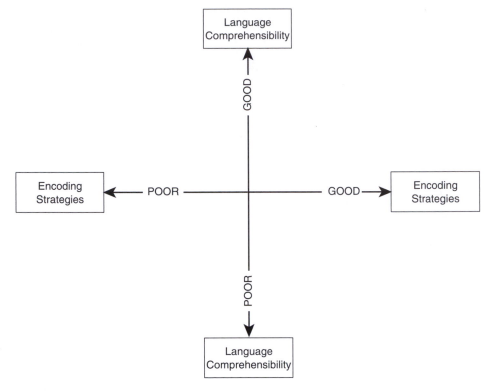

Figure 5.1 A simple view of early writing

In Figure 5.1, encoding skills take the place of decoding skills. These are usually spelling and handwriting or word processing though the use of a scribe or electronic writer also enables many writers to encode their ideas. Comprehension which is central in reading is replaced by comprehensibility: the ability to communicate in ways understood by a listener or reader. So, in this model of writing 'language comprehensibility' denotes the ability to make yourself understood to a listener. This involves vocabulary, understanding of phrase and sentence structure and the conventions of presenting ideas. It also demands a level of knowledge of what is to be communicated. Children move gradually towards language comprehensibility as their vocabulary extends, their utterances involve strings of words and they become aware of the needs and rights of the listener. Language comprehension is usually more developed than language comprehensibility in young children because it is easier to understand the material composed by an experienced speaker than it is to compose speech.

Once children are able to speak in comprehensible phrases and clauses they are ready to compose text. The sentence, though the base unit of writing, is not the way we structure most of our speech. Spoken language is often made up of incomplete utterances and single words. As they become familiar with text, children will structure material to be written in appropriate ways. Here's an example of this; a four year old child is talking about a picture and then composing a sentence about it.

Danny: My trankoline. In my garden. And that's me. And Tyler. And Ally. Big big trankoline for jumping. Like this. JUMP very high. High as this.

Teacher: That's very high jumping on your trampoline! What shall we write to go with this picture?

Danny: Get a trankoline and you can jump very high.

Another factor which makes speech a shaky basis for writing is that the elements of facial expression, gesture and intonation which help the speaker aren't available in writing – Danny supplemented his dictation with some very vigorous jumping!

Kress (1996) explores the complexities of writing showing it is far more than the translation of speech to another medium. Though the language comprehensibility developed through interactions is essential, the language comprehension drawn from reading is also important. This enables the child to recognise the narrow band of the broad spectrum of everyday talk which is translatable into writing and is valued in the school system. Rich, varied and extended interactions with others and with texts set the conditions in which writing can thrive.

The other aspect of this view of writing is the encoding skill needed by the writer. This is an interesting example of writing from a six-year-old child who was struggling with encoding his plentiful ideas.

IFlowaBe

ISleouFlwr

In this form the writing made little sense. However, Martin's writing begins to be comprehensible if you recognise that he has indicated the start of important words by using a capital letter and has started a new sentence on a new line. Divided into conventional word units, the text reads

I fl ow a be

I sle o u flwr

Now, if you are told that Martin has a strong East London accent it is fairly easy to work out that he is writing

I fell out of bed

I slept on the floor

In this example, it can be seen that Martin has actually got no real problems with the phonics used to encode speech; he lacks an understanding that it is not his accent which is encoded in conventional writing. Unlike many children he has yet to learn to translate his normal speech patterns into the desired school pronunciation before segmenting the words and translating phonemes to graphemes. He also has no notion that encoding requires representation of units of meaning isolated by gaps.

In writing, language comprehensibility and encoding blend together to create text that communicates the intended ideas to the intended audience. Inexperienced writers' texts will be comprehensible long before they are accurate. Through all the primary years of education, writers are moving towards being able to produce appropriate, accurate texts of many different types. They will reach our goals for them as writers if they are taught carefully and empathetically.

Roles when teaching writing

The realist

Perhaps our most important role when teaching writing is to be honest about its difficulties. Our teaching of writing must always recognise that the relationship between speech and writing isn't as simple as it may seem. Good speakers may not necessarily be great writers; the problems of text creation may overwhelm them. It is greatly to children's disadvantage if we gloss over the difficulties because they may come to believe that, as they find writing difficult, it must be their fault. It really isn't: English is an enormous, capricious, slightly eccentric language which is very difficult for the writer.

Teacher as scribe

Though there is much less individual scribing of text in EYFS and KS1 than in the past, all teachers will act as scribe during shared text creation. When scribing, it is important to write exactly the words given by the children. They are using their language comprehensibility skills to compose; you are providing encoding skills. Frequently the text you are given will need more shared work which is undertaken when you work as an editor. Keeping the two processes apart gives children the chance to see the original text clearly and evaluate it, enabling them to participate more fully in text editing.

It is worth noting that very young children or inexperienced writers usually speak at a speed which you can't keep up with and offer phrases which are inappropriate to written forms. Pontecorvo and Zucchermaglio (1989) researched children's dictation and noted that as they gained experience they learnt to monitor the scribe and speak at a dictation pace using conventional phrase structures. This suggests that scribing allows children to develop knowledge about how written language is structured and the ways it differs from spontaneous speech.

Teacher as editor

Editing is not the same as marking. It is part of the process of writing rather than a response to a product. The teacher identifies parts of a draft which are unclear or unsuitable for the purpose. Bearne (2007) shows that effective writers take responsibility for their own writing. By sharing the role of editor with children, the teacher is modelling the framework of questions and reflections on text which will gradually be internalised as children move towards independence. In this example Shiam (student teacher) is helping five-year-old Poppy compose a sentence.

Poppy: At a weekend me and Granda Woof flied my kite in a park and and it kept bumping along the ground and I runned along fast and a dog chased after the kite and it did bite it.

Shiam: That sounds really exciting. Let's think what we should write.

Poppy: 'I flied my kite in a park'.

Shiam: I'm not sure that's as exciting as what you said before. I think we should write about the dog too.

Poppy: 'I flied my kite in a park with Granda Woof and a dog did bite it'.

Shiam: Who's Granda Woof?

Poppy: My mummy's daddy. He used to have a dog and my other nanny and granddad doesn't.

Shiam: People might not know 'Granda Woof' means 'granddad'. Would it be better if we put granddad?

Poppy: Yes. Use the grown up word.

Shiam: Ok. Listen to what you've decided. Think if it sounds like book language. 'I flied my kite in a park with Granddad and a dog did bite it'. Happy with that?

Poppy: ' … and a dog bited it.'

Shiam: I think 'bit it' sounds better.

Poppy: Bit it. Yes … grown up.

Though Shiam is offering his expertise, he is also encouraging the child to reflect on her work and make decisions about meeting the needs of the reader. It is noticeable that Poppy is already developing notions of 'grown up' vocabulary and book language.

Teacher as reader

Writing is meant to stimulate, inform or entertain the reader so our response should be in those terms. Assessment is a separate issue which will be considered later. Our first response should be a consideration of how well the text worked, in terms of what it was trying to do. This is Tess's response to Adam's writing:

> I thought the way you described the forest was great, particularly 'grasping fingers' and 'skeletons of the summer'. They made me realise that the story was going to get sinister. And I liked the way you characterised the little sister trying to help put up the tent with her thumb in her mouth. I could see her doing that. There was one bit that confused me – when the narrator comes back and sees 'You will die' written on the tent in blood. Where did the blood come from? I thought one of the characters must be dead but they were all alive.

Adam later edited his story so that the murderer decapitated a squirrel and used the body to write on the tent. This raises another issue for the teacher as reader: whether your taste should be reflected in your comments. It would seem that, if the instruction was specifically to write a story which you are likely to enjoy, it is fair to comment on the choice of subject. If fiction has been written for a different audience, then you must accept your preferences may not be universal. However, there may be times, as with reading, when the professional responsibilities of a teacher lead you to respond in certain ways.

Reading Tess's comments has probably made you question how this depth of response would be possible with a class of 30. If you consider your role as reader only at the end of the process this is a valid worry. Adam read his story to the class and Tess's comments were part of a writing conference where everyone had the opportunity to respond. Her expertise offered children guidance about how to act as critical reader of their own work, leading them towards independence.

Teacher as publisher

Cohen and Riel (1989) noted enhanced performance and motivation when children knew they were writing for a real, distant audience. Publishing just involves making the writing public. In its simplest form it may be on a display for others to read and enjoy or made into a book. There is also the potential, with due care, to publish on the internet. Whatever the form of publishing, the fact that the writing is to be made public justifies close focus on accuracy and appropriateness.

This is one local school's audit of the published writing undertaken in a week:

- invitations, messages home, letters and cards (reception)
- lists of ingredients, joke book, notice about a lost jumper (Y1)
- letter about visit, display of tongue twisters, class agreement for wet playtimes (Y2)

- anthology (Y3)
- time capsule descriptions of school, letters home (Y4)
- book reviews for library, emails to authors (Y5)
- replies to letters from Y7 pupils, posters, performed a play they had written for younger children (Y6)

Teacher as proof-reader

Editing was described as using adult expertise with compositional aspects of writing. Proof-reading focuses on the secretarial aspects of spelling, punctuation and conventions of written standard English. Hall and Robinson (2003) argue that too great a focus on independent accuracy inhibits the desire to write. It is justifiable to use your expertise to identify those things which the child should have been able to do correctly: things which you know have been taught and were relevant to the instructions.

If work is to be published, it is appropriate to work on harder errors together; if it isn't to be published these errors give you indications of the next steps for the individual. Far too often, the only response given to children's writing is a generic comment with indications of what is wrong without any idea of how this can be made right. This is not proof-reading: it is just a way of ensuring that the child learns to dislike writing.

Teacher as coach

A sports coach will always focus on a specific skill and give detailed advice and useful examples. The same approach is sensible when teaching writing. Even a few minutes' intense individual attention can help a child address a weakness or further develop a strength. CUREE's (2006) influential report also showed the value of coaching in motivating children. This is of great value when teaching writing, as its difficulties and complexities can be very daunting. A child who feels a failure will quickly learn to avoid writing.

Peer support in writing

Each of the roles described above should be part of the teacher's normal techniques. As they become part of the expected rhythm of the teaching sessions, children can be encouraged to support each other in their writing, adopting the approaches which you have modelled. Peer tutoring may be formal or a casual extension of the paired or group interactions which are at the heart of English lessons. The process is beneficial for the coach as it will extend knowledge about language through giving explanations as well as being helpful to the writer. Here are 11-year-old friends Imogen and Mollie discussing Imogen's use of imagery.

> *Mollie*: I think it's good that there's similes for the monster but I think there's maybe too many … too different. Like you've put fur like bonfire ash and teeth like scimitars and a smell like a rotting pond and claws like sabres.
>
> *Imogen*: But that makes it exciting.
>
> *Mollie*: I think it would be more exciting if you chose just one for that paragraph and another for the bit where it grabs Robin. Like the scimitar one there and have just the best one first.
>
> *Imogen*: The bonfire ash.
>
> *Mollie*: That's my favourite but … fur isn't frightening.

This courteous and constructive peer tutoring is only possible because all the girls' teachers have modelled similar responses to writing.

After the primary phase (KS3)

In secondary school, students who are struggling with literacy will receive dedicated help with spelling and text organisation and composition. All students will use writing across the curriculum with all teachers taking responsibility for literacy development, for example by teaching new genre features through exemplification, modelling and shared composition. All teachers will also be aware of what has been learnt in the primary school and will expect students to draw on secure knowledge and skills independently and accurately. In English lessons, new genres will be explored and further language features taught. These may then be consolidated, practised or extended across the curriculum.

Chapter summary

- Writing starts with thinking and talking. They are also important at key points in the process
- Writing is the most demanding of the language forms because it requires several skills and types of knowledge being synthesised
- Teachers need to be active participants in all parts of the writing process
- Children need to be able to make decisions (and need to be taught to do so)
- Motivation can be enhanced by making writing purposeful and relevant to children's reading preferences
- Both the writing processes and the products need consideration
- Compositional and secretarial skills and knowledge need to be balanced in instruction and teacher response
- It is a key aspect of progress across the whole curriculum so must not be undervalued
- Writing should be enjoyable and rewarding for everyone

Further reading

Bearne, E. and Wolstencroft, H. (2007) *Visual Approaches to Teaching Writing: Multimodal Literacy 5–11*. London: SAGE.

Cremin, T. and Dombey, H. (2007) *Handbook of Primary English in Initial Teacher Education*. Leicester: UKLA/NATE.

Cremin, T. (2009) *Teaching English Creatively*. Abingdon: Routledge.

Graham, J. and Kelly, A. (eds) (2009) *Writing Under Control: Teaching Writing in the Primary School* (3rd edn). Abingdon: David Futon.

References

Bearne, E. (2007) 'Writing'. In T. Cremin and H. Dombey (eds), *Handbook of Primary English in Initial Teacher Education*. Leicester: UKLA/NATE.

Bearne, E. and Warrington, M. (2003) 'Raising boys' achievement', *Literacy Today*, 35: 18.

Bruce, H. (2002) *Literacies, Lies, Silences: Girls' Writing Lives in the Classroom*. Oxford: Peter Lang Publishers.

Cohen, M. and Riel, M. (1989) 'The effect of distant audiences on children's writing', *American Educational Research Journal*, 26(2): 143–159.

Collingwood, J. and Collingwood, M. (1990) *Hannah More*. Oxford: Lion.

Centre for the Use of Research and Evidence in Education (CUREE) (2006) *Mentoring and Coaching for Learning: Summary Report of the Mentoring and Coaching CPD Capacity Building Project* 2004–5. London: CUREE.

ESTYN (2006) School Inspection School Number: 6692388 Ysgol Y Bedol.

Farr, M. (1999) *Advances in Writing Research, Volume 1: Children's Early Writing Development*. New York: Ablex.

Grainger, T. (2005) 'Motivating young writers to write with purpose and pleasure'. In P. Goodwin (ed.), *The Literate Classroom*. Abingdon: Fulton.

Graves, D. (1994) *A Fresh Look at Writing*. Portsmouth, New Hampshire: Heinemann.

Gough, P. and Tunmer, W. (1986) 'Decoding, reading, and reading disability', *Remedial and Special Education*, 7(1): 6–10.

Hall, N. and Robinson, A. (2003) *Exploring Writing and Play in the Early Years*. London: David Fulton.

HMI (1980) *A View of the Curriculum HMI Series: Matters for Discussion No. 11*. London: Her Majesty's Stationery Office.

Kress, G. (1996) *Before Writing: Rethinking the Paths to Literacy*. New York: Taylor and Francis.

Lewis, M. and Wray, D. (1998) *Writing Across the Curriculum: Frames to Support Learning Reading*. Reading: University of Reading Press.

Martello, J. (1999) 'In their own words: children's perceptions of learning to write', *Australian Journal of Early Childhood*, 24(3): 32–37.

National Commission for Writing in America's Schools and Colleges (2003) *The Need for a Writing Revolution: The Neglected 'R'*. New York: College Entrance Examination Board.

National Literacy Strategy (2000) *Grammar for Writing*. London: DfEE(0107/2000).

Pontecorvo, C. and Zucchermaglio, C. (1989) 'From oral to written language: pre-school children dictating stories', *Journal of Reading Behaviour,* 21(2): 109–126.

UKLA (2006) *Raising Boys' Achievements in Writing*. Royston: UKLA.

Woodward, K. (nd) *The Teaching of Writing in Primary Schools: Could Do Better* [Online]. Available at: www.standards.dfee.gov.uk/literacy/glossary

Wray, D. (2006) *Teaching Literacy Across the Primary Curriculum*. Exeter: Learning Matters.

Wyse, D. and Jones, R. (2001) *Teaching English, Language, and Literacy*. Abingdon: Routledge.

CHAPTER 6

ACCURACY AND PRESENTATION: THE SECRETARIAL ASPECTS OF WRITING

- accuracy • difficulties • handwriting • links to oral language
- presentation • punctuation • rules • secretarial aspects • spelling
- teacher response • technology

This chapter aims to:

- consider aspects of writing which some children find particularly difficult
- examine ideas about keeping a balance between compositional and secretarial aspects of writing
- suggest ways of responding to children's writing during the writing process and when it is finished
- consider strategies to help children to learn to spell accurately and confidently
- suggest ideas about teaching handwriting
- provide an outline of the issues relating to sentence structure and punctuation

There is a real problem with writing: children find it extraordinarily difficult to match the excellence of their oral language when asked to write. For far too many children writing is daunting, frustrating and far from pleasurable.

Yet we know that the desire to communicate ideas and the ability to engage the audience are clear in oral work so the issue for teachers must be to focus on ways of transferring these skills, knowledge and positive attitudes to the written media.

Millard (2001) found that some boys disliked virtually every writing activity they were asked to complete in school. Yet other children, most frequently girls, seem to enjoy every kind of writing. Possibly, identification of the issues with writing should focus more on the processes of transferring ideas from the writer's mind to the finished product rather than the nature of the activities – if the ideas are there in children's speech, drama and drawing, perhaps the issue with writing is the joyless chore of getting the ideas onto the paper.

Fisher (2002) saw handwriting as being a particular problem. In a case study cited on the National Strategies website (http://nationalstrategies.standards.dcsf.gov.uk/node/245003) Wicks identified a major problem being the unfamiliarity with the sentence structures required. Wood et al. (2009) noted the demands made upon inexperienced spellers and the difficulties presented by the language. These three areas – spelling, handwriting and written sentence structure – seem to have been the main areas of difficulty for many years. The Cox Report (DES/Welsh Office, 1989) identified these as key aspects of language to consider in the development of a national curriculum. He described them as the 'secretarial aspects' of language asserting that, while very important, they should not take precedence over the true purpose of writing which is to convey thoughts, knowledge and ideas to a reader.

Society's focus on accuracy

It is worth considering why accuracy in writing is given such a high priority in a society where the secretarial aspects of adult writing are usually left in the capable care of the word processor. It would seem that the 1870 Act that made education compulsory was partly inspired by the need to educate children to work as clerks in industry and empire. Clerks needed to be able to read and to write accurately and legibly (Hastings, 2004). There were few jobs in which the ability to write a breath-taking haiku or terrifying ghost story were in demand, but thousands of workers who could write accurately and neatly were needed. Right from the outset, secretarial skills were prized. At the time, this was probably an excellent thing; the difficulty is that we seem to have carried this demand through many generations of schooling even though technology has moved so far forward. Primary schools sometimes seem not to have noticed the invention of the typewriter (invented just before the 1870 Education Act) let alone the word processor. It seems extraordinary that in 1914 school children went on strike partly because their teachers were instructed not to teach them to type (Nevitt, 1992), yet we still haven't really got a grip on the ways in which technology eases our routes into writing.

Before the primary phase

Writing in EYFS

A good EYFS setting should be full of writing. As well as child-initiated activities, EYFS teachers will usually model writing every day, showing children the purposes of writing and demonstrating key skills and knowledge. Speaking and listening will encourage children to extend from early telegraphic structures to conventional sentences which they are taught to compose differently for different situations. The early phonics work at EYFS should lead to children having a toehold on phonetic spelling. Many settings will ensure that children work on their fine motor control so that they can make the hand movements required for writing. A good EYFS setting will also focus on the recording of achievement and progress in early writing so that children believe themselves to be writers and choose to write.

Most children leaving EYFS will know:

- the sounds of English speech are represented by fairly predictable symbols
- writing involves choosing the symbols which represent the words you want to use
- writing is horizontal and leaves spaces between words
- some symbols in writing do not represent sounds (punctuation)
- successful writing can be read

Spelling

The emphasiss plaiced on acuracy inn spellling seams verry extrordinary. You will have been able to read the preceding sentence almost as quickly and easily as if it had been written conventionally. You may have felt that it is intrinsically wrong to misspell deliberately and may be uneasy about inaccuracy being used to make a point. People are offended by misprints in books (ask any publisher) and may think the worse of someone who spells inaccurately. Spelling our gloriously eccentric language accurately seems to matter immensely to us so it is important that we teach children the knowledge and skills which gain access to, and acceptance in, professional life.

A very abbreviated history of spelling

Our history is one of invasions, exploration and cultural changes – all of which add to or change the language. Tudors spelled with a cheerful creativity; for example, the young princess Elizabeth amused herself by trying out different spellings of her name. It was not until the common availability of printed text in English that spelling began to settle down. The publication of dictionaries also impacted on spelling. Johnson set out to *describe* a language rather in the way that a zoologist might describe an ecosystem. However, dictionaries were soon used to *prescribe* the language – to show how a word should be spelled rather than how it was observed to be spelled. Unfortunately, though English spelling began to standardise, English pronunciation continues to change, so words which would once have been phonetically regular no longer sound as you would expect from their spelling.

Information about word derivation and families needs to be taught at Key Stage 2. This could be enlivened by these topic related activities.

- Invent some dinosaurs. To show the way Latin and Greek base words are used in English, analyse dinosaur names (there are several excellent sites which give the derivations) and use them to create new dinosaurs. For example a saltoelesmasaurus would be a leaping lizard with scales like beaten metal.
- Tudor names. Explain to the children that the Tudors thought it immensely witty to spell names in different ways. Children could experiment with versions of their name which are still comprehensible.
- Voyages of discovery – children should invent something wonderful brought from a new land and create a name for it as unlike English as possible. They then spell the name as they wish and hide it. In a ring pass round the imaginary object saying its name. Very soon the word will soften and change to fit in with the phonemes of English. This could then be spelled as it now sounds and compared with the original.
- World dictionary. Loan words taken from other languages (I don't know why we call them that as I doubt if we'll give them back) often show their origins by unusual spelling patterns. Over a term you could add these words to a world map showing their origins.

All these activities teach children about spelling rather than teaching strategies for learning words. Developing knowledge about spelling is important as it puts the difficulties into perspective.

Teaching spelling

The important thing is that spelling is taught accurately, confidently and consistently in ways which recognise the difficulties of the area and take account of children's needs. All children in their primary years need to be taught to spell. There is no case for simply sending them home every week with a list of words but without strategies to learn them. Testing spelling does not teach children to spell; it teaches most of them that they are poor at spelling. Once children come to believe this, everything gets much harder for them and their teachers.

Systematic synthetic phonics

Lessons should focus as much on spelling (encoding) as on decoding for reading. However, as Oudeans (2003) identified, children's use of phonics for spelling lags behind reading. This is because phonics in reading is immediately open to checking – when you've blended a word it is likely to sound like a word you know. In spelling there is no parallel checking device for beginners. This is not a reason for discounting the value of systematic synthetic phonics for spelling but a pointer to the need for both teacher support and the acceptance of comprehensible misspellings which draw on the information which the child has learnt. For example, *ellifunt* is a good attempt for a five-year-old and should be praised as a significant achievement. It is, however, an unacceptable spelling for a more advanced writer and would need to be addressed.

Spelling by analogy

Children's first realisation that words can be grouped by pattern as well as meaning is often based on recognition of the patterned sounds of rhymes and jingles. Analogy won't always work in English: if I can spell *meet* I can probably work out *feet* but not *heat*. But, the fact that a method of spelling won't always work is no reason to discount it. No method is going to work all the time.

Look, cover, write, check

This is the equivalent to the use of 'Look and say' in reading because it is based on the strong visual memory of many young learners. The main disadvantage is that it teaches only a single word at a time unlike phonic methods which allow children to generalise. Hebblewhite (2008) notes the weaknesses when it is still used in schools where systematic synthetic phonics has become the prime way of teaching early reading. The difference of approach is likely to cause children problems if 'Look, write, cover, check' is the prime method of teaching spelling. However, as many of the most common words of English are irregular, this is a sensible method of learning the early **tricky words**.

Learning the rules

Everyone knows the rule about '*i before e except after c*'. If you learn the rule like that, it isn't going to be a great deal of help. What about *achieve*? The 'i' is certainly before the 'e' but the common version of the rule doesn't work. Equally *science* appears to break the rule. This isn't because the rule doesn't work very well; it is because it hasn't been taught very well. The rule should be '*i before e when the sound made is 'ee' except immediately after c*', which works very well. (There is a cluster of rule breakers including weird, seize, vein, heir, neighbour etc. I usually save these for Halloween and indulge in some horror story work using them.)

I've used this example to show the difficulty with rules in English spelling. As the language has been pieced together from different origins and has changed over time, it is important to know something about the type of word you want to spell and its source. An example of this is the 'rule' that many adverbs end in *ly* and many place names end in *ley*. For this rule to work, you need to be able to identify the type of word. Another rule which works fairly well is that you only get silent letters in very old words (because pronunciation has changed since the written form was established). This again demands that the writer has broad knowledge about language.

These are some rules which work fairly well:

- A plural is made by adding 'es' when the plural adds a syllable, e.g. 'watch-watches'
- Suffixes sometimes double the final letter. This is most often true in *one* syllable words with *one* vowel and *one* letter after the vowel e.g. bat-batty, sit-sitter, sin-sinning
- Suffixes again – if a word ends in a vowel, you often drop it before adding a suffix
- Prefixes never alter the root word (a wonderful rule because it always works)
- Words (except names and recent additions to the language) don't end in j or v
- One syllable words are very unlikely to end in a single f, l, s or z
- 'Q' is followed by 'u' and another vowel

Knowing your weak spots

- If you know you can't spell a word it isn't a problem to you – you can always find a reference source. Good spellers know their weak spots. It is a sensible strategy for children in upper Key Stage 2 to start to keep a list of their particular danger words.
- Some fortunate people have an excellent kinaesthetic memory which means that, as they write or type a word, it feels wrong if misspelled. In this case, spellers know more than they are aware of.
- Repeated misspellings cause the real trouble. They are the words which we have learnt wrongly. Teachers have to watch carefully for these words and point them out so children can begin to work on them.

Mnemonics

These are rhymes or acrostics used to spell words, for example, students recently taught me two different ways of remembering how to spell 'necessary': *it is necessary for a shirt to have one collar and two sleeves* (the tricky bit of the word being the single c and double ss) and *never eat cake; eat salmon salad and remain young*. Mnemonics can be criticised for the same reason as look, cover write, check: they teach a single word rather than giving access to a group. They are immensely useful as a final resort.

Isolating the tricky bits

We can all spell bits of even the most difficult words so it is a waste of time to learn the whole word by rote, for example *diarrhoea* (which a parent, very appropriately, wrote as 'dire rear' on an absence note) starts off fairly easily with *dia*. The *ea* ending is also easy; it is just the middle bit which is nearly impossible to predict but easy to learn in isolation. Engaging children in analysing the difficulties within words, finding the tricky bits, and devising their unique solutions helps them take control of their spelling.

Use a synonym

This is an admittance of defeat and should certainly seldom be encouraged. Children use synonyms when accuracy seems to outweigh creative perfection. Though substituting a synonym is a poor stratagem if used directly, looking up a synonym which you can spell in a thesaurus is a brilliant way of accessing words which you can't spell independently.

Errors and misconceptions in spelling

It is well worth analysing the mistakes children make as these will give insight into the strategies being used. For example *girl* is frequently wrongly spelled as *gurl* (which shows over-reliance on phonic knowledge: it uses a more likely letter combination) or *gril* (which shows overuse of visual information: *gr* is a much more common letter pattern than *gi*). Every error gives you the opportunity to consider the best strategy for moving towards accuracy.

Wing and Baddely (1980) identified the links with errors in decoding words as readers when they identified the most common types of spelling error made by adults as being:

- Omission (a boy *caled* Luke)
- Additions (was *hopeing* to get)
- Substitutions (a toy *polece* car)
- Inversions (for his *brithday*)

To this analysis of adult errors we could add *non-attempt* and *inappropriate whole word substitution (the shapes were square, triangle, ring and rectangle)* in children's spelling.

Teaching approaches

Spelling should be taught as part of every discrete phonics lesson at KS1 and as part of writing at all times. The most successful approach is probably in shared and guided writing where a very brief spelling activity set in a meaningful context enables you to model successful strategies. The key thing is to move children towards independence so that they are thinking about best approaches.

Just as when a child is reading you only 'give' a word which is beyond the scope of existing strategies, so with spelling you only 'give' words which children have no way of reaching for themselves. It is wise to remind a child of the best strategy to use then ask her to make an attempt.

It is also worth:

- Setting up a spelling area with thematic word lists, thesauruses, dictionaries, electronic spell checkers and lists of tricky words
- Before independent writing tasks, encourage children to choose words they probably want to use but aren't sure they can spell
- Giving lists of theme words
- Talk about spelling

> *Laura*: I loved the description of the family 'careering down to the air-raid shelter'. Perfect word but so hard to spell. How did you go about it?
>
> *Matt*: Sounding out. Then to check I used the computer – no red line – so had to be right.

- Praising comprehensible attempts then working on them individually
- Allowing young children to attempt just the first phoneme or syllable
- Demonstrating your own need to check words. Though student teachers find this very scary, it is important to dispel the myth that educated adults find spelling easy

 What are the arguments for and against having a basket of spellcheckers available in every primary classroom?

Handwriting

Like spelling, handwriting carries a historical burden. It would be easy to dismiss handwriting as an anachronism which doesn't merit much thought. As adults, we seldom write important documents by hand so we could argue that our focus as teachers should be on equipping children for an adult life in which handwriting is going to be used for shopping lists and hurried notes or as a beautiful art form. However, while handwriting remains so important in the education system, it has to be taken seriously.

Medwell and Wray (2008) found that poor handwriting can impact on children's compositional skills and their motivation. This is particularly the case for boys whose fine motor skills often lag behind those of girls and who, in an attempt to be neat, may adopt postures and movements which they find painful. The solution is to make sure that children are taught at the beginning that handwriting is a matter of making the correct movements rather than creating even, properly sized letters and words. If the movements are correct, the writing will soon become fluent, regular, easy to read and painless for the writer.

Children need to understand:

- Clockwise and anti-clockwise movements – making the right movement is essential in handwriting
- Many of our letters start with an anti-clockwise curve: a, c, d, e, f, g, o, q, s
- Another important group start with a downstroke: b, h, i, j, k, l, m, n, p, r, t, u, y (in most styles)
- The other lower case letters are the ones which start with a slanting downstroke: v, w, x
- Z doesn't fit into any of these groups and both e and s are slight anomalies
- If children start a letter at the right point and know the first movement, they are unlikely to go far wrong

Joining letters

People make this seem very much harder than it needs to be. Joins are simply light lines between the finishing point of one letter and the starting point of the next. If letters are formed correctly, joining them is simple. If the join isn't easy to make, most sensible handwriting styles leave the letters separate. It has been accepted for some years that a joined style of writing (cursive) improves spelling because it encourages children to approach a whole word as a single complex movement. However, Karlsdottir (1996) found no difference in spelling accuracy in children taught print or cursive styles. It could also be argued that print, being more like the typescripts children read, enables easier reviewing and editing. As systematic synthetic phonics is taught as the prime approach to reading it also seems valid to use a handwriting style which separates graphemes as units rather than linking them through the whole word.

Left-handedness

The Left-handed Children organisation recently conducted a survey which showed that 88% of left-handed people had problems at school with smudged work and 38% with writing slowly; 71% found writing painful. There are many things a teacher can do to help a left-handed child with writing. These include:

- Providing a slope for writing so children don't to have to lean over the paper
- Inviting a left-handed adult to show the correct hand positioning and movements
- Allowing the child to slant the paper for writing
- A left-handed pen won't solve problems but it will help. Pencil grips are also helpful but need to be introduced with care as some children may feel humiliated by using them

- Monitoring hand position. Many will develop the habit of holding the hand like a claw above the writing as this enables them to see what has been written. Though understandable, it will cause pain so a better position must be taught
- Watching carefully for reversed letters: clockwise movements are much easier than anti-clockwise movements for left-handed children
- Seating the child at the left of others so elbows don't get entangled
- Accepting that writing may take longer for a left-handed child and may not look very beautiful
- Configuring the computer mouse to left-handed use. Left-handed children may find the keyboard much easier than handwriting but they may find this easier with the mouse on the left

Talk to a left-handed adult about his or her experiences in primary school. Try to find out what was particularly difficult, the feelings this provoked and the ways in which the school tried to meet specific needs.

Sentence structure

Sentence structure causes problems for three main reasons. If children are asked to write in ways which haven't been thoroughly explored through speech and reading, they are going to have difficulties. Difficulties are also caused when children take so much time to write a sentence that they have forgotten how it started. The other reason for problems is insufficient encouragement to read and edit – the child simply putting down the words but taking no responsibility for checking them.

Atkinson's (1992) research on writing was very influential in our teaching of syntax (sentence structure). One major point was that structure should be seen as an aspect of composition: a way of conveying the desired meaning. Harris (2003) also links structure to purpose showing how the young writer needs to know the decisions to be made relating to structure. So, accuracy in this area isn't as easy to determine as it is in spelling, which is so reassuringly right or wrong.

Expert reflection

Sally Hughes: Links between sentence structure and mathematical calculations

My son's primary school encourages parents not to refer to calculations as 'sums'. Alternatively, children are encouraged to complete their 'number sentences'. This comparison leads me to question the parallels between linguistic sentences seen as a *unit of language* and mathematical sentences seen as a *unit of mathematics*. In that sense, the following 'number sentences' are 'units of maths':

[5 + 5 =___   7 + ___ = 10   10 minus 4 = ___]

So can the comparison between linguistic sentences and mathematical 'sentences' be taken further? Do they each follow rules and norms governed by the rules of grammar/mathematics? They probably do. However, a more powerful likeness comes from comparing expressions in mathematics to linguistic sentences. Consider the following expression:

[10 + 5 × 6]

To find the correct value, mathematical rules need to be obeyed, rules that govern the order that the operations within the expression should be carried out. In this case it's a matter of knowing that multiplication takes priority over addition. This leads to the correct answer of 10 + 30 = 40. However, this might confuse children who 'read' this mathematics sentence from left to right. Therefore, a *logical* answer would be 15 x 6 = 90, found by adding then multiplying. However, the term *logical* deserves its italic status. The logic of the 'read from left to right' misconception can only be justified if reading is viewed as a practice to be followed without comprehension. Perhaps this sentence illustrates this:

[You can have some chocolate buttons if you eat all your carrots.]

The comprehension of this sentence depends on the reader's ability to comprehend the nature of the condition, the 'if'. The reader needs to comprehend the meaning of the condition 'you eat all of your carrots', before they can comprehend the full meaning of the sentence. If asked 'Can the subject have some chocolate buttons?' readers who understand the linguistic rules in place would probably conclude that the subject can have chocolate buttons once all the carrots have been eaten. The correct meaning is comprehended when the grammatical rules of conditional statements are understood. This is like 10 + 5 x 6. The correct value (meaning) of the expression is understood only when mathematical rules of priority of operations are understood.

(*Sally Hughes is Subject Leader for Mathematics in Secondary Education, University of Chester*)

Children need to be taught about sentence types and sentence complexity in order to make the decisions needed to write effectively. For example:

- *Simple sentences* convey meaning with clarity and power
- *Complex sentences* demonstrate an authority over the material which is particularly valuable in discussion and persuasive genres
- *Compound sentences* are a bit of a transitional form because they are used mostly by children who have decided that simple sentences seem immature and want to lengthen sentences so they use a number of conjunctions

The other main consideration is the purpose of the sentence. Sentences can be statements, questions or orders; children seldom find it difficult to write these accurately if they have been covered thoroughly in oral work and reading. Exclamations are easy too but some argue that they aren't really sentences. It is valuable to work with children changing similar content into each of these forms to show how elements are manipulated to show the audience the change of purpose.

> Fred saw a monster *(statement)*
>
> Who saw a monster? *(question)*
>
> Look at the monster, Fred *(instruction/command)*
>
> Monster! *(exclamation)*

Though this is splendidly straightforward, one of the quirks of English is that in spoken language we dislike giving direct instructions. We often soften them with an introductory 'please' which makes it hard for children who are taught that instructions start with an imperative verb. We also present them as statements, 'I'd like you to look at the monster' or questions, 'Are you looking at the monster, Fred?' This can cause problems to children who are uncertain whether to write according to the form or the purpose.

Punctuation

As a student teacher, you are going to have to explain the use of full stops, commas, semi-colons, colons, apostrophes, speech marks, quotation marks and brackets.

- Decide the mark about which you feel most confident; shut yourself away from spectators and video your explanation. How did you do?
- Look at the list again. Which punctuation marks have been omitted? (You need to be confident with these as well)

You will probably need to revise and augment your subject knowledge – nearly everyone does. There are several excellent texts for student teachers which explain all necessary material in detail.

Waugh (1998) noted that punctuation gained less attention than spelling in both research and guidance for teachers. This is possibly because punctuation is so closely tied to teaching about sentence structure, whereas spelling is, largely, an isolated skill. Hall (1998) showed that the teaching of punctuation needed to start in reading so that children understood its value and didn't see it as an unnecessary complication to writing. Punctuation gives children particular difficulties because it is specific to text, taking on the roles of pause and intonation change in spoken language.

As with spelling, a little bit of history makes some of the issues with punctuation clearer. It was first used by dramatists in Ancient Greece to guide the actors to the correct way to speak the lines (McDonald and Walton, 2007). This commonsense approach (*I'm putting a comma here because I want my reader to pause*) makes excellent sense to children but it doesn't go far enough in explanation to enable writers to handle punctuation successfully.

The rules of punctuation are arid but necessary. To go back to the example in the paragraph above, '*I'm using a comma because I want my reader to pause*' leads to the next question: *Why do you want the reader to pause there?* This is the sort of question which we need to explore through shared writing. The answers will always be that the comma is used to make the sentence clearer.

- It is used in lists to separate the items.
- It is used to show when something, of less relevance, has been added to a sentence.

The comma is one of the most difficult pieces of punctuation to teach because writers need to make judgements about when it is helpful. This means that there may not be consistent exemplification in children's reading. Many writers have a quirky approach to commas because they want to depict idiosyncratic speech or a distinct authorial voice (Jane Austen was lavish with them.) Other punctuation marks are much easier: all the ones involving a dot either end sentences or show when complete sentences have been linked. Full stops, question marks and exclamation marks are all easy to teach so long as children are secure in their understanding of sentence structure. Admittedly, many children will go through a phase of being overgenerous with exclamation marks!!!!!!! (like that – they soon grow out of it).

Semi-colon and colon are slightly harder to teach. I approach this by explaining that the dot means that the sentence could be ended but that I am warning the reader that I've decided to run two sentences together. The semi-colon links closely related complete ideas; the colon gives information about some causality. (Usually you could substitute a colon with 'therefore' or 'because'.)

After the primary phase

Accuracy and presentation at KS3

At Key Stage 3, students will be expected to spell all common words accurately and to have good strategies to locate correct spellings for new or subject specific terminology. Teachers may assist them with vocabulary lists or displays and will, dependent on school policy, identify misspellings. Students are unlikely to be

(Continued)

(Continued)

taught more about handwriting though most adolescents make conscious decisions to change from the styles of their childhood. They will certainly learn and be expected to draw on a broad range of ICT based presentation skills. Sentence structure and punctuation will develop through the close focus on genres valued across the curriculum. In some schools these are led by focused work in English or literacy lessons. Secondary colleagues across the whole curriculum are increasingly undertaking shared writing activities and guided work as ways of ensuring that students become aware of the writing demands of the subject and know how to approach these.

Chapter summary

- Accuracy in writing and clarity of presentation are vehicles for conveying meaning.
- The English spelling system is complex so children need a range of strategies to spell well
- The demands of presentation can impact on children's motivation as writers
- Teachers need to teach value strategies, model desired characteristics and support children's attempts
- Children need to be taught how to make decisions about the sentence structure and punctuation which will convey their meaning most effectively
- Presentation is the final element of the model of learning which starts with speaking and listening and moves through reading and composition
- Times are changing: we need to change with them to prepare children for the real world

Further reading

Medwell, J., Moore, G., Griffiths, V. and Wray, D. (2009) *Primary English: Knowledge and Understanding* (4th edn). Exeter: Learning Matters.
O'Sullivan, O. and Thomas, A. (2007) *Understanding Spelling*. London: The Centre for Literacy in Primary Education.
Wyse, D. and Jones, R. (2008) *Teaching English, Language and Literacy* (2nd edn). Abingdon: Routledge.

References

Atkinson, M. (1992) *Children's Syntax: An Introduction to Principles and Parameters Theory*. Oxford: Wiley–Blackwell.
DES/Welsh Office (1989) *English for Ages 5–16 (The Cox Report)*. London: HMSO.
Fisher, R. (2002) 'Boys into writing'. In M. Williams (ed), *Unlocking Writing*. London: David Fulton.

Hall, N. (1998) 'Young children and resistance to punctuation', *Research in Education*, 60: 29–39.

Harris, P. (2003) *Writing in the Primary School Years*. Australia: Social Science Press.

Hastings, S. (2004) 'Handwriting', *TES magazine*, 12 November.

Hebblewhite, D. (2008) *Teaching Spelling: How To* [Online]. Available at: http://www.teachingexpertise.com/articles/teaching-spelling-how-5079

Karlsdottir, R. (1996) 'Print-script as Initial Handwriting Style II: effects on the development of reading and spelling', *Scandinavian Journal of Educational Research*, 40(3): 255–262.

Medwell, J. and Wray, D. (2008) 'Handwriting – a forgotten language skill?', *Language and Education*, 22(1): 34–47.

McDonald, M. and Walton, J. (eds) (2007) *The Cambridge Companion to Greek and Roman Theatre*. Cambridge: Cambridge University Press.

Millard, E. (2001) 'Boys, girls and writing', *Literacy Today*, 28.

Nevitt, R. (1992) *Burston School Strike (Oxford Playscripts)*. Oxford: Oxford University Press.

Oudeans, M. (2003) 'Integration of letter-sound correspondences and phonological awareness skills of blending and segmenting: a pilot study examining the effects of instructional sequence on word reading for kindergarten children with low phonological awareness', *Learning Disability Quarterly*, 26(4): 258–280.

Waugh, D. (1998) 'Practical approaches to teaching punctuation in the primary school', *Reading*, 32(2): 14–17.

Wicks, C. *Improving Standards in Writing Through Developing Sentence Structure and Punctuation* [Online]. Available at: http://nationalstrategies.standards.dcsf.gov.uk/node/245003

Wing, A.M. and Baddeley A.D. (1980) 'Spelling errors in handwriting: a corpus and distributional analysis'. In U. Frith (ed.)., *Cognitive Processes in Spelling*. London: Academic Press.

Wood, C. (ed.) and Comelly, C. (ed.) (2009) *Contemporary Perspectives on Reading and Spelling*. London: Routledge.

CHAPTER 7

INCLUSIVE LEARNING AND TEACHING OF ENGLISH

• autism • bilingual • dyslexia • first language • gifted and talented
• inclusion • individual needs • progress • support strategies

This chapter aims to:

- identify key features of successful inclusive practice for literacy
- explain current approaches to teaching children who are learning English as an additional language
- consider ways of enabling dyslexic children to make progress
- advise on teaching children who are struggling with literacy
- examine the provision for gifted and talented language users
- give practical advice about engendering an inclusive atmosphere

This chapter doesn't include before and after sections because provision varies a great deal.

Introduction

Teachers who are fully committed to the achievement of all the children in their classes will be great teachers of inclusive English and literacy. There are no magic techniques for teaching literacy to children who have atypical needs, knowledge or prior experiences. There are certainly skills, necessary knowledge and ways of understanding some key issues which will help but, at the heart of every truly inclusive classroom is a teacher whose attitudes ensure that every child thrives. This means, more than anything else, that every decision made by the teacher is informed by the certainty that every child can make significant progress towards handling the language challenges of adult life. Children who are secure, happy, appreciated and challenged will succeed; though the routes and targets may be different for some children, these basic conditions for learning do not change for children who are not learning in typical ways. Many student teachers find that working with children with additional needs or children who are learning English as an additional language is uniquely rewarding because they see a difference in a short time and can recognise the good effects of their work. Their attitudes have led them to study, seek advice (every experienced teacher will be happy to give it), try, reflect, look, listen and think. Many student teachers have looked back on placements working in an inclusive classroom and have realised that while they have been teaching the children, the children have also been teaching them.

Children who are learning English as an additional language

> I couldn't understand anything that was happening to me. At my school in India I had been doing well and now I was in the bottom group. My mum every night would say 'How was school today?' and I never told her it was horrible. First I thought everyone in England must be really clever then I began to listen and understand and I realised that the children in my group weren't clever so why was I there? I was so ashamed I wanted to give up but I also wanted to show them I was clever too. On the carpet I wanted to answer the questions but it took too long for me to hear the words and translate them in my head, then think of an answer and then translate it back. So I sat there and didn't put my hand up. I remember one day I was so angry with colouring in a worksheet that I broke all the crayons. (*Najima, student teacher*)

This is Najima's recollection of her experience in primary school as a newcomer to English. She makes the point very clearly that her time in school could have been much more constructive if her teacher had understood her needs and made a few simple adjustments to the ways of teaching. Najima also shows the frustration and humiliation of being voiceless, powerless and unsupported. Hopefully, teachers' knowledge has improved now so the children now starting to learn English in our schools have a much more constructive experience.

Though these sections focus closely on the learning of English and not on the creation of a culturally and linguistically inclusive ethos in the class, these aspects are also essential. No child who is marginalised or unhappy will be very receptive to teaching, so in order for English teaching to be effective, the school must be welcoming, informed and prepared.

Being bilingual

Children who have very little English may well be **bilingual** as many will already be users of more than one language. This was shown by Bindu expressing her frustration at not being able to communicate with a new class member.

> I don't know what to do. I've tried talking to her in Guajarati and Urdu. So I tried Hindi: everyone knows Hindi. I think she's just shy.

However, the term 'bilingual' is best used cautiously as it implies an equal ease with two languages, the assumption in most documentation being that one of them is English. Gregory (1997) uses the valuable term 'emergent bilinguals' for those who are at the early stages of learning English as an additional language. Just as reading and writing emerge through opportunity, encouragement and focused teaching, so English will emerge if teaching and circumstances are favourable.

True bilingualism is advantageous in many ways. Professor Antonella Sorace's recent research (see Buie, 2010) suggests that bilingual people have developed powerful systems to keep the languages separate. She believes that this facilitates multi-tasking in other circumstances and enables greater concentration. Other benefits may include more creative and flexible thinking, higher achievement and ease of learning more languages. There are also important benefits in terms of esteem, family and community links and work options and choices (Kelly, 2007). Though 'commonsense' might suggest that children find it difficult to handle learning more than one language at a time, the occasional inconvenience of confusion between vocabularies is very much outweighed by the advantages of bilingualism.

The first few weeks

It is certainly daunting the first time you are faced with the sudden arrival of a child with whom you share no language. Of course, that last statement isn't completely true: though you do not share a spoken language, the child will be an astute reader of body language and interpreter of your tone of voice so it is essential to ensure that everything you do inspires confidence and helps the child feel welcome. Some practitioners recommend teaching a formalised set of signs and gestures to bridge initial language difficulties. Though this is advocated by some Local Authorities and supported by research indicating that it is found to be valuable with young children (e.g. Madigan, 2005), there may be arguments against moving beyond a few universal symbols, particularly with primary aged children. Firstly, the child's priority will be to be like her peers as soon as possible. To do this she needs to make a start on the language of classroom, playground and community. Secondly, a focus on signing may encourage the teacher to perceive the child as having special needs. This may lower expectations for reaching full potential.

There will be a need for visual material to ease the new learner into school routines (probably with photographs and signs) but it is also good to teach some key words as early as possible. If at the end of the first day the child is using three words, you have both done very well. Good target words are:

- No (to keep safe)
- Toilet (to have personal dignity and allay common fears)
- Thank you (to be liked and accepted)

Beyond these emergency words many new learners will start with a period of intense listening in which they will probably not start to speak English (Siraj Blatchford and Clark, 2000). At this time, children will be observers in literacy lessons but, though not responding linguistically will increasingly show, through non-linguistic response, that understanding of English is growing. At this time the model of English must be excellent so, though this may seem odd, it is far better for children to be included for guided work in groups of average or high attainment as the child will learn as much from the language of her peers as the language of the teacher. The language of high attaining children will teach far more than the language of groups who are struggling. At this time it is important to enhance understanding in literacy lessons by:

- using additional visual aids
- using dual language texts where possible (if this isn't feasible, it is often possible to ask someone to translate and produce an audio version in the first language. Remember that dual language texts are only valuable if children can read)
- asking first language speakers to give previews of the literacy lessons for the week. It is so much easier to work out what is happening if you already have an idea of what is likely
- using an online bilingual dictionary service to translate key words (such as Babylon.com)

The silent period is likely to be prolonged if you try to pressurise a child into speaking so, though you should consistently invite a spoken response you should never insist on it. At the same time ensure that there are several activities every day in which the child can participate and know that she has succeeded. These may be paired work in first language, listening games or simple actions. With a class of 11-year-olds I found this was a good time to revise some handwriting (much needed as they were reaching the stage of thinking that illegibility was highly sophisticated). We had riotous handwriting relay races every day in which our new class member soon became a ruthless competitor. From the very beginning, new English users must be seen as communicators who use whatever forms they find comfortable to participate in interactive learning.

Continuing support

Though much of the support for children learning English as an additional language is focused on the earliest stages, it is often later on that support is really needed. The evidence of under-attainment in English tests at KS2 and KS3 suggests that our current policies are not fully meeting the needs of the pupils in our schools. Pressure on specialist resources may mean that children who have achieved enough English to 'get by' in class, flounder in the complexities of the literacy curriculum and have difficulties with language demands in other subjects.

 These features of good teaching should enable children to thrive in literacy:

- Oral rehearsal with talk partners before writing
- Clear explanation of new language features and key terminology
- Multi-media presentation of information
- Single objectives for each piece of work
- Focus on understanding of text in reading
- Setting of tasks which offer age-related cognitive demands and meet language needs
- Allowing time for rehearsal of answers
- A respectful atmosphere where all responses are valued
- Clear monitoring of progress and awareness of next steps
- Insistence on task completion (set shorter tasks if necessary)
- Acknowledgement of achievement
- Focus on language demands across the whole curriculum

In an interesting case study published by NALDIC in 2008, Sue Boulter highlights the continuing need to assess children's understanding of key terminology. She cites the wonderful example of a child thinking that 'conquer' means ' ... that you are coming to collect conkers from trees in this country' (2008: 1). This is a very sensible answer if you have had to continue your English development through the everyday transactional language of the classroom and playground. As Boulter argues 'the accumulation of unrecognised misunderstandings may then lead to underachievement and low expectations' (2008: 2). When this is considered with the frequently cited suggestion (TDA, 2006) that it takes a new learner between five and seven years to become fully competent in English, the need for continuing planning and provision becomes very clear.

First language teaching

There is a strong case for the encouragement of continuing teaching in children's first languages. As well as the cultural issues, the sense of identity and the valuing of existing knowledge, Kenner (2004) shows that the more any child understands of the first language, the greater the understanding of English. This, at first, may seem unlikely. It would appear sensible that, if children are to function well in the English system, the focus of teachers' work should be on the rapid acquisition of English. However, for the first couple of years of learning English, children will either translate the words and phrases of English to gain meaning or will, later, check their attempts to gain meaning from English against their conceptual knowledge based in their preferred language. If the development of the first language is stopped (as some well-intentioned families and teachers suggest) at the age of five, two years later the seven-year-old will only have the language of a five-year-old to use to come to understand the demanding Y3 curriculum. If the first language is stopped, children's cognitive development will be slowed, leading to under-achievement across the curriculum.

Re-read Najima's reflection on her experiences of learning English as an additional language. Identify ways in which the school could have helped her more.

When in school, discuss with your teacher or mentor what they do to include newly arrived children in literacy lessons.

Phonics and children learning English as an additional language

Rose (2006) suggests that children who are learning English as an additional language can benefit from systematic phonics teaching in the same way as their peers. The report emphasises that speaking and listening should come first with young **EAL** learners and that 'systematic, high quality teaching, detailed assessment and early intervention are as important for learners of English as an additional language as they are for all other children' (2006: 25). This is always the key message regarding teaching EAL learners: good teaching is effective. No methods which would not be of value to the rest of the class are valid (just because the child is at an early stage of learning English.)

If children are starting to learn English in Key Stage 2, the advice that speaking and listening are the logical entry routes into English may need to be modified. Even very young children new to English and to the English school system are very likely to have a silent period (Fumoto et al., 2007) but this is usually longer the nearer the child is to puberty. For such children, the silent phase is a time of very active listening and learning as the new language features are placed in the context of what is already known. If the child's established written language is based on phoneme–grapheme correspondences and the child is able to read in the established language, then phonic information is transferred fairly easily to the context of English. In such cases the child may be able to decode words before she is ready to attempt the highly complex linguistic task of composing and speaking an English phrase or sentence. It is very important to note that this decoding is not an indication that the child is drawing meaning from text. For example it is fairly easy to pronounce *Qoslij Dativjaj* without being aware that it is the way to wish a Klingon a happy birthday!

It is valuable to consider what the child knows about how language works. Though there are now comparatively few logographic languages (ones where the written symbol is based on meaning rather than pronunciation, for example, Hanzi), if a child has learnt to read in such a language, the concept of grapheme–phoneme correspondence needs to be taught before any phonics programme. Even in a phonically-based language, the linguistic noises are not going to be the same as those used in English. Bongaerts et al. (1995) undertook work on the critical period for language acquisition which suggests that young children adapt to the sounds of a new language much more easily than older ones. A child new to English phonics at the later years of KS2 is going to need help to pronounce phonemes accurately.

The last point to make specifically about phonics is the organisation of groups. A couple of months ago I was disheartened to see a seven-year-old Polish boy trudging off to the reception class for 'Letters and Sounds'. I can think of few more effective ways of putting a child off learning than to belittle him in the eyes of his peers, convince him he is stupid and take no account of his developmental or cognitive development. The way to start him on English phonics was not to have him jumping over golden rivers with a group of four-year-olds. It may be more convenient for his class teacher not to have to meet his needs within the classroom but convenience is never a valid criterion for a teaching decision. The right of the child's individual needs to be met with understanding and respect is far more important than the teacher having an easy time.

There is a strong commitment in all our schools for inclusion of children who are learning English as an additional language, yet the government is also moving towards a focus on time-limited one-to-one coaching for vulnerable learners. In what circumstances could such support be valuable for a child who does not use English at home?

EAL and languages teaching

There is no reason for apprehension about including children in learning an additional language. Those still at an early stage of learning English may muddle words occasionally but this is soon overcome. In many ways EAL learners will be advantaged as they are able to draw on experiences and knowledge which monolingual children do not have, so learning another language may have benefits to self esteem as well as increasing the essential knowledge about language. The advantages of inclusion are clearly identified by the DCSF (2007).

> Children for whom English is a second or additional language can be greatly encouraged and supported by language lessons. They are able to take pride in their existing linguistic skills and see languages other than English being valued. They can build on their experience of using a number of languages in their daily life and contribute to the Intercultural understanding of their fellow pupils. Their plurilingual experience may help them to learn the new language or languages. (2007: 12)

This suggests that when the whole class is learning a new language, EAL learners will have a real contribution to make. Additionally, the methods advocated for modern foreign language teaching, interaction, games and a great deal of oral and aural work, may well give a template for valuable approaches across the curriculum. Children may be much less wary of contributing because the pace will be right for them. Though we are still at the beginning of such work, it will be interesting to see whether the equalising nature of MFL lessons enable children to progress rapidly and generalise their confidence across the curriculum.

    Expert reflection

Barbara Pickford: Factors affecting the literacy development of Gypsy, Roma and traveller children

Government statistics show that ascribed Gypsy, Roma, Traveller (GRT) pupils attending schools in England are the lowest attaining of all pupils in the education system. The attainment of many Travellers throughout school, both primary and secondary, lags far behind that of their peers. At their current rate of progress it is estimated that it will take almost 100 years for them to 'catch up' and attain levels similar to their peers.

Recognising that each Traveller pupil and family is unique, there are, however, many shared barriers to learning faced by Traveller children and young people attending school.

One difficulty faced by a large number of Traveller children in learning to read is the low level of literacy within their own immediate and extended family. Perhaps not so much value is put on the need for literacy within some Traveller families if they themselves have had little formal education; there may not be much modelling of the use of reading materials or availability of reading materials at home.

Mobility is perhaps a more obvious barrier. Depending on the travel pattern of their family, some Traveller children can attend a number of different schools for

(Continued)

(Continued)

varying amounts of time during just their primary education. This makes access to intervention programmes very difficult.

A less obvious barrier might include the amount of space available to a family for the storage of reading materials at home. A family living in a trailer (caravan) has limited space available for essential items such as food and clothing.

An awareness of these barriers is very important so that they can be addressed but what could be a much greater inspiration to a Traveller parent and child than seeing their rich culture and heritage recognised and displayed within the school environment? How much greater an incentive to learning to read so that you can celebrate the lifestyle and share in the history of generations of your family?

(Barbara Pickford is Team Leader, EMTAS, Children & Young People's Services, Cheshire West and Chester Council)

Progress in English for children who have special educational needs

It is very likely that in every class you teach there will be children who have special needs. Due to the complexity of English many special needs impact significantly on learning. They slow the progress children make in the acquisition of the basic aspects of literacy and the opportunity to draw on these skills to access the full curriculum. True inclusion is not about the physical presence of a child with additional needs in the room (far too often I have watched children who only seem to interact with a specialist teaching assistant in literacy lessons) but should involve skilful individual adaptation of learning objectives and teaching methods within the context of the general work of the class. This careful planning and teaching ensure that the child makes progress in her own terms.

The 'long tail of underachievement' (Brooks et al., 1996) has been cited frequently as a characteristic of our education system. It means that, as teachers focus on moving the class as a whole forward, some children gradually fall behind as our teaching methods do not ensure that they meet their potential. Once children have fallen behind, it is very difficult to catch up. Sadly, our system may have condoned the tail in the past with teachers making assumptions such as children who can't keep up never will keep up. I remember a meeting when I was teaching in London where a colleague was vociferously blaming the families for the poor standards of the children in her class. Dan Taverner, an inspiring LA adviser, remarked characteristically gently: 'You know, I always think it's a good idea to teach the children who are in your class, rather than the children you wish were there'. Excellent advice: I hope I've always kept it.

The next sections will give a very brief introduction to two of the most frequently occurring conditions which are likely to impact upon learning literacy.

These have been chosen as they exemplify the differing approaches needed according to children's needs. In teaching a child with an identified special need it is essential to research the need in depth as well as finding out as much as possible about the child as an individual learner.

Dyslexia

There is probably going to be somebody in every classroom who has some dyslexic characteristics. If it is you, the teacher, you can bring a real sense of empathy to your teaching and you will certainly have learnt strategies which will be valuable to the children you teach. You will also show the most important characteristic of **dyslexia**: although it cannot be overcome even with great teaching and high aspirations, its impact on literacy learning can certainly be minimised.

The word 'dyslexia' is possibly the educational equivalent of a doctor saying you've got spots: it is often a description of symptoms which could be caused by different underlying problems. MRI scans indicate that classic dyslexia relates to difficulties with phonological processing rather than, as thought for some years, processing visual information (Vellutino et al., 2004). Though some people who have typical 'dyslexic' difficulties are helped by coloured overlays or spectacles, they probably have Meares–Irlen syndrome (Irlen, 2005) which gives similar difficulties with word recognition and spelling but fewer of the related characteristics such as poor motor control. However, many people who have visual processing issues also find phonological processing very difficult.

Because dyslexia is so complex in cause and outcome, there is never going to be a quick-fix solution; what will be essential is a partnership between learner, teacher and family in which all are committed to maximising progress. Equally importantly, disruption in early education, family stress, movement to a different accent area and prolonged absence from school can all cause problems with reading or spelling development which look very like dyslexia. Pure developmental issues such as the establishment of laterality can lead to some things which could be identified as dyslexic behaviours, such as the reversal of letters. These complexities show that diagnosis is difficult and, as the outcomes can be life changing, it is the responsibility of specialists. Don't ever leap to conclusions from your observations but, if you feel a child may be dyslexic, keep your eyes and mind open and seek advice.

Children who are on the dyslexic spectrum may find these things particularly difficult:

- Rhyme (establishing patterns based on linguistic similarities)
- Distinguishing between some letters such as b/d , g/q, m/w, s/z
- Recognising or writing a word which has recently been decoded
- Remembering phoneme–grapheme correspondences

- Identifying right and left
- Understanding puns and jokes
- Following complicated instructions
- Combining knowledge from different sources to spell

However, many children will find some of these things difficult at some time. Perhaps the best definition of a specific language difficulty or dyslexia is finding some aspects of language very much more difficult than peers. It is important to avoid simplistic diagnoses as they don't do any good. At one meeting on dyslexia the speaker asked us whether we would find it difficult to thread a needle while standing on one leg or to read a map upside down in a foreign language. When we all agreed that we would, we were told that we were dyslexic and that showed how widespread the problem was! Of course we weren't: some characteristics had been taken to an unjustifiable extreme to demonstrate a point.

Early diagnosis is now much more likely so teachers can begin to address the needs of dyslexic children at KS1. Valuable strategies include:

- Emphasising the pleasures to be gained from reading and writing. These have to be immediate not some distant aspiration.
- Focusing on kinaesthetic memory when teaching grapheme–phoneme correspondences: tracing in the air, dancing the shapes, making letter patterns in different media while enunciating the related phoneme.
- Choosing good quality, entertaining texts with strongly patterned repetitive language.
- Choosing texts which merit the time spent on them, perhaps by being funny, exciting or closely aligned to children's interests.
- Relating reading consistently to meaning by using the illustrations, predictions and sentence structure to check phonic approaches.
- Modelling reading and writing to make your knowledge about language evident.
- Using oral and aural activities to access text and to ensure the dyslexic child has at least one really successful moment every lesson.
- Involving the child fully in paired and guided work of suitable cognitive challenge.
- Liaising closely with family so that every opportunity is taken to ensure success in reading and writing out of school.
- Teaching word processing skills as well as handwriting.

As children get older, if early experiences are not successful, they are likely to be burdened by low self esteem (in all its disruptive manifestations) and a feeling that they cannot succeed. The worst thing that can happen is for the child or family to believe that dyslexia inevitably causes failure and therefore excuses giving up. Though it is quite understandable that a family wants to shield their child from distress, low literacy levels in adult life are such a burden that everything must be done to work together on confidence and attainment.

The current policy shown in NPS and through the *Independent Review* is that, if children are still struggling with the early stages of reading at KS2 they need careful and age appropriate focus on phonic approaches. There is definitely logic to this: reading and spelling are heavily dependent on grasping the alphabetic bases of the English language. However, it is sometimes necessary to take the child's previous experience into account. If there has been an accumulation of failure in the early years and Key Stage 1, it may be worth opening one of the back doors into reading by focusing greatly on language comprehension and prediction. When a confidence has been established using these methods, phonics can be brought in firstly as a checking device as this focuses on initial sounds and then whole word blending as a prime stratagem when working with unfamiliar text. Any decisions about individual programmes must be made in consultation with the SENCO and specialist support agencies.

At KS2 it is also valuable to:

- Focus on modelling comprehension skills in reading at inferential and appreciative levels.
- Work individually with the child on a text before whole class work.
- Encourage full contribution to all oral activities.
- Agree individual targets and success criteria with the child.
- Create wordbanks for reading and spelling across the curriculum.
- Shorten tasks but insist on completion.
- Work together to create strategies for demanding activities.
- Minimise impact on other curriculum areas to ensure success while giving time to reinforce language skills.
- Never put additional language work in place of an activity the child enjoys (one of my class once bit an educational psychologist who tried to take her out of a science lesson).
- Work on the child's knowledge and interests to make the work purposeful.
- Get in touch with adults with dyslexia as models and mentors.
- Use opportunities across the curriculum to enhance metalinguistic awareness. For example a lesson on the Tudors could include experimentation with spelling as it was at the time considered witty to be able to spell in many different ways.

 Please read Tessa's account of her childhood struggles with dyslexia. As a teacher her experience is going to equip her with valuable insights. What does her account tell you about how it feels to have dyslexia? What does it suggest as helpful teaching attitudes and strategies?

When I was in junior school I was very aware that I wasn't quite the same as everybody else. I looked the same and sounded the same but during lessons I didn't feel the same. My friends zoomed past me with the reading books and I was left in the bottom group struggling, and hating every minute that my teacher made me read and re-read the same books over and over. But how can you expect a child to read well when you're telling them there is one D one O and one G, and I am seeing two of everything. I didn't realise until I tried to write things down that the teachers were right, there was only meant to be one, but I could see two.

 This is how I saw words formed.

Other parts of my life were harder too, I had really bad balance, was very uncoordinated and had very poor hand–eye coordination. I can remember feeling very embarrassed that at the age of nine I was still unable to tie my shoe laces.

But as I grew up the word dyslexia became part of my life, not a bad part, just part of me, that as I got older I was more able to understand, to work with instead of against. People telling me that I couldn't do certain things made me more determined to do them, and do them well. I always remember telling people at a young age I was going to be a teacher, and slowly but surely people letting me know that being dyslexic this was very unlikely. But here I am, year 2 in my early years teaching degree, and although its hard work and sometimes things are just that little bit harder for me than everyone else, I am more determined to succeed than ever before.

By Y3 many dyslexic children will be aware that conventional reading instruction isn't helping them to make progress. When a programme is individualised to meet a child's needs, we may either give intensive instruction in the areas which cause difficulty or seek to strengthen the areas which the child finds easier. In what circumstances would each approach be preferable?

Children on the autistic spectrum

Children who are diagnosed as being on the autistic spectrum are increasingly being taught in mainstream classrooms. The term **autism** covers an enormous range of difficulties and characteristics from difficulty in understanding jokes or another point of view through to, as an extreme, an inability to interact either through language or gesture. Whereas children with dyslexia share the characteristic of finding word recognition processes uncharacteristically difficult, children on the autistic spectrum (or with a diagnosis of the related syndromes such as Asperger's or semantic pragmatic disorder) may usually have problems with the other axis of the Simple View of Reading: language comprehension processes. These may cause issues with each language mode, for example:

- understanding intention or tone when listening
- understanding the needs of an audience or engaging in discussion when speaking
- understanding causality, language patterning or implication when reading
- understanding how to explore imaginative purposes or characterisation when writing

Researchers have become increasingly interested in breaking down the characteristics of language difficulties associated with autism which will enable teachers to understand more fully how to help children make progress. In the past much research focused on problems with pragmatic processing as this was a frequently reported characteristic. This is a typical example:

> When we were getting ready for our holiday we tried to involve Michael with everything. We explained the importance of passports and on our last day I said, 'The passports are in the drawers of the bedside cupboards. Please get them'. Of course, he came down with all the drawers.

Eigisti et al. (2007) have found children with autism have a poor understanding of syntax. This could explain some of the pragmatic processing problems. For example in the example above, Michael's issue is largely with the pronoun 'them' which he assumes to refer back to the noun immediately before it. Just as with dyslexia, patchy ability makes it difficult to use another system to check, so Michael lacks a way of checking whether his understanding of what is wanted is correct. He doesn't have the empathy to realise that it is unlikely that his father wants the drawers. Eigisti et al. go on to suggest ways of enhancing syntactic understanding through direct, carefully focused teaching; this could include clear exemplification in relevant contexts and use of structural framing.

Peppé et al. (2007) also found that children with autism's difficulties with poetic language were related to lack of understanding of the specific structures being used. Similarly, Wang et al. (2007) found that specific instruction to attend to facial expression improved autistic children's brain activity in the areas which respond selectively to the face and voice. This study has great implications for teaching children how to detect a speaker's intentions and validates teachers' realisation of the value of very clear facial expression and body language. Each of these studies gives new insights into the complexities of language processing for autistic children but also gives a message about careful, appropriate direct teaching being beneficial. This teaching must always be based on expert needs analysis and individual target setting; research shows what is likely to be valuable but it is essential for the group of professionals concerned with the individual to make decisions about the best ways to ensure progress in communication and literacy.

There are also shared characteristics which make other aspects of literacy work very difficult. Children may feel safest in an unvarying routine which makes it hard but not impossible to bring variety and spontaneity into teaching. They may also have sensory difficulties which can impact on handwriting (this often involves prolonged contact with textures seen as threatening). The difficulty with understanding the actions and responses of others, classmates or characters in books, all make the convivial bustle of a good literacy lesson very daunting. However, Chiang and Lin (2008) have found that children with autism in mainstream schools have more interaction with other class members than those had by similar children in special education, so though your classroom may sometimes be baffling and daunting to a child with autism, it may still be the best setting for continuing language development.

 Careful, informed teaching will certainly enable children on the autistic spectrum to make progress. It is particularly important to:

- think carefully about the language of instruction. For example: 'I'd like everyone to line up at the door' would probably be interpreted as 'She is telling me about things she likes. There is no need to respond'.
- be careful with the use of metaphors and similes. 'The sun is like a huge fried egg' got the response 'Eggs do not radiate heat and light and the sun is not made of albumen', in a lesson I was observing.
- be very careful when modelling sentence structure as autistic children will find it hard to cope with ambiguity.
- avoid inference and irony as both will be difficult. This will be equally important in oral work, reading and writing.
- ensure that you identify every new aspect of subject knowledge. Children will have to be taught explicitly rather than taking the opportunity to learn by implication or example.
- offer a secure pattern of expectations in literacy lessons but, in consultation with the specialist teachers, do not allow this to stagnate. If nothing changes, no progress can be made.
- prepare the child for changes. For example one local teacher sends the main texts home a week ahead. Social story books are also an excellent way to help a child accommodate change (see below).
- be flexible. If the child loves Thomas the Tank Engine, use it to teach reading.
- be aware of hyperlexia which is often related to autism. Children with hyperlexia can decode far in advance of their understanding and may give the impression of being excellent readers.
- set very clear instructions for oral work. 'Discuss how the three bears felt when they got home' isn't going to be easy. 'Look at the picture of Daddy Bear. Tell the people in your group if Daddy bear's face is angry or happy,' can then lead to further questions about what has happened in the story to change the character's emotions.
- give opportunities for decision-making but do not demand response.

Many teachers use social stories, developed by Carol Gray in the 1990s, to help autistic children cope with difficult situations. Intended to enhance social understanding, the carefully structured use of sentences written in a set form for a specific purpose (descriptive, perspective, directive, affirmative) within these stories gives a framework for increased understanding of syntax, and a focus on the perspectives of others. Chatwin (2007) also showed that social stories can be very motivating for reading and writing development as they focus on the individual's needs and interests. This is an account of one student teacher's successful use of a social story.

I was nervous about teaching Christopher who has Asperger's syndrome so my mentor suggested that I made a social story about my placement and gave it to him before I started. I put in photos and thought about what would scare him. My class teacher gave me advice. This was my book:

Mrs Cooke is learning how to be a teacher. She is going to teach me and Beech class. Mrs McGowan is going to be in the classroom. Mrs Hillier is going to be in the classroom (teacher and learning support worker).

Mrs Cooke is going to teach me about plants. She is going to teach me maths and English.

Mrs Cooke knows I don't like having dirty hands. She will not make me get dirty. She knows I get worried about the toilet. She will let me go to the toilet when I want to. It is okay if I am nervous with Mrs Cooke. I will remember that she doesn't know me very well so I will tell Mrs Hillier if I get worried.

It will be all right when Mrs Cooke teaches me. When I finish my work I can read my Dr Who book.

Making the book helped me to understand Christopher. He took the book home before I started in school and I think it reassured his parents because it showed that I had tried to find out about autism to understand their son. During my placement Christopher added two pages.

Mrs Cooke says 'good job' when I do good work. ... Mrs Cooke is not teaching me next week. I will be sad.

It was the best moment ever when I read Christopher's last page! I think that the book helped us both and it is definitely something I would do again.

Many children who are on the autistic spectrum love the Thomas the Tank Engine books and videos. (There is an interesting amount of research and a fascinating debate about this on the internet.) Think about what makes these stories so attractive to children. How could they be used as a gateway to real inclusion in literacy lessons?

Many autistic children struggle with drama and reading and writing fiction. Does imaginative engagement with language have enough value in adult life to merit focus when teaching an autistic child?

Gifted and talented speakers, listeners, readers and writers

Describing responsibilities for meeting the needs of the gifted and talented, Siegle (2007) identified three key roles for the teacher or school:

- providing opportunities for the ability or talent to emerge
- recognising it
- helping to move it to exceptional levels

Each of these aspects is important for the teaching of literacy – talent will not emerge in environments where children's activities are tightly prescribed and the objectives determined solely by the teacher. The traditional WALT and WILF sharing of objectives may be too restricting for some literacy work and for some children. (One very able child recently redefined the terms as: 'We already learnt this' and 'What I'd like to forget'.)

Recognising talent may depend on your attitude: one teacher's talented pupil may, unfortunately, be another's complete pain. Eyre (cited in DCSF, 2008) developed the 'Nebraska Starry Night individual record sheet' which identifies 18 key characteristics of gifted children which include using humour, seeing the big picture, making connections, questioning, observing, showing curiosity, being independent, being recognised by others, sharing and volunteering knowledge and insights. Gifted and talented children do not just do the same things as the other children 'but a bit better'; they may work in different ways and become frustrated when these aren't accepted or nurtured. They may also find it very difficult to work out when their contributions will be appreciated as their ways of thinking are not something which they can switch on and off as appropriate. Originality may not be welcomed and eagerness to contribute seen as showing off.

If talent in English is not identified and treated sensitively, children quickly learn to mask it. This is Ozzy's account of the wisdom of hiding his reading ability when he was in the reception class.

> *Ozzy:* It was really good because it was all playing with the cars and water and the play dough. Then she started with cards with words on and the kids who read the words had to do reading and writing not play. So I didn't.
>
> *Teacher:* Could you read before you started school?
>
> *Ozzy:* Not everything. Not in English. In Turkish, I think, yes.
>
> *Teacher:* What about now?
>
> *Ozzy:* (I could read) ... anything if I wanted.
>
> *Teacher:* But you don't?
>
> *Ozzy:* Not in school. It's boring.

As Siegle (2007) suggests, we have the responsibility to enable children to develop their talents to exceptional levels; this does not mean precocious curriculum coverage or asking children to undertake work beyond their emotional or developmental level.

Individualising English for gifted and talented children should not be about moving them on to the next stage of a linear model as this is simply a deferral of boredom until someone else is teaching them! Differentiation by output is of little value if children are just expected to do more of a simple task. The child is likely to question, rightly, why she should do three pages of something a bit tedious when you seem happy for everyone else to do one page. It is far better to keep in mind the fact that giftedness is much more about the processes a child brings to an activity rather than the resulting product.

Tasks need to be adapted to accommodate children's specific strengths. These are likely to be independence, desire for enquiry, ability to see different perspectives, imagination and absorption. This is an example of a student teacher managing a perfect 'twisting' of an activity which meets a child's needs while including her in the work of the task.

> We were working on describing words in traditional stories (Y1) and I knew Linnet would need something different because she has a fantastic vocabulary. So I gave her the copy of the story (Baba Yaga) and told her she could choose only five words to change the story from frightening to funny. She quickly found five adjectives to change and then experimented with her friends' reactions to different new words. The next day she came in to school and said that she had changed her mind and instead of changing the adjectives she wanted to use her five words to add 'and the toilet was disconnected' to the part where the house began to move. She explained that 'if you make that bit funny, all the sinister words twist themselves round and seem funny too'. (*Laura, BEd student*)

In this example, there are some typical aspects of a gifted writer in the making. Linnet is stimulated by good teaching but then takes the task further. Dissatisfied with her first solution she keeps thinking about the problem until she is satisfied she has the best response. She is able to explain her decision very astutely, demonstrating a sophisticated understanding of how a writer can influence reader response. She also has enough confidence in the student teacher to try to express her new insights, knowing they will be respected. It is also interesting that Linnet's response is firmly in the emotional range of a six-year-old, for whom there is nothing funnier than a toilet.

Do you believe that exceptional linguistic talent is inherited or is it created by families and schools? How will your belief influence the way you teach?

Chapter summary

- Good inclusive teaching is more about teacher attitude than specific techniques
- Individualised provision is dependent on observation and observation gathering
- Though there may be general characteristics relating to an additional need, all children are different
- Inclusion in literacy is about being involved as much as appropriate with the full curriculum and the full language life of the class
- Individual targeting is central to progress
- All children bring knowledge and understanding to their language learning; some children also bring burdens
- Because success in education often depends on success in literacy, you have to prioritise it

Further reading

Birkett, V. and Barnes, R. (2003) *How to Support and Teach Children with Special Educational Needs*. Hyde, Cheshire: LDA.

Brookes, G. (2002) *What Works for Children with Literacy Difficulties? The Effectiveness of Intervention Schemes*. London: DfES.

Haslam, L., Wilkin, L. and Kellett, E. (2006) *EAL: Meeting the Challenge in the Classroom*. London: Fulton.

Primary National Strategy (2005) *Speaking, Listening, Learning: Working with Children Who Have Special Educational Needs*. London: DfES.

Scott, C. (2008) *Teaching Children English as an Additional Language: A Programme for 7–12 Year Olds*. Abingdon: Routledge.

Tunnicliffe, C. (2010) *Teaching Able, Gifted and Talented Children*. London: SAGE.

References

Bongaerts, T., Planken, B. and Schils, E. (1995) 'Can late starters attain a native accent in a foreign language? A test of the critical period hypothesis. In D. Singleton and Z. Lengyel (eds.), *The Age Factor in Second Language Acquisition*. Bristol: Multilingual Matters Limited.

Boulter, S. (2008) 'Why EAL learners need specialist support teachers: a case study for policy makers to note', *NALDIC News*, 27: 1–2.

Brooks, G., Pugh, A. and Schagen, I. (1996) *Reading Performance at Nine*. Slough: National Foundation for Educational Research.

Buie, E. (2010) 'Bilingualism brings host of mental benefits, claims academic', *TES*, 12 March.

Chatwin, I. (2007) 'Why do you do that? Stories to support social understanding for people with ASD'. In B. Carpenter and J. Egerton (eds), *New Horizons in Special Education*. Stourbridge: Sunfield.

Chiang, H.M. and Lin, Y.H. (2008) 'Expressive communication in children with autism', *Journal of Autism and Developmental Disorders*, 38(3): 538–545.

DCSF (2007) *Key Stage Two Framework for Languages*. London: DCSF.

DCSF (2008) *Gifted and Talented Education: Helping to Find and Support Children with Dual or Multiple Exceptionalities*. London: DCSF.

Gregory, E. (1997) *Making Sense of a New World*. London: Paul Chapman.

Eigisti, I.-E., Bennetto, L. and Dadlani, M. (2007) 'Beyond pragmatics: morpho-syntactic development in autism', *Journal of Autism and Developmental Disorders*, 37(6): 1007–1023.

Fumoto, H., Hargreaves, D.J. and Maxwell, S. (2007) 'Teachers' perceptions of their relationships with children who speak English as an additional language in early childhood settings', *Journal of Early Childhood Research*, 5(2): 135–153.

Irlen, H. (2005) *Reading by the Colors* (2nd edn). New York: Perigree.

Kelly, C. (2007) 'Making language diversity matter'. In T. Cremin and H. Dombey (eds), *Handbook of Primary English in Initial Teacher Education*. Leicester: UKLA/NATE.

Kenner, C. (2004) *Becoming Biliterate: Young Children Learning Different Writing Systems*. Stoke on Trent: Trentham.

Madigan, S. (2005) *Using Symbol Communication to Support Pre-school Children with English as an Additional Language*. University of Warwick.

Peppé, S., McCann, J., Gibbon, F., O'Hare, A. and Rutherford, M. (2007) 'Receptive and expressive prosodic ability in children with high-functioning autism', *Journal of Speech, Language and Hearing Research*, 50(4): 1015–1028.

Rose, J. (2006) *Independent Review of the Teaching of Early Reading*. London: Department for Education and Skills.

Siegle, D. (2007) 'The time is now to stand up for gifted education', NAGC Presidential Address, *Gifted Child Quarterly*, 52(2): 111–113.

Siraj-Blatchford, I. and Clark, P. (2000) *Supporting Identity, Diversity and Language in the Early Years*. Buckingham: Open University Press.

TDA (2006) *Every Child Matters – English as an Additional Language and SEN*. London: TDA.

Vellutino, F., Fletcher, J., Snowling, M. and Scanlon, D. (2004) 'Specific reading disability: what have we learnt in the past four decades?', *Journal of Child Psychology and Psychiatry*, 45(1): 2–40.

Wang, A.T., Lee, S.S., Sigman, M. and Dapretto, M. (2007) *Metaphorical vs. Literal Word Meanings*. General Psychiatry Archive US Library of Medicine, National Institute of Health.

CHAPTER 8

INFORMATION AND COMMUNICATION TECHNOLOGIES IN THE TEACHING OF ENGLISH

• audiences • collaboration • editing • internet • new literacies
• problem solving • publishing • reading • safeguards • speaking and listening
• word processing • writing

This chapter aims to:

- incorporate exciting ICT use into your teaching of literacy and English
- describe some ways in which ICT can help the English curriculum to develop
- draw on children's knowledge of and enthusiasm for ICT in their learning
- enhance the processes of writing using ICT
- extend the range of text sources and audience accessible to children
- recognise issues of safety relating to ICT use in English and Literacy

ICT has the most enormous potential to enhance literacy learning for all children. It can link the classroom to experts from all over the world, remove the drudgery from writing to give every child a voice, extend the vision of what counts as text, enable children to research any topic from a huge range of resources, converse with unknown audiences, talk around the world … The potential is almost unlimited but it has been just 'potential' for far too long. Since the mid 1980s there have been computers in primary schools and educational researchers have written with vision and passion about being on the brink of a new world in which communication would be transformed into something rich, exciting and relevant enabling children to meet the demands of a technological world and be ready to move ICT forward to further and even more amazing developments.

Far from leading society forward in working in new literacies, our teaching has lagged behind the opportunities many children gain at home. Here's Ben's account of a crisis with his homework when he was ten.

> We had to write a letter about persuading the council to give us a new skatepark. So I did it on the computer. My mum helped me make my own letter template with a header like a business letter. Mrs **** said it was good but I had to copy it into my own writing. I was really cross about it and so was my mum. It is politest to do letters on the computer because it is easier to read and it looks like you are taking it seriously.

Many teachers might feel that this sort of computer-based homework is unusual and may be worried that it is open to abuse, but it may be valuable to think about the more typical uses of ICT in children's lives outside school in order to consider how the knowledge which children bring to school can inform their work in English. Children at home regularly play games on their computers and consoles; most games involve immersion in some form of character as a narrative unfolds. The shape of the story is probably going to be directly relevant to writing though it is presented in a different form. This challenges our notions of story but also teaches the way in which all narratives are structured with decisions and consequences, twists and surprises. This is wonderful, transferable knowledge: we would be delighted to draw on what children learn from reading fiction at home; we should be just as happy to build on their knowledge of playing fiction.

Many children will also be using ICT to write in new ways and for new audiences and to converse informally. They are developing great information location skills with something as simple as their Sky+ menu. It would be possible to write a very long list of all the new ways in which children brush up against literacy in their lives beyond the classroom and, for many children, a rather shorter list of the ways that ICT enriches and extends literacy in school. It is therefore important to consider why relatively little has moved forward. Montieth (2004) considered the issue of the slow pace of curriculum change relating to ICT and suggested that, when teachers reflect on their beliefs about teaching and learning, they can challenge their assumptions. This enables them to make changes which move the curriculum forward. It could be that student teachers, immersed in a computer-rich environment from early childhood, are the people who have the vision and open-minded approaches to the subject which takes the curriculum forward.

Before the primary phase

Most children will have started learning about ICT in literacy in the home from something as simple as the symbols on a kitchen device or as exciting as the TV handset. These first experiences help the development of the concepts of reading symbols and the permanence of recorded forms. Many children will also use programmable toys and games which talk or read. In EYFS ICT is brought into role play and, through the use of cameras, children begin to build up visual narratives and sequences (Price, 2008). Talking books may also be made with or for the children. Children's creative responses are developed through interactions with visual texts and group writing activities. Programmable toys are used to enhance group problem solving. In all these activities the emphasis will be on group interaction and the parallel development of spoken language. It is worth noting that some Early Years practitioners are opposed to the inclusion of ICT in the curriculum, arguing that it takes the focus from the real to the virtual (House, 2010) and may have a detrimental impact on sensory development.

Current use of ICT in literacy

Andrews (2004) surveyed ICT in literacy lessons and concluded that most of the use of the computer was for 'low level' work. Though this does not develop children's understanding of the power of computing or enhance the literacy curriculum, this is not to condemn all such uses. For example, there are large swathes of the existing curriculum which are necessary but are not intrinsically very interesting. For example, phonics in spelling requires focused, accurate teaching and a great deal of consolidation. If some of the necessary practice is based on the many commercial computer games available, this may motivate children and make such learning more palatable. This may be particularly valuable when children are still working well below age-related expectations. It is far better that the child gains the necessary additional experience working on a computer with software written to appeal to a child of her age, than being sent to work with much younger children in another class.

There is a case for such computer-based work when the teacher has considered all the possibilities and decided this is the best implementation to ensure achievement and enjoyment of an aspect of learning. This could perhaps be seen as the spoonful of sugar which makes the medicine go down. If the medicine is necessary, the sugar is justifiable. However, to continue on the Mary Poppins theme, the computer must never be the nanny in the corner which keeps the children occupied. Unless there is new learning, necessary consolidation or application to a new context, there is no validity for the activity. If the prime reason for using a computer in literacy is perceived to be that it is motivating, it is probably worth considering what makes even a low-level computer software program an attractive tool for learning in literacy.

- It is usually multi-sensory
- It is usually exciting
- It usually allows the user to set the pace of learning
- It offers positive feedback
- It is infinitely patient
- It makes no assumptions about the user
- It never has a bad day (unless the system crashes!)
- It gives complete attention
- It gives access to high-status activities, prized in society

It could be that, rather than feeling that the simple drill and practice programs used in so many literacy classrooms have little merit, they have a role to play in helping us to see which of their characteristics offers ideas for moving forward with our teaching away from the computer.

One Saturday, keep a tally of all the different ICT based technologies which you use (use 'has a chip in it' as a definition). Identify the technologies which have involved you in reading, writing, speaking or listening. For example, the microwave will count because there is writing on the buttons. Take this list into school and ask children:

- Whether they have used each item
- What they use it for
- What they think it has to do with their language skills

Then shadow a child's ICT use in school for one day and consider the language learning. Use this list to show yourself gaps which could be filled and links which could be made.

ICT in speaking and listening

Papert is best known for his ground-breaking work on empowering children's thinking through ICT. This transcends subject boundaries to a consideration of the most important aspects of learning. He asserted 'good discussion promotes learning' (1993: 87), showing that ICT has an important role in enabling children to express, develop and extend ideas in collaboration with others. In many ways Papert's work links closely with the consideration of dialogic learning (in Chapter 2). By showing how high-quality problem solving activities facilitate good discussion, he sets a context in which oral language can be extended and enriched.

Here is an example of three five-year-olds working with a student teacher, a glove puppet and a Bee Bot. Their task is to instruct the puppet how to program the Bee Bot to go through a tunnel. (The task has been set this way because the student teacher wanted the children to compose instructions rather than experiment with the programming.)

Kesta: Go it forward three!
Ollie: That's not enough. One, two, three. Three'd only be to here. Go forward a hundred.
Kesta: NO.
Saul: Three and another three. Let's try that and if it … [*unclear*] … enough we can do some more.
Ollie: It'll only go to here. It'll stop in the tunnel. Do a hundred.
Saul: A hundred is as far as the playground.
Kesta: A hundred is too a big number. Make it … [*unclear*] … the wall and break it. Go it forward ten. My house is number ten.
Puppet: What do you want me to do?
Kesta: Go it forward ten!
Saul: Bee Bot, go forward ten times.

The computer application is facilitating the discussion here because the task seems very real to the children. They are aware of the limits of the robotic toy's programming; this acts as a stimulus to their own language as they adapt their vocabulary and syntax to forms which will be understood. Mayesky (2008) makes a strong case for activities which engender creative approaches to learning in young children including those in which young children collaborate to reach creative solutions. One of the valuable things about using robotic toys in this way is that the solutions are testable and therefore empowering for the participants.

Though this example comes from work with young children, similar ideas can be developed for other age groups. A 'Strictly Come Bee Bot Dancing' competition engaged BEd student teachers in an intense discussion which involved forming hypotheses, considering other factors, testing, refining and reaching conclusions. (Admittedly, it also involved intense rivalry, dastardly tricks and general mayhem, but these are not necessarily things to avoid. In this case they all involved astute, closely focused language as students built on ideas about how to win.) Discussion can certainly be enriched and focused by the inclusion of good ICT activities in literacy lessons and what is noticeable about such discussions is that much of the work, though focused on the computer or application, does not involve touching it. The language richness comes in the decision-making because the children are controlling the computer rather than it controlling them.

Speaking, listening and responding can also be enhanced and extended through ICT. While CDs and the television offer opportunities for listening to a wide range of models of spoken English in both home and school, there are also further activities which schools can provide. One of the most valuable is the facility to listen to and edit performances which can be offered by the increasing range of very easy to use audio and video recorders available. These take the children's ICT use beyond the low level because they enable something which cannot be done without them: it is usually hard to reflect on speech because it is not captured. When speech is easy to record, children can become much more independent as they become their own listeners. They can reflect on the effectiveness of their performance rather than needing to rely on the comments of others. This will always involve listening and may go onto editing, rerecording and polishing for final electronic presentation. The recording of speech moves oral language into the permanence of text with all the implications of this. So, to be equipped with the knowledge and skills valued in the world beyond the school, children's speaking and listening skills have to be a strong focus, not just as the foundations of reading and writing but as valuable assets of themselves.

As well as these formal, permanent forms of speech which require composition usually associated with writing, children are now enabled through live links to talk and listen to people way beyond their usual circles of communication. Due to children's vulnerability and the potential dangers of the internet, teachers are careful to observe the protective guidelines in place. Once certain of the safety of the activity, there are huge benefits to children to, for example, using webcams to chat to a favourite author online or to video pen-pals in schools across the world.

For children who are learning English as an additional language, speaking and listening in computer-based applications allows the learner to hear excellent models of English which can be repeated as often as needed. It also allows children who are making their first attempts at composing responses in English the chance to think carefully and rehearse answers without the embarrassment of keeping the class waiting. However, a particularly valuable ICT is the scope to extend children's understanding through continuation of first language. In one school, this is done through a live link to a first language speaker who then offers an immediate translation of new terminology and explains difficult concepts. In other schools, children hear a pre-recorded home language trailer for literacy lessons so that they know the content, the activities and the key learning outcomes.

ICT and reading

At its simplest, ICT ensures that children have access to written information on every possible subject and from a range of sources unimaginable to past generations. In particular, when working with non-fiction in literacy or across the curriculum, the barrier between the text written specifically for children's learning and the abundance of real-life sources has broken down almost entirely. Children access the same material as the rest of the population and learn from it in new ways. This necessitates the broadening of our teaching of critical reading skills so that children are taught to challenge the authority of text rather than assume that everything they find is reliable, thorough and unbiased. When working with non-fiction, the reader has to retain her disbelief and ask questions about who is writing, the basis of their authority and the purposes of the text. These higher forms of comprehension were traditionally left until students were older but now, with the ease of access to text which has not been screened by a publishing company, need to be taught to children at primary school. It is notable that the renewed literacy framework placed much more focus on text evaluation in recognition of the increased urgency of such learning. School computers will have safeguards in place to ensure that children do not access inappropriate material but, due to risks, if internet searches are needed for homework, it is advisable to recommend sites or suggest that the work is undertaken with an adult. This broadening of text availability gives teachers a dilemma: though we have a duty to protect children from unreliable or unsuitable material, we also have a responsibility to ensure that they learn to identify safe, constructive ways of reading on the internet.

There are other ways in which ICT enhances reading without going to the internet. When a group of BEd students recently discussed how they would equip a classroom with ICT resources to advance literacy, some opted for a document projector (described by one as being just a camera on a stick) as being even more useful to them than an interactive whiteboard for literacy teaching. They chose this because it allowed a class of children to see any text and removed the necessity for using a Big Book. This would enable them to choose a text that was ideal for the desired learning and that specific class. They also saw potential for speaking and listening work across the curriculum and work on editing and composing texts. Turpin (2011) has undertaken a case study into the use of visualisers (document projectors) in secondary school which indicated a particular value in enabling the class to review work being undertaken and offer guidance and ideas about the next steps. Though document projectors are not yet frequently available in primary schools, they certainly appear to have great potential for work with children talking around text and interacting during the processes of writing.

Talking books can be motivating for many children because they enable them to learn about how books work and enjoy the subject matter without being limited by their decoding skills (Wood et al., 2005). This allows the development of comprehension skills which later inform independent reading. They may also be a great asset for children learning English as an additional language if, as is often the case, they can speak the text in other languages. In the past, many teachers had reservations about talking books because they were sometimes of dubious literary merit and therefore only motivated children to enjoy them, not to use them as a bridge into other texts. With the increasing availability of ebooks for children these concerns may diminish. However another factor to be considered is the quality of the experience of reading beyond the taking of meaning from print. Children's books particularly are beautifully crafted, aesthetically pleasing objects which appeal to most of the senses (small children automatically seem to think that anything that looks, feels and smells so good must be delicious). Evans (2009) argues that the aesthetic pleasures of reading are important: these can't be gained in the same way from a talking book. They are useful additions to the reading opportunities given to children and may have an important role motivating those boys attracted to everything which involves electricity and buttons but are unlikely to be subject to the deep affection we all feel for our favourite books from early childhood.

Interactive storybooks are a wonderful tool for group reading and discussion because they give children the opportunity to influence events, making the decision-making very purposeful. Gamble and Yates (2008) identify the significance of book-based interactive texts in involving the child directly through second person voice ('you' rather than the more usual 'I' or 'she/he'). This gives an immediacy which may be particularly attractive to those less able to lose themselves in other forms of literature. These texts, when presented in an ICT format, bridge the traditional categories of story and game so have great strengths in making decision-making from textual cues very real. If you take the extreme example that, if the reader doesn't predict wisely, the character dies, it is clear that these texts bring a depth to comprehension. However, there is one small proviso which is worth considering: young readers have to learn about the permanence of text as one of the building blocks of early reading. They develop relationships with the security of books, knowing that a loved story will use the same words and sentences to travel to the same ending on every reading. For this reason, interactive books are usually not introduced until children have moved beyond the early stages of reading and are able to recognise that the choices they offer are very special.

One of the most constructive uses of the interactive whiteboard in literacy is for guided group reading as children, rather than having their own copy, will be working together with the same text. This encourages the interaction and collaboration which enables children to learn from each other while the teacher is able to focus on the specific teaching point needed by the whole group. In this extract, the group is working with Ellie (BEd student teacher) together to reconstruct a traditional story which has been chopped up into exposition, complication, climax and resolution. Her aim is to ensure that children can identify these parts and recognise their purpose in a story. They will then move the elements around on the whiteboard and work together on editing one section before working on a section each on individual laptops before bringing them back to the rest of the group on the IWB.

Ellie: First of all we're going to look for the exposition. Can anyone remember what bit this is in a story?

Molly: The beginning

Ellie: Yes! Do you remember we said it was when the writer exposes the setting and the character. Read it in your head and hands up when you've found the characters.

Jaina: [*reads*] A poor fisherman and his wife.

Ellie: Good job, Jaina! Can you highlight that and take it to the top? So we have our characters. Now I'd like you to read to find the setting. Quick as you can! Go.

Mark: [*reads*] lived in a tumbledown hut by the side of the sea.

Ellie: Fantastic, Mark. Can you highlight and drag to its proper place? Good job. Now, last thing: this is the million pound prize one. Who's thinking this is going to be a realistic story and who thinks it's going to be a traditional story?

[*General agreement that it's a traditional story.*]

And what do you get in a traditional story, from when it used to be storytelling out loud, to let everyone know it was going to begin?

Jaina: Once upon a time.

Ellie: So, so close, Jaina. Well remembered. 'Once upon a time' is an example of an …

Jossy: Aperture.

Ellie: Double wow, Jossy! Everyone look for an aperture. I'll give you a clue. It isn't 'Once upon a time.'

Jossy: I already found it before you said. [*reads*] Long, long, ago.

Ellie: Double wow with a cherry on the top! Pop it in the proper place. Well done. Now let's read the beginning together.

All: [*reads*] Long, long, ago, a poor fisherman and his wife lived in a tumbledown hut by the side of the sea.

Ellie: Lovely. What should we look for next in a traditional narrative?

Mark: Complexication?

Ellie: Almost – it's an easier word. One we've talked about. Complication …

Though it would be possible to do this activity away from the interactive white-board, it would not be nearly as effective as it would be very difficult to all read together and to reinforce the elements of a story beginning and manipulate text together.

New ways of reading

Though this section has considered the ways in which ICT can enhance reading in the existing curriculum it may be even more important to consider what needs to be taught to enable children to read fluently in the new literacies which surround them. Leu (2002) defined new literacies as the knowledge, skills and strategies which enable readers to use information and communication technologies as they emerge. He makes the important point that these cannot sensibly be listed because, as the technologies change, so the nature of reading expands to encompass them. This process means that we should be lifelong beginning readers for every new technology but, as with every form of reading, motivation to learn is determined by perceived value of doing so. For example my son has learnt that, when texting me, he has to modify the way he writes because I don't understand his usual text vocabulary: my reading has failed to evolve to meet new demands.

This is not speculation for the future. Technologies which challenge our concept of reading are already available in our classrooms. An example would be talking books. Bennett (2004) considers the value of these books in reinforcing, consolidating or supplementing existing skills at each stage of development of reading in the primary years. For example, a book could be set to enunciate separately and then blend phonemes on a problematic word for beginning readers – modelling desired strategies. As children progress the talking book could exemplify intonation and flow to convey the meaning of text. This may lead to questioning whether, with technology capable of taking over part of the act of reading, teaching should move from the mechanics of decoding towards much greater focus on information location and comprehension. Children will certainly start to question why they should make the effort to learn skills which can be done for them. Reading is changing and the curriculum needs to accommodate this.

Are we reading when we watch a movie based on a book?

Expert reflection

Richard Bennett: Reading and writing in 2030

If, in 1991, I'd been asked to predict what reading and writing would look like in 2011, I wonder if I would have been able to anticipate Web 2.0 developments such as *Youtube*, *Wikipedia*, *Facebook* and *Twitter* or the introduction of the smartphone, the iPad and the e-Book. But, to what extent have these developments actually influenced reading and writing today? Probably, by 2030, the impact of these developments on publishing and the accessibility of information will begin to show. Portable devices will undoubtedly be the principal means by which we access text but I doubt paper-based media will disappear – it's just too handy! Although these devices are able to read text aloud, we will still want to read it ourselves. Try looking at any text without immediately decoding it – unless you are profoundly dyslexic, it's almost impossible! In terms of writing, one would hope that reliance on the QWERTY keyboard will have diminished. But there will still be a need to input text, probably through voice recognition. Maybe the office environment in 2030 will resemble a present-day call centre, with dozens of people babbling away into headsets rather than clicking away at keyboards. However, just as I have spent considerable time composing, editing and reframing this short paragraph, it is difficult to imagine what will replace the engagement a writer has with a page of text.

(*Richard Bennett is Senior Lecturer in ICT in Primary Education, University of Chester*)

ICT and writing

It is in the teaching of writing that the gap between school and society's use of technology is already clearest. The word processor has become a standard tool in professional life and with the increase of home working (house sellers are being advised to turn a spare bedroom into an office to attract buyers – see Spencer, 2010) children may have a strong idea of how adults compose high status, important text. Though the renewed Primary National Strategy placed a great deal of emphasis on children composing 'on screen' there is not a great deal of evidence that word processing is becoming an everyday tool for writing in primary schools.

English (2008) notes that many primary teachers use word processors only for the final parts of the writing process, the creation of an accurate neat copy suitable for publication. Additionally, Ofsted (2009) concluded that ICT suites could detract from computer use across all subjects by reducing the opportunities for consolidation of skills. They found that children often used the suite to enable them to present work attractively rather than to further their learning. Though this study considered all subjects and both primary and secondary sectors, the relevance to writing is very clear. Writing is a complex process, requiring time and a number of differing activities. It cannot be compressed into the time when the class is timetabled to use the computer suite so, in order for learning to advance, schools may need to move to new solutions. Here's Ashleigh's solution from her final school-based placement.

> We had three computers in the shared bay and one in the room linked to the whiteboard most of the time. The other teachers agreed for me to have the shared bay for a week and I borrowed a laptop so there was one for each group. Our unit was adventures and mysteries. I wanted all the literacy groups to write an adventure. They came up with a title and we put these on top of a monitor. Every day the group discussed what was going to happen next in their story, then they told that bit orally. Then two composed at the computer, in turns all through the day. They got fifteen minute turns and were allowed to come in to write for half of lunchtime too if they wanted. The last half hour of the day was a time for reading the adventure out loud and doing editing. I did this for guided work with a group each day. One day G came in with his sister's memory stick with a whole next paragraph. Friday was publishing day. All the groups read each other's work and made suggestions about "wow" words and things that weren't clear or interesting. The group made changes and made sure everything was accurate. Then they all made the stories look brilliant. In the ICT suite we made book covers. It was a good way of doing it because the children enjoyed it and kept thinking about their work and making it better. I was surprised by just how often they read each other's stories and made suggestions, and they talked a lot outside of the lessons. I would definitely do this again.

Ashleigh's planning shows recognition of the value of access to the computer throughout the process. She also recognised that teachers need to be creative, making the best use of resources, rather than seeing the pragmatic factors as valid barriers to learning.

Pragmatism is also used in discussions about the value of word processing for young writers. These often centre on speed of writing and concerns about the use of uppercase letter forms on keyboards. Berninger et al. (2009) found that children's transcriptional skills were often slower when using a keyboard than when writing by hand. Rather than suggesting that this means ICT use is detrimental to writing, it indicates a need to teach on the basic transcriptional skills which when mastered enable children to move to using the computer to create, mould and polish text. There would seem to be a case for applying Rose's (2006) 'fast and first' advice to keyboard skills. If we teach children to use a keyboard efficiently from the earliest years, devoting at least as much time to it as we do to teaching handwriting, they will then be able to benefit from ICT use in their writing.

- Should we teach children how to text?
- What is the difference in learning between recreating a story on paper and as an animation?

Beyond the word processor

McArthur (2006) notes that, though young writers are more willing to edit their work if it is word processed, the editing usually involved minor changes, not those which could enhance meaning. He concludes that the value of computer use in writing depends on the scope of the teaching. Merchant (2004) noted similar points in relation to children's movement into digital writing. He emphasises the constricting nature of a traditional, genre-led curriculum as this leads to children being asked to write digitally the same sort of things as would be found in paper texts using the computer as little more than a typewriter. His research enabled children to draw on models from other forms of narrative such as console games and Pokemon cards as ways of thinking about structure and presenting their ideas. This work suggests that teachers' subject knowledge and the perceived constraints of the curriculum may limit the effectiveness of computer-based writing. As new entrants to teaching, readers of this book are very likely to use and enjoy all sorts of ICT-based forms of writing outside school: please bring them into the classroom – it would do us all a power of good.

Writing areas are common in EYFS and Key Stage 1 but are seldom seen in KS2 classrooms. If there is no writing area, discuss with your teacher the viability of setting one up. If she is happy about it, brainstorm with the children what they would like in it, explaining that it is going to be an area where they can choose to do any type of writing for anyone they choose. It's a good idea to set categories such as:

- Easy to manage
- Possible
- Fantasyland

Allow the children to be very imaginative in their replies so you get an idea of the boundaries of their concepts of writing. Set up the area, including as many of their ideas as possible and ensure that there is access to it every day. Monitor the kinds of writing undertaken and the audiences chosen.

Would we lose anything important if all reading and writing in the classroom made use of ICT?

If we broaden our views of what counts as reading to include the multi-modal texts prevalent outside the school, this is certainly going to impact on work in school. It should certainly include web pages, emails, multimedia presentations, talking books, control technology instructions, databases, flowcharts and mind-mapping diagrams. The pace of change outside the school is so rapid that it would be possible to write a longer list every few months. However, equipping children to use every new device or piece of software is impossible and it is probably not even desirable. What we should be doing is giving children confidence in themselves as readers and writers, the ability to develop and use strategies independently and above all enquiring minds and a desire to communicate. If these things are in place they will handle change with ease and may well go on to be the creators of even more exciting advances.

These are some ways in which we can move children forward with computer assisted writing.

- Use the computer and interactive whiteboard in most shared and guided writing activities, modelling the editing capabilities and extra features such as emboldening and the facility to move text easily. It's also valuable to show the use of the thesaurus, spell and grammar checking.
- Every available computer should be in use for every writing task across the whole curriculum. There'll always be one child willing to take responsibility for the fiddly bits, such as saving to a memory stick to get the work printed if not all the computers are networked. (A local school has 'Computer Commandos' in Year 6 who volunteer to do this for every class.)
- Do everything possible to get children familiar with the QWERTY keyboard. Chalk one on the playground, make individual whiteboards with it printed on them, play tiddlywinks with them. Anything which gets them beyond the hunt and press stage.
- Encourage experimentation in which children move beyond the replication of paper-based models of writing.
- Email has a place in the classroom. There have to be safeguards but, once these are in place, it is an excellent way to encourage real writing for real audiences.
- Publish children's writing on the internet.
- Plan for group writing, editing and reviewing. One of the great features of digital writing is that it is accessible for everyone because it is legible.
- Look at the technologies in the home and consider how they could inform or energise or extend work in school. For example a student teacher

recently worked with her Year 5 class to produce electronic Greek gods and heroes Top Trump cards with pictures, sound effects and text. Top Trump games then informed the creation of talking books.

- Remind yourself that the potential of ICT in writing is a great opportunity and not something to be afraid of.

After the primary phase (KS3)

Students at KS3 will be expected to use internet sources to research material across the whole curriculum. Work on information location strategies will be enhanced either in dedicated ICT sessions or in each curriculum area. Students will also be taught how to evaluate the status of sites and the purposes of the texts. In English visual and electronic texts will be explored as part of the curriculum, enabling new forms of response. Students are often encouraged to use ICT for writing in course work due to the ease of adapting editing and redrafting. They are also taught to choose the most effective form of presentation for written work and to use a range of desktop publishing applications effectively. There are also likely to be computers available for additional study beyond the curriculum.

Chapter summary

- Though ICT can be used to make the existing curriculum attractive, its importance is in transforming the opportunities for learning English
- ICT has valuable roles in all language modes
- Not all commercial software for English is of a great quality. Teachers must evaluate all English software with great care
- Children will need to be ICT literate to thrive in our society
- Children's ICT use in the home probably includes rich opportunities for language development. School must build on this knowledge
- Teachers need to ensure that children's safety is ensured in all ICT work

Further reading

Barber, D., Cooper, L. and Meeson, G. (2007) *Learning and Teaching with Interactive Whiteboards: Primary and Early Years (Achieving QTS Practical Handbooks)*. Exeter: Learning Matters.

Bennett, R. (2004) *Using ICT in Primary English Teaching*. Exeter: Learning Matters.

Bennett, R., Hamill, A. and Pickford, T. (2006) *Progression in Primary ICT (Teaching ICT Through the Primary Curriculum)*. London: Fulton.

Rudd, A. and Tyldesley, A. (2006) *Literacy and ICT in the Primary School: A Creative Approach to English*. London: Fulton.

References

Andrews, A. (ed.) (2004) *The Impact of ICT on Literacy Education*. London: Routledge Falmer.

Bennett, R. (2004) *Using ICT in Primary English Teaching*. Exeter: Learning Matters.

Berninger, V., Abbott, R., Ausberger, A. and Garcia, N. (2009) 'Comparison of pen and keyboard transcription modes in children with and without learning disabilities', *Learning Disability Quarterly*, 32: 123–141.

English, R. (2008) 'Using ICT to enhance the teaching of English'. In D. Waugh and W. Joliffe (eds), *English 3–11: A Guide for Teachers*. London: Fulton.

Evans, J. (2009) 'Creative and aesthetic responses to picture books and fine art', *Education 3–13*, 37(2): 177–190.

Gamble, N. and Yates, S. (2008) *Exploring Children's Literature*. London: SAGE.

House, R. (2010) 'Is technology harmful?', *Education Plus Scholastic*, July.

Leu, D.J. (2002) 'The new literacies: research on reading instruction with the Internet and other digital technologies'. In J. Samuels and A.E. Farstrap (eds), *What Research Has to Say about Reading Instruction*. Newark, DE: International Reading Association.

Mayesky, M. (2008) *Creative Activities for Young Children*. New York: Delmar.

McArthur, C. (2006) 'The effects of new technologies on writing and writing processes'. In C. McArthur, S. Graham and J. Fitzgerald *Handbook of Writing Research*. New York: Guilford.

Merchant, G. (2004) 'The dagger of doom and the Magic handbag: Writing on screen'. In J. Evans (ed.), *Literacy Moves On: Using Popular Culture, New Technologies and Critical Literacy in the Primary Classroom*. London: Fulton.

Montieth, M. (ed.)(2004) *ICT for Curriculum Enhancement*. Bristol: Intellect Books.

Ofsted (2009) *The Importance of ICT: Information and Communication Technology in Primary and Secondary Schools 2005–8*. London: Ofsted.

Papert, S. (1993) *The Children's Machine: Rethinking School in the Age of the Computer*. New York: Basic Books.

Price, H. (ed.) (2008) *The Really Useful Book of ICT in the Early Years*. London: Routledge.

Rose, J. (2006) *Independent Review of the Teaching of Early Reading*. London: Department for Education and Skills.

Spencer, P. (2010) *Phil Spencer's Top Selling Tips* [Online]. Available at: http://www.home.co.uk/guides/articles/selling_tips.htm

Turpin, M. (2011) *Using Visualisers in Schools – Looe, Cornwall* [Online]. Available at: http://www.avermedia-europe.com/blog/post/2011/02/04/Using-Visualisers-in-Schools-Looe-Cornwall.aspx

Wood, C., Littleton, K. and Chera, P. (2005) 'Beginning readers' use of talking books: styles of working', *Early Years: An International Journal of Research and Development,* 39(3): 135–141.

CHAPTER 9

ENGLISH AND LITERACY BEYOND THE CLASSROOM

• beyond the curriculum • clubs • display • family participation • library
• performance • publishing • special events • Theatre in Education
• World Book Day

This chapter aims to:

- explore some ways of enriching children's language learning
- consider how the school environment can further the curriculum and demonstrate a love of language
- describe some ways of making close, constructive relationships with families and the community
- suggest opportunities to offer special activities beyond the curriculum

Excellent schools are much more than a collection of classrooms where English and communication, language and literacy are taught very well. They are vibrant communities of language learners, both adults and children, which come together to plan, organise and enjoy memorable events beyond the conventional curriculum. These memorable events can be the times where the

English language comes alive for children, giving them a taste of the beauty, excitement and fun of its richness (Beverton and Sewell, 2002). Where the curriculum is organised to give children what they need to become confident, competent language users, what happens beyond the curriculum can be what makes a child's experience of language very special. This chapter will consider the school beyond the classroom, the special events which schools can offer to children, the voluntary activities which can occur beyond the curriculum and the links between the school, its families and its broader community.

The language rich environment: displays

A school should be a place where a love of language oozes out of the woodwork. The impact of high quality displays is far greater than the celebration of children's achievements or the provision of resources for learning. Beadle (2005) describes his impression of a visit to a primary school when he was researching ways of enhancing the learning environment for high school students:

> Here there seemed to be an ethos, a belief system, around the fripperies on the walls; a genuine sense that an exciting environment makes for an excited child. You could tell that the children loved, and felt loved by, the place in which they learned, and this affected how well they learned the stuff they were meant to learn, and how happy they were doing so. (2005: 1)

This quotation shows a recognition that the 'interior design' of the school is just as much a statement of personality and beliefs as are the clothes which we choose to wear. Most importantly, Beadle recognises that the environment sets the tone of the education which occurs within it. Exciting places encourage excitement. Happy places create happiness in the children (and teachers) and an environment focused closely on opportunities for learning will help children to learn. Excitement, happiness and focus are essential to children's learning: a great environment can reinforce all three.

Though children will not develop as English learners simply by being placed in a language rich environment (they do not learn through osmosis) it can certainly do a great deal to reinforce, contextualise and celebrate language learning. Ofsted reports frequently comment on the quality of displays and their efficacy as tools for learning. For example, one inspection report in 2009 noted:

> Innovative ways of providing academic guidance have been introduced, with many displays in classrooms explaining exactly what pupils have learnt, celebrating the progress between one piece of work and the next, particularly in English. (2009: 4)

This quotation shows one important aspect of using displays effectively: they need a commentary to explain their value and their purpose. In many schools this commentary is offered by the children. For example, a local school had an excellent display of work on the Ancient Egyptians in the foyer. As I walked past it, an Echo Bot strategically placed behind a sarcophagus asked politely: 'Would you like to look at our work about Egypt? We learnt a lot about how people lived and … (spooky voice) died. Yr 5 made this display; we hope you enjoy it'. This seemed an excellent way to engage the whole school community in the work of one class. (An Echo Bot is a simple recording device with a movement sensor so it can play back a message when it detects someone coming close to it.)

Displays of children's work can be both a means of celebrating achievement and an important form of publication which makes writing purposeful (Everybody Writes, 2010). Because they are accessible to many readers, children can see a purpose in being very careful with the secretarial aspects and the aesthetic qualities of the work. But, if children are asked to be careful with presentation because children from other classes and visitors to the school will read their work, then it must be displayed at a height where it can be read or it is in danger of becoming no more than an attractive rectangle to be glimpsed while passing by.

Many teachers are concerned about displaying inaccurate work which may be a real achievement for the writer but may not be viewed sympathetically by a reader. This issue can be resolved by not always focusing displays on polished finished products but by also giving insights into the whole process of writing from idea onwards. In this sort of work, there is a clear justification of unpolished drafts. The issue is particularly important in the work of young children who find editing very unrewarding and who may be encouraged to draw on partial phonic knowledge to begin to communicate through writing. Alex (PGCE student teacher in Y1 placement) solved this effectively.

> The children had Duplo but there were arguments about how many people could play with it. Clyde wrote a sign which said '2 ppl cn play her'. I was worried about whether to allow this but my teacher said it was fine. She suggested that I encouraged children to use the words around the classroom to develop their writing. A month later Clyde made a new sign which said '3 childrens can play here'. He used the words on the wall to make it right. He said that it was all right for three children to play because they were much older now!

Here, Clyde saw the need to edit and did so without prompting. A combination of valuing emergent work, allowing decision-making and providing models of accuracy has allowed development.

Displays often incorporate learning resources for the children such as key terminology for a topic or unit of work, 'tricky' words, desired vocabulary and examples of targeted language structures. These, along with the ubiquitous graphemes charts of Key Stage 1 are often the basic backdrop for effective literacy teaching. If they send out tentacles beyond the individual classroom, then the sense of progression in language development is made evident to all children. For example, alphabet footprints down the corridor give the youngest children a chance to hear the older ones recite the 'rhyme' which they will need to learn soon. Older pupils have a reminder of the importance of recalling this information in new contexts and the whole community has a visual message about the value of core knowledge.

The purposes of display are usually to celebrate good work, ensure that it reaches a wider audience and to offer a model for other children to emulate. To meet these purposes displays must be smartly presented and changed quite frequently. Poorly mounted, dog-eared displays on faded paper only convey the message that no one cares much about the quality of writing or the achievements of individuals.

The language rich environment: special areas

Many schools will have areas specially designed to encourage literacy beyond the classroom. These can be anything from a permanent stage area in the playground to comfortable, freely accessible places for reading. Each part of the school and its grounds can be a focus for particular language activities and, when these are used imaginatively, they can bring learning to life. This example is work undertaken in a wildlife area.

> I had to work with the same group for guided speaking and listening every day. It was quite hard to think up new ideas for activities sometimes so I asked the children what they wanted to do and they decided to do work outdoors. We pretended to be aliens who had landed in the playground and we sent messages back to our ship describing the things we saw. The best one was Adam. He said that a ladybird was a miniaturised tank that was invading the thistles. I think this activity got them to look closely at things and describe them imaginatively. (*Gwen, BEd student*)

 When on a placement, walk around the school and its grounds. In every accessible place (not the private staff areas or other classrooms) list how the children use language there. Then consider whether the area has the potential to be used as a site for a literacy activity which could not be undertaken the same way in the classroom. Always check with your teacher mentor before planning such work.

Another area which should be special in every school is the library. It should not be a glossy showplace designed for prestige but an area where reading in all its forms is celebrated and nurtured. Children need to have as much access as possible throughout and beyond the school day so that they can discover the pleasure of being cocooned in a great story or the invigoration of chasing an investigation through to a satisfying conclusion. This does not need to be solely book-based (many primary schools are deciding that a book-based comprehensive non-fiction library can no longer be afforded) and, perhaps it shouldn't be, as so much of children's reading will be electronic as they move towards adult life.

Whatever the size of the library, children must be taught how to locate the texts they want. (The skills of locating information within a book will be taught as part of literacy.) Most school libraries use a simplified version of Dewey Decimal for non-fiction texts and some thematic or readability-based way of organising fiction, poetry and play scripts. Clear labelling and accessible storing will ensure that resources are used well once the access systems are taught. Like in so many other aspects of teaching literacy, effective teacher modelling and demonstration is essential to effective learning. This should be a real pleasure: curling up in an armchair reading, having found the perfect book may not seem like teaching but, for many children it will be the most potent image of the value of reading they have ever seen. They will probably want to join you on the chair; they may suggest that you share the book or talk about it; they will certainly pick it up as soon as you put it down.

In 2008, Booktrust undertook a survey of what makes a school library effective. They found these key factors:

- Ensuring the leadership of the head teacher and the commitment of designated library staff
- Involving children in the day to day running of the library
- Integrating the library into the school and encouraging collaboration between library staff and teachers
- Maximising the opening hours of the library
- Making innovative use of space and ensuring the availability of resources to provide a wide range of quality stock
- Using evidence to evaluate the effectiveness of the library (2008: 1)

Though some of these aspects are at the level of whole school policy, for policy to be effective, it must be known and followed by all members of staff, including student teachers on placement. For example, it is valuable to become familiar with the systems of the library on an initial visit and, as part of medium-term planning, ensure that some teaching occurs in the library. Many schools have links with libraries in the local community and these should be used with enthusiasm as specialist children's librarians have great experience and knowledge which will benefit both you and the children you are teaching.

 Will the school library exist in 20 years? Will the classroom exist in 30 years?

Working with children of different ages

However stimulating the classroom environment, children really enjoy the opportunity to work in the playground, the corridors, the hall and the computer suite and other specialist rooms. These are shared areas where the display work and facilities may not be designed specifically for them. These are a great strength as the school maps out the literacy journey for all its members whether it is a six-year-old stopping to enjoy and begin to understand a Year 6 exhibition of work or the Y6 children giving considerate appreciation to a KS1 class assembly. Children are members of the whole school language community, not just their own class and will gain a great deal from being immersed in the breadths of its language, cultures and opportunities.

There are many opportunities for children to work beyond the classroom. These include gaining the views of other classes about an issue, performing for them and listening to their performances, reading with older or younger children and writing books or other media for other classes. Very often this involves older children writing for younger audiences but there is no reason why this cannot be reversed. For example, in one of our partnership schools, the Year 1 children composed rules for the playground for the whole school.

Reading buddies and paired reading work can be powerfully motivating and may enhance progress. Butler (1999) found that children preferred to read with other children as they were less concerned about critical responses. The study also suggested that the activity was beneficial for both children even if their abilities were very different. The less advanced child benefited from the guidance given while the better reader found that having to explain a point consolidated and clarified learning. Nes (2003) found that the fluency of all children in her study was improved by paired reading opportunities. Though her data focus on the needier readers in the paired reading activity, it could also be that the more advanced readers, when modelling the fluent reading skills which enabled their reading buddies to make progress, were given unusual opportunities to consolidate and extend their own skills.

If reading buddy systems seem to work so well, it is surprising that the same model hasn't been used more frequently to enhance writing and speaking and listening. Gélat (2001) studied the value of peer interaction in writing some of the more challenging genres at Key Stage 2. Her work suggested that paired work was more effective than the constraining structures of direct teacher instruction. Her work involved pairs of similar ages and development. This now happens frequently within the classroom but it would certainly be valuable to go further than this and to encourage shared writing across ages and the introduction of writing buddies to give additional support to young struggling writers.

Special events

Many schools participate in big events such as World Book Day which have done so much to promote the fun and importance of books. By offering activities which are outside the normal curriculum, schools enable children to view books and reading in new ways. For example an author visit often has a great impact because children realise that a book was written by a real person who probably went through exactly the same difficulties that they encounter as writers. It is strange that one of the questions authors are mostly frequently asked at this event is how much they earn from writing. Perhaps this is an underused way of motivating children to write: they are aware that we develop skills in childhood which will make us economically secure as adults! So, by showing that people make their living writing, we might help children realise that it is worthwhile. Publishers sponsor and subsidise author visits because they are aware of their enormous potential for encouraging reading (and book purchase). If children meet an author, enjoy a reading and develop a loyalty from a special event, they may go on to encountering other authors through their books.

Of course the main purpose of Book Day activities is to promote reading in the school and the home. For this reason, the activities planned should be about celebrating the pleasures of reading; it should not become 'wear your Batman pyjamas to school' day. Many successful schools use the national events and fun activities to make a direct link to the books they admire. So for example, if teachers dress up as characters, they will give readings from books or teach in role. Family participation is most successful if it starts at the planning stage and is an invitation to a pleasurable activity not a last minute test of ingenuity or dress-making skills. One local school working with the PTA organised a Saturday book trail where 20 people hid round the village ready to read and talk about books to the families who found them. This kind of activity is particularly successful because the school goes out into the community rather than expecting the community to come to it.

 Expert reflection

Anne Plenderleith: What children gain from theatre

Theatre inspires, excites, challenges and develops the imagination of children and young people.

Albert Einstein, the physicist who developed the special and general theories of relativity winning the Nobel Prize for Physics in 1921, captured the fundamental need for imaginative beings in a nutshell:

> Imagination is more important than knowledge. For knowledge is limited to all we now know and understand, while imagination embraces the entire world, and all there ever will be to know and understand.

Theatre allows children to imagine, empathise, explore and play in a safe environment, and playing is the foundation of creative and artistic activity, as well as helping them to develop life skills for the future.

Theatre can nurture a young person's ability to question and make connections, to develop the capacity for independent, critical thought, to have the ability

(Continued)

(Continued)

to put themselves in someone, or something, else's skin. Utilising theatre skills and techniques for themselves can inspire children and young people with new ambition and confidence. Exposure to excellent theatre and high quality practitioners can build children's aspiration, breaking the cycles of poverty and deprivation so often caused by low self esteem, educational under-achievement and lack of social engagement.

Creative, thinking and empathising young people will use their imagination and creativity to question, fuel and feed the arts, helping to build and re-shape their world by taking it in new and innovative directions, building a strong, healthy, imaginative, articulate and confident society.

Theatre, and all it encompasses, can be a key that unlocks and opens doors for children and young people to a world of infinite possibility.

(Anne Plenderleith is Producer, Clwyd Theatr Cymru, Theatre for Young People)

Cross-curricular approaches to literacy beyond the classroom

The activities described above have all focused closely on enhancing the core literacy curriculum by breaking out of the classroom. However, every special activity and event will offer chances to enrich language learning, often in memorable ways. For example, there are several splendid Theatre in Education organisations which focus on science learning. If children see and enjoy these, they are inevitably learning more about drama as well as science. They could analyse what they've learnt from the production about the effective presentation of material through drama and later present their own science drama on a different theme for other classes or for a family assembly.

Historical participation days at museums, houses or sites are planned to give empathy about a period, and enable children to learn from role play by listening, questioning and observing. These are all core skills of literacy as well as historical investigation. Additionally, these events give unique opportunities to make the history of the English language seem relevant and to teach a deeper understanding of the etymology which is so important for understanding and for spelling. I frequently see groups of children marching behind a Roman centurion as they learn about the history of Chester. I was very amused to hear one class chanting 'Sinister, dexter. Sinister, dexter,' as they marched. I hope this led to a discussion of the ways in which word meanings evolve over time.

Though every activity beyond the classroom is an opportunity to further children's language, it would be wrong to allow the literacy learning opportunities to swamp the original intention of the activity. Readers may recall from their own primary education the realisation that, whatever the event, they were sure to be asked to write about it. Nothing could be more certain to spoil the enjoyment of the special occasion. Teachers must choose original, exciting ways of capturing the literacy potential (Kress, 1995) and not resort to yet another dull recount which will do little to advance literacy.

Extracurricular literacy work

It would be tempting to think that, as literacy takes such a prominent position in the curriculum, children will have no need to do more voluntarily. However, the curriculum cannot allow full opportunity for children to follow particular interests so there should always be scope for these to be fostered beyond the conventional curriculum. Enthusiastic young writers, readers, actors or listeners have as much right to have their talents fostered as sportspeople. A recent survey of the opportunities for extracurricular literacy activities across partnership schools found children were offered:

- *Readers' groups.* These tend to be age or genre specific so that children all read material they will enjoy. Some seem to have been created specifically to foster boys' interests in voluntary reading while others give a sense of purpose by allowing group members to make choices for the school library or classroom. Some schools are setting up reading groups for very young able readers while others make the group an opportunity for strugglers to read without pressure or embarrassment in a comfortable setting. There's also a lot to be said for family/parent reading groups which encourage a love of reading in the home.
- *Writers' groups.* These also seem to be based on encouraging specific groups to take part. One very successful school advertises a termly programme of events which vary from fan fiction to poetry; children simply choose to take part in the events which appeal to them. They also had a 'play in a day' event which involved children of all ages and started with a title at nine in the morning and finished with a performance at the end of the school day. This event, like those of most successful writers' groups, brought school and community together to write for a real purpose.
- *Drama groups.* Though these are sometimes permanent clubs, often they form for a specific production and then rest for a few months. One school which has a permanent club has sections for different age groups and an established pattern of activities which includes a monthly presentation of scenes from a new fiction book. They also contribute to the schools' work on anti-bullying with short dramas for younger children.

These groups are probably what would be expected but we have also found more unusual groups such as:

- *Publishing company.* A group of children meet to choose material for the school to publish in an annual magazine, on their website and as little books for the classrooms and for sale at school events.

- *The arguing club.* The teacher who ran this wanted to have a debating society but the children found this a bit too formal. They meet every fortnight to argue in a reasonably restrained way about contemporary issues. They also discuss school problems and report their ideas to the governors.
- *Calligraphy club.* This was originally created to give handwriting practice to children who found it difficult. It became very popular and now involves adults as well as children.
- *Word processing club.* This is run by the school secretary and community volunteers and aims to ensure that every child can use a keyboard effectively by the end of Key Stage 1.
- *Movie club.* This speaks for itself really. Children meet once a week to watch a DVD together and to discuss it. They also go to the cinema together once a term. Popcorn is involved.
- *Story club.* This is a lunchtime club for Key Stage 1 children where, once a week, a member of staff tells a story. Children then have a time to retell the story in groups if they would like to do so.
- *Comedy club.* Children get a chance to try to be stand up comedians. The teacher who runs this had to make rules about content as children often repeated unsuitable material from the television. They now run a monthly competition where every competitor has two minutes. The organising teacher reports that children who seem shy often do very well.
- *Performance poetry/rap club.* This also involves competitions. (Children seem to find short-term focused activity with a clear aim particularly engaging.)
- *Puppet theatre club.* This is aimed at children who are reluctant to take part in other drama activities, possibly due to shyness. The children make puppets, improvise and write formal plays for performance within the club.

All these activities mean a lot to the children who take part. By choosing to join a literacy based club, they are committing to the importance of the subject in their lives as something to be enjoyed. The teachers who offer their own time are also forming new relationships with the children and frequently going out beyond the familiar safety of the school to bring new relevance to their approaches. Several of the teachers who run these clubs said that the ideas generated by the members often feed into the curriculum. They give opportunities for teachers to experiment and gain confidence just as much as they are for children. The best teachers of literacy are those who are prepared to listen, think and learn throughout their careers. Running an extracurricular activity can be an excellent form of professional development.

Choose the 'club' from the list above that you think you'd most enjoy setting up and running. How would you go about it? (If you have some good ideas, remember them for job interviews.)

Family participation in literacy development

Throughout the primary phase, family and community will continue to have great influence on the child's language development. The National Literacy Trust has recently published the results of a major survey of the levels of participation in children's reading and its impact on their development. They assert that:

> Young people who get a lot of encouragement to read from their mother or father are more likely to enjoy reading, to read frequently, to have positive attitudes towards reading and to believe that reading is important to succeed in life than young people who do not get any encouragement to read from their mother or father. (2010: 4)

If the relationship between encouragement and success is so clear, it is vital that schools do everything possible to create strong, constructive relationships with families to support literacy. Dearing et al. (2006) found that close family involvement in school was most beneficial to the most vulnerable learners. This implies that, when the family lacks confidence in the best ways to support literacy development, the school can have great impact on learning to ensure progress. However, teachers frequently report that the very families who would probably gain most from support are those who are hardest to reach through conventional invitations.

Wolfendale's pioneering work on family participation focused on inner London boroughs in which there were a high proportion of vulnerable families. Her consistent assertion (1999) that schemes which were based on an equal partnership between family and education system were likely to be the most successful, has influenced many successful initiatives across the country. Teachers need to go out to families and listen to them rather than expect them to come to the school and be told what to do for their children. Though teachers may know a great deal about children and education in general, the family will always know most about the individual child. To form strong partnerships with homes, teachers need good ears and open minds.

 Schools can be very frightening places for adults who did not enjoy their own primary education or did not make good progress. Imagine you are a single parent with a school age child and a baby. You do not have a car and have little spare money. You had a poor attendance record at school and left with no qualifications. (This is a dreadful stereotype but, because it is extreme, it will help you to think imaginatively about ways of reaching out.) You were invited to a meeting at the school to teach you ways of helping with early reading but did not attend. You are very concerned that your child is successful and happy at school.

Think about:

- The barriers which prevent this parent attending meetings at school. These may be practical or emotional.
- What the school could do to make this parent feel welcomed and appreciated.

- The ways an individual teacher could increase the parent's confidence in helping the child.
- Ways in which schools could go into the community or reach individual families.

We can never give up on the family because invitations are not taken or work sent home is not completed. The family remains the child's prime educator and, unless schools and families work together, our impact on children's enjoyment and achievement will not be great. This is one example of a teacher reaching out to a family in unusual ways to ensure that everyone worked together for the child's benefit.

Paul enjoyed Reception and made a good start on reading and writing. But he grew quieter and less happy about giving ideas in literacy all through Year 1. By Year 2 he seldom spoke in lessons – we were very worried and hoped to be able to talk to the family at parents evening. No one came and letters home weren't answered. There were no entries in the reading log. I bumped into Paul's mum one Saturday in the local supermarket. They were worried too. It turned out that none of our notes had reached them and they thought that children didn't take their books home. We had a cup of coffee, then Paul's mum said that she thought she knew what was going on but didn't want to tell me because it wouldn't be fair. I was sorry but we left things like that.

Two weeks later Paul's dad was in the playground at the end of school. He asked if we could talk so we walked round the playground together and he told me that he thought the problem was that he couldn't read or write. He thought Paul was trying to be loyal to him by not reading and writing either. He said he knew he had to learn to read with Paul but it scared him a lot and, if he failed, then it would make things worse.

I agreed to help and for the next month we did supermarket reading together every Saturday morning. We wrote a list together in the café, found the things on the shelves and then had a cup of tea all together when the shopping was finished. Paul's dad started to realise that he could read quite a lot. He started to come with a list and then, after a month asked me if I could find out about proper classes he could go to.

I think he is one of the bravest people I have met in all my life. (*Angie, Y2 teacher*)

Though Angie praises Paul's father, she deserves a great deal of credit herself for identifying a problem, going out to the family, helping in ways which they could cope with and, most importantly, not being judgmental. Fortunately, such demanding responses won't always be necessary but it is always important to see the issue from the child and family's point of view rather than being dogmatic about what everyone should do to help with literacy development.

Did your family's participation in your development as a language user focus on the school?

These are some basic ideas which could ensure that the simplest forms of family participation such as reading at home and completing literacy homework are successful.

- There should be plenty of time to complete any work. It should never be set one day and expected back the next as many families have busy schedules.
- Teachers should ensure that they know about important factors such as religious festivals or spending time with a non-resident parent as these could put particular strain on work completion.
- Work at home is always in addition to work covered in school. For example, it is inappropriate to send home a list of spellings for the family to teach but it is fine to send home words with a note that these have been taught, the strategies that will help the child to remember them and a request to check that the child still knows them.
- Books get lost. It isn't the end of the world – at least you know there is one book in the house. Children who lose books must not be penalised.
- There needs to be a balance between the security of routine and the drudgery of ritual. This can often be achieved by giving children the opportunity to choose between activities to undertake at home. In this way they become active partners in the home–school relationship rather than its subjects.
- Teachers need to get to know the families so that the work is carefully judged to meet their needs. For example many schools use different bookmarks to ensure that the reading at home is pleasurable and valuable. These often read: 'your child can read this book to you'; 'please read this book together'; 'please read this book to your child' and 'please talk about this book.' These can be bilingual if appropriate. This system allows the child a much wider choice of books as the teacher, knowing child and family, can choose the most appropriate bookmark.
- Families are diverse. It is often fine for a child to work with an older brother or sister or someone beyond the nuclear family.
- The relationship must be mutually respectful. The way in which teachers write in homework or reading diaries can often give a clear impression of the way in which the family is viewed. It is always insulting to use 'suitable for Key Stage 1' handwriting when writing a note to adults. The diary needs to explain clearly what the school would like to happen and needs to respond professionally and thoughtfully to comments from the family.
- Attendance at school meetings on reading is often very low. Some schools make DVDs of the meeting to go home. One teacher noted recently that parents nearly always come if their child is performing so she incorporates drama into her presentations on reading (casting very carefully to maximise attendance).
- Family participation in literacy does not need to be instigated or controlled by the school. Teachers need to take the opportunity to find out what is happening rather than dictate what should be happening.

- Children should never be used as go-betweens. If the school needs to get a message to the family, a direct approach is important.
- Good classroom practice in literacy is the most important factor in ensuring strong family participation. If a child goes home happy, eager to talk about the exciting achievements of the day and keen to build upon them at home, the family will find it very rewarding to become fully involved in furthering the achievements.

Chapter summary

- Children's language learning doesn't just occur in the classroom
- The school's beliefs about literacy should be obvious in the whole environment
- Special events are very valuable
- Extra-curricular activities help children develop special interests
- Family participation needs to be mutually supportive and respectful

Further reading

Cremin, T. and Dombey, H. (eds) (2007) *Handbook of Primary English in Initial Teacher Education*. Leicester: UKLA

Evans, J. (ed.) (2004) *Literacy Moves On*. Abingdon: Fulton.

Nutbrown, C. (2005) *Early Literacy Work with Families: Policy, Practice and Research*. London: SAGE.

References

Beadle, P. (2005) 'Look what I can do, mum', *The Guardian*, 12 April.

Beverton, S. and Sewell, G. (2002) 'Implementing whole school policies for Key Stage 2', *Education 3–13*, 30(1): 24–29.

Booktrust/LISU (2008) *Successful Primary School Libraries: Case Studies of Good Practice* [Online]. Available at: http://www.booktrust.org.uk/Resources-for-schools/School-libraries-research.

Butler, F.M. (1999) 'Reading partners: Students can help each other learn to read!', *Education and Treatment of Children*, 22(4): 1–12.

Dearing, E., Kreider, H., Simpkins, S. and Weiss, H.B. (2006) 'Family involvement in school and low income children's literacy performance: longitudinal associations between and within families', *Journal of Educational Psychology*, 98: 653–664.

Everybody Writes (2010) Exploring Writing Beyond the Classroom [Online]. Available at: http://www.everybodywrites.org.uk/ (accessed 10 August 2010).

Gélat, M. (2001) 'Peer interaction, cognition and argumentative writing (Key Stage 2 children)'. EdD thesis, The Open University.

Kress, G. (1995) *Writing the Future: English and the Making of a Culture of Innovation*. London: NATE.

National Literacy Trust (2010) *Literacy in the Home and Young People's Reading*. National Literacy Trust.

Nes, S.L (2003) 'Using paired reading to enhance the fluency skills of less-skilled readers', *Reading Improvement*, 40(4): 179–192.

Ofsted (2009) *Blackpool Church of England Primary School Inspection Report 325807*. London: Ofsted.

Wolfendale, S. (1999) '"Parents as Partners" in research and evaluation: methodological and ethical issues and solutions', *British Journal of Special Education*, 26(3): 164–169.

CHAPTER 10

PLANNING TO ENSURE PROGRESS IN ENGLISH

• activity • group work • guided work • independent work • individual work • lesson plan • medium term plan • phase • prior learning • roles of the teacher • shared work • targeting • unit of study • whole class work

This chapter aims to:

- show some of the information needed to plan great English lessons
- discuss some issues of learning through activities
- link planning to assessment
- consider how we plan English for whole classes, groups and individuals
- describe progression through the language modes for a unit of work

Every literacy lesson needs to be planned with great care to ensure that children learn effectively and with pleasure. Many student teachers find the idea of planning independently extremely daunting, rightly so, as determining the most constructive next steps in children's education is a huge responsibility. Planning needs to start not with what will be taught but why this is considered the wisest next step. The National Curriculum sets out a logical hierarchy of broadly age-related learning subdivided into the language modes (attainment targets). The Primary National Strategy took this outline and added valuable detail to each step so that teachers had guidance on what should be taught in each year and how to approach the teaching. Though this model brought great strength to the literacy curriculum there was also a consistent undercurrent of concern that any detailed curriculum for literacy was intrinsically prescriptive and took away teachers' decision-making. It was also thought that, in attempting to describe the desired progress of the average child, the needs of atypical learners were not met. Alexander (2004) voiced concerns about the impact of the strategy, which has been very influential on the way in which the primary curriculum is evolving.

Before the primary phase

Planning communication, language and literacy at EYFS

There is a common misunderstanding that planning at EYFS involves teachers creating a free-flow in which exciting activities capable of helping children to progress in their language development are set out and then children choose to do them or initiate their own linguistic activities. This is an oversimplification of a very sophisticated model of planning in which teachers structure a block of time (often a week) to ensure that every child has frequent, meaningful learning activities in all language modes. These are then consolidated through child-initiated activities which are based around interests and preferences. The teachers and practitioners lead the key activities and then participate as appropriate in the play, skilfully moving children forward to meet identified targets. For example, a teacher may read a book which is then made available for children to look at. If a child then chooses the book, gathers some toys around her and then uses reading-like behaviour to retell the story, the teacher may well join the group of toys to involve the child in a conversation about the text, identifying what she enjoyed about the retelling and possibly focusing on key words. She will use the information gained about progress to plan the next overt teaching work

Decisions before planning

The Primary National Strategy was never compulsory in schools (as it was never part of governmental legislation) and it was certainly never intended to remove the right, or duty, of individual teachers to make planning decisions about the best next steps for classes or individuals. Most teachers found, and still find, it an invaluable resource and a reliable structure which forms the basis of planning but does not remove the need for the development of a unique approach to literacy planning based upon:

- Previous teaching
- Previous learning (these are not necessarily the same thing) and attainment
- Individual needs for successful inclusion
- The school's medium and long term plans
- The links with other subjects
- Links with the teaching of phonics

This list shows that the traditional model of research, planning, teaching, assessment and evaluation cannot easily be broken apart to find a starting place for the process. Planning is heavily dependent on assessment, evaluation and research of typical development, curriculum hierarchies and individual subject matter. When student teachers are planning lessons or units of study in literacy it is important that as much of the information suggested above is discovered as possible in order to ensure relevance and progression.

 How much should teachers rely on published schemes of work for English?

Additionally, factors to do with the individual teacher's beliefs about teaching and learning and their strengths, knowledge and preferences will influence planning (Zeichner, 1999). These factors link to both evaluation and research, so the teaching cycle becomes the way in which teachers continually refresh, augment and enhance their skills and knowledge. Preferences, in particular, require very careful evaluation to ensure that they do not limit or distort the opportunities given to children. If, for example, a teacher finds fiction genres more interesting to teach than non-fiction ones, there might be a temptation to devote more time to these or teach them with more flair and energy. This could easily disadvantage the boys in the class as those who may tend to prefer non-fiction. Moss (2007) argues for the need to be attuned to the complexities which impact on preference-making of this kind in literacy planning and teaching. This is Val's (teacher mentor) consideration of one of her dislikes.

> When I was mapping out the year's work, I knew I was going to have a student in the summer term and I thought it would be good to leave 'persuasion' for them because it's a big unit and it uses a lot of skills from previous units, then I thought, 'Face it, Val, you're passing it on because it is difficult and boring'. It wasn't fair to leave it to the student. I threw away everything about persuasion I did last year and started again with the planning and I loved teaching it.

This reflection shows a teacher's realisation that avoidance of initially unattractive or daunting material is detrimental to children's progress (and that it isn't fair to leave the hardest material to the least experienced teachers). However, dislike of an author or text may be a very good reason for finding an alternative as it is extremely difficult to keep a positive approach to such material.

Planning units of study

When this background information has been discovered and the rationale behind the planning decisions clarified, decisions can be made about what should be learnt. Many schools will be guided by the units of study of the Primary National Strategy as they ensure that the statutory requirements of the National Curriculum for English are met through logical steps in inter-related themes (Primary National Strategy, 2010). This section is based on planning for a unit of study of the strategy though the principles are relevant to any medium term plan. (A plan is for a unit of work lasting between two and four weeks.)

A unit of study is nearly always related to a genre. By the end of the unit of study children will be able to recognise it, identify and describe its key features and bring these to their work in understanding and creating text. These general learning outcomes are amplified, refined and made specific to lessons as the children move through their learning. The activities undertaken are the ways of ensuring the learning rather than being the purpose of the unit. So, a unit on writing play-scripts may culminate in the children writing a script but completing the activity is not the purpose of the unit; it is a way of demonstrating that the teaching has been effective and the learning has taken place. Many student teachers allow the activities to be the starting point of their planning. This is because they are, rightly, determined to plan for children to do enjoyable and relevant things. However, if the activities come first, the learning is not sufficiently obvious to ensure precision and clarity in teaching and assessment. Your role is to make sure that children learn by doing interesting, engaging work, not to ensure that they complete activities.

Most teachers will plan to work for a fortnight or three weeks on a single unit of study. This can be divided into speaking and listening, reading and writing rich phases. Units usually start with speaking and listening as a main focus as this is the most accessible language mode for most children. It enables the teacher to familiarise the children with the genre by drawing on her own skills and knowledge. Very often, this initial work will remind children of previous learning which the new material may extend or may be a sideways move, for example from stories with familiar settings to stories with unfamiliar settings where similar narrative structures give a secure basis for new consideration of setting, characterisation and vocabulary extension. The first phase therefore enables children to recall and build upon existing knowledge, ensuring immediate success and feelings of achievement. These are important because initial success will encourage children to believe that they will enjoy and make progress as the work continues.

The speaking and listening phase is, however, much more than a foundation for reading and writing. One great thing about speaking is that it enables children to explore new concepts and develop new skills without the messy impedimenta of reading or writing. It is in this phase of the work that the key ideas such as why the genre is valuable and how to have maximum impact on an audience are set in the learners' minds. This can be shown from a speaking and listening activity planned by a student teacher. The theme is persuasion and the children have been given a die with 'however', 'but', 'additionally', 'also', 'nevertheless' and 'furthermore' written on the faces. Their task is to argue for and against a new supermarket in the town. The work is successful because the subject is something the participants know about and which interests them.

Gemma: There's Tescos and Aldi and you can get shopping delivered so we don't need another supermarket. [*throws die*] Also . . .

Louise: Also ... the other shops might shut down. [*throws die*] 'Also' again . . .

Katie: Also ... it would be good to have somewhere new.

Gemma: If it's 'also' it has to be another something against.

Katie: Alright ... also it would be bad to have somewhere new because of the old people and they like everything to be like it always was when they were young! [*throws die*] But . . .

Louise: But ... they don't have to shop at the new Sainsbury's. They can still go other places. [*throws die*] However . . .

Gemma: However ... my Nan says if we have a Sainsbury's then the market will shut down and she always goes every week.

The girls in this example are doing exactly the right thing for the first part of any unit – becoming familiar with the concepts and language use. Later in the week they did some drama work on the same theme before having a formal debate. Through this they learnt important speaking and listening skills which would be transferable to other contexts across the whole curriculum as well as rehearsing the language structures which they'd need to understand the persuasion texts they were asked to read and to compose their own written arguments.

The second phase usually focuses on reading as this gives children the opportunity of studying expert use of the new genre. This takes them a step forward from their spoken successes by extending vocabulary, sentence structure and knowledge of genre conventions. The learning objectives are to do with identifying the key aspects of texts and contrasting them with others written in a similar style or for a similar purpose. They learn to make judgments about effectiveness of writing and support these with arguments drawn from the texts they read. Importantly they are also learning to create their mental 'writing frame' or planning structures to help them to structure their own work. If these are developed by children through consideration of material they have read, they are more likely to be remembered. This leads them to be accessible for writing on other texts or in different curriculum contexts.

Just as the speaking and listening phase often involves some reading and some preliminary writing or note-taking, so planning the reading phase will certainly involve children listening to and talking about texts. Group or paired work, whether guided or independent, enables children to draw on the strengths and ideas of others to further their learning. Many student teachers are more at ease planning individual work, possibly in the belief that class man-agement will be easier. This is seldom the case; children enjoy talking and are very good at it so it is far better to plan for interaction about the subject than to try to prevent talk off the subject.

With young children there will have to be some focus in the reading phase of the unit on the mechanics of early reading such as the consolidation of ways of decoding learnt in the discrete phonics sessions. This will always be an important consideration in the planning as it supports the focus on gaining meaning from text. As reading will still be daunting for many young children, planning often focuses on the key aspects of the text which link with decoding skills. This is Danny's example of working on descriptive language in stories with familiar settings with the lowest group in a Year 2 class.

> My objective was for them to find the describing words in a story but I knew that they find it very hard to read for long. So I asked them to tell the story using only the pictures and then for each picture, decide on one of the words they would expect to find. Then they had to see if the author had used the same word. They were so pleased when they had decided on 'gloomy' as the best word for the forest and the author had written 'dark'. They thought their word was better. If I'd just asked them to read it, two of them would have found 'dark' difficult but they read it easily because they'd talked about the best words. (*Danny, Y4 BEd student*)

The writing phase of a unit of study is planned to draw on the material covered in the two previous phases. This enables the planning to separate the most daunting aspects of writing – what to write about and how to do it effectively – from the writing processes of composing and editing text. By the beginning of the third phase children will already be equipped with a solid understanding of the purposes and conventions of the material to be written and a good idea of the consistent key features of the text type. Though this diminishes the difficulties of writing, this is still the most daunting part of the planning because it is necessary to ensure the learning objectives are met while offering support to the children.

The learning objectives must lead the way in which the writing phase is con-structed as otherwise it is easy to be entangled with the issues of accuracy and presentation. Though these are always important, as poor spelling, handwrit-ing or word processing skills will prevent the writer's material being communi-cated to its intended audience, they are the continuous secondary foci of all writing work, not the prime purpose of the unit. The final learning outcomes for most blocks of work will be that children:

- can describe the key linguistic aspects of a given genre
- can locate them in their reading of the genre
- can use these in their own writing to communicate ideas effectively
- can evaluate the effectiveness of writing (their own and that of others) in conveying the desired message

Many teachers will want the final activity to offer evidence of individuals' learning so the focus will be on independent writing. This may mean that the knowledge of children who find writing difficult may be underestimated because the final product may not give good examples of the learning. This can be overcome if there is adequate planning for shared and guided work, group or paired writing and discussion about both the writing product and processes. This is part of Katy's (student teacher on final placement) discussion with Liam at the end of a block of work on myths.

> *Liam*: I think my own myth was good because it explained why there's high and low tides (his myth was called *'How Anansi tricked the whale with the salt pot'*). But the not so good bit was the end. It needed explaining why it goes on happening every day, not just the two times.
>
> *Katy*: We found that myths do that – linking the story to the present day, didn't we?
>
> *Liam*: I could of put 'and every day the thirsty whale gulps in a great mouthful of water and that's the low tide but it is still too salty so he spits it all out of his blowhole and that's the high tide'.
>
> *Katy*: I think that would help the reader. We can add it if you want. What about the language you used?
>
> *Liam*: Casual connectives so it made sense.
>
> *Katy*: Causal – they tell us the causes why the things happened.
>
> *Liam*: Yeah, causal. I did some of them in it. It was hard to make it sound like it had been written thousands of years ago when the myths got made. Harry's was good. The way he shouted 'behold' when he read it out – you jumped!
>
> *Katy*: He scared me! Maybe it's something to remember for next time.

This extract shows that Liam's final piece of writing did not, in his opinion, show the sum of his understanding of the material he'd covered (what piece of writing ever really does?). His lack of stamina in writing has left the work unfinished and unpolished. His evaluation shows that he fully understands key aspects of the unit and can identify effective language use. Because the planning included this evaluation opportunity, Katy can see the successes of her teaching much more clearly and Liam is able to recognise his own learning.

It is always worth considering whether the planning really needs to move the children towards a final, independently written product. For example, if studying performance poetry the culmination would logically be a performance. In this unit, children's writing may occur earlier in the annotation of a text for performance or in editing or adding to a poem to be performed. Even when writing is the final product, it need not necessarily be individual. For example, list poems may include contributions from all the class which groups edit to create different poems. In planning for writing the teacher needs to balance the need to develop individual skills, including stamina in writing, with the need to find the best ways of ensuring that every child is enabled to reach the central learning outcomes.

How much of our planning should focus on consolidation and extension of previous learning?

Planning individual lessons

The structure of the typical phonics lesson at Key Stage 1 is considered separately, so the focus here will be on the ways of planning a typical literacy lesson. This is likely to include these components which maximise learning:

- Some whole class shared activity in speaking, listening, reading or writing
- Some direct teaching of a new concept or skill
- Some time in which the teacher works with a group of children of roughly similar ability
- Some time in which most children work independently either individually or as a member of a group
- A time when the class comes together again to identify achievements and consolidate learning

The proportions of time spent in each activity depend on the content of the lesson. It is always worth working with the rule that children can sit still on an uncomfortable carpet for no more in minutes than their age in years (try it yourself!). It is always sensible to plan for at least ten minutes for writing or very little will be achieved. When planning the time allocations in the lesson, teachers must ensure that children have enough time to complete the work set. If work is persistently allowed to be left incomplete, its value will be diminished for the children. Pretty soon there will seem little point in even trying to finish, which is why some children are so skilled at wasting time while appearing to get ready to work.

 Would our teaching of English be better or worse if the photocopier had never been invented?

Shared work

The whole class shared work usually begins the lesson so it sets the tone for everything which follows. It should make reference to previous learning so that children have this reactivated; it also needs to address any misconceptions noted in previous work. The learning objectives should be shared with children in language which they can understand and it is fair to explain what will count as demonstration of the learning. The session needs to be fully participative which does not mean asking questions of individuals in turn while the others fiddle and fidget. Full participation means all the children involved in the work all the time. It can be achieved through paired work and feedback, and through oral work which requires thoughtful empathy or decision-making.

The shared activity will include adult modelling of the key learning. Children participate by assisting in the decision-making, offering ideas or suggestions for improvement. By including questions in this part, the teacher is showing the sort of internal questioning the children will need to undertake as they move towards independent work. In this example, Laura (student teacher) has paused in her retelling of Aladdin to reflect on word choice.

> *Laura*: 'Still clinging onto the rope, Aladdin swung the lamp around him to see what might be in the cave'. Now, I think I've got to make a decision. If I tell you about all the treasure, it will slow down the story but I need to get you imagining this wonderful cave full of glittery treasure. Any ideas? [*pause*] Talk to your shoulder partners.

[Children talk for a minute and a half]

> *Laura*: Anyone worked out a good way to do it?
> *Josie*: Use a simile. Like a butterfly wing, something . . .
> *Kyle*: Sunrise. Being inside a sunrise.
> *Laura*: I love that idea. Being inside a sunrise. 'And as he swung his lamp, he felt as if he was in the centre of a sunrise. Every wall and the ground and even the stalactites . . .' I'm not sure if it's a good idea to explain why it felt like that. When you do your retelling of this bit, you need to decide whether to explain.

The next part of the lesson flows usually naturally from the shared activity (though it is fine to change the order of elements to enhance learning). In the lesson quoted above, Laura went on to build on previous work on similes, showing how to use them to develop character by making sure that the simile chosen was within the character's experience. This led to direct demonstration of the work she was going to ask some groups to do independently: a tag retelling with each child speaking in role as a different character. At the end of this direct teaching she had the children in exactly the right frame of mind to work independently: aware of the learning, certain of what they were expected to do, enthusiastic about doing it and sure the activity was worthwhile.

Guided work

Guided group work seems to be the least-loved element of literacy teaching, though it has the most power to ensure that children progress. It is based on a direct Vygotskian approach that what children can do working with an expert, will soon become attainable without help. (Don't assume that you have to be the expert – it could easily be a friend.) As in the shared work, all children are active all the time (up to 20 minutes) and the teacher is fully engaged in direct teaching not supervision. As the children are grouped loosely on the evidence of previous attainment, teaching can be very precise. This is an extract from the same lesson where Laura is now working with the fourth attainment group of five in her Year 4 class. (Children were mostly working at level 2 for reading and writing but level 3 for spoken language.)

Laura:　This time I'm going to describe the treasure cave as if Abanazar was seeing it and if my simile doesn't seem right to you, you stop me and we'll think of a new one together. 'The treasure cave looked like a jewellery shop . . .' Do you like that?

Cherie:　No. I think we should say 'was glittery with a thousand jewels and gold necklaces'.

Laura:　That's very vivid and I can see it in my imagination. But we were learning about similes today so I'd like you to use a simile. Saying it was similar to something the audience would know about and the character would know about. Can you think of a simile, Cherie? Start with, 'it looked like …

Cherie:　A butterfly.

Laura:　That's a great start. Thank you. Can we add a describing word?

Georgia:　Twinkly.

Ethan:　Butterflies are little! This big. And the cave has to be huge.

Laura:　Can you make our idea better?

Ethan:　'The walls looked like a pirate's treasure ship.'

Laura:　That's a great simile but I'd like to work with Cherie's idea for a minute. Can we keep yours for later?

Later in the same discussion Laura used Ethan's idea to consider whether Abanazar would know about pirates. This example shows good guided work because the children are working with the teacher to extend their understanding in ways which they could not manage without her help.

Independent work

While teachers work with a guided group, the rest of the class will be expected to work independently. Goodwin (2005: 9) defined the independent reader as a child 'who has strategies for tackling the unknown'. The purpose of the independent working time in a lesson is to enable the child to draw on the taught strategies and to make them her own. This implies that children, when working independently, need to be decision-makers so that they are drawing on strategies, consolidating them in new contexts and understanding their use. Far too often, independent work is planned which does little more than guarantee that children can work without interrupting the teacher.

The other aspect of planning independent group work which merits thought is how we ask children to sit in most primary classroom. Tables are put together in ways which facilitate interaction but children are often asked to work individually. If children are encouraged to work together or, at least, consult each other if there is a problem, each individual's strategies are shared with others and may be learnt. It is far better to plan for interactive work than to be distracted from working with a group by trying to impose a spurious silence.

Planning for a plenary should be simple. It should be a time when the children come together again to reflect on their learning and to consider how it could be taken forward across the curriculum. It should be a time when learning is articulated and when achievement is celebrated. It isn't a muddled 'show and tell' because the focus, as ever, is on the learning rather than the task. Here's a great example from Pete, a postgraduate student teacher:

> *Pete*: So we were aiming to learn how to persuade someone by using contrasts. What did you manage? People at the window table? Matthew, can you be spokesperson?
>
> *Matthew*: We thought. . . you can make the other things, possibilities, look bad by making fun of them. Like 'of course, you might prefer to go on a caravan holiday in the cold and wet and the mud and with no proper toilets to going on our magnificent cruise'.
>
> *Pete*: Do you think that's a good method of persuasion?
>
> *Matthew*: Yeah, but it's bad as well because you are saying it's either this or that and actually there are lots of other things not just cruises or caravans.
>
> *Pete*: So perhaps it's something you shouldn't do because it isn't fair?
>
> *Leo*: People do it. Often. Like those insurance ads. So now we can see it, we are like immune.
>
> *Matthew*: But if I was wanting to sell a cruise, it's clever to do it.

Some teachers believe that younger children find this sort of reflection too difficult and therefore tell the children what has been learnt. However, if children recognise their learning they are in a better position to make progress. This is the same student working with Y1 children.

> *Pete*: What did we try to put in our heads today? [*Pointing towards a brain diagram on which the objective has been written*] Who could read it for me? Lisette?
>
> *Lisette*: 'To find the difficult parts of some tricky words.'
>
> *Pete*: Thank you. How could I know if it is in your head now? Sophie?
>
> *Sophie*: You could, after play, go 'spell me said' and I'd go 'S is easy. D is easy. The middle is tricky and and it's 'ai'.'
>
> *Pete*: So it's in your head! And because you are going to surprise me some time today, I'll know it's there. Everyone, tell your shoulder partner when you think you can surprise me. Whisper or I'll hear.

Planning for individual needs

Planning for specific needs is covered more fully in Chapter 8. Every lesson should be constructive for all participants and, to ensure this happens, teachers reflect on previous attainment and difficulties to carry these forward to the planning of lessons. It may be valuable to consider three possible levels of previous attainment which will need some individual approach in planning.

If a child completely failed to grasp the concept, the teacher will need to consider whether the knowledge and skills necessary for the learning were in place. For example, no child could grasp the value of similes if she did not understand how and why authors include description in writing.

Understanding the reason for difficulty will show what is needed to overcome it and will identify the things which need to be included in planning for the child to progress. This is often necessary when a child has been absent for a time. However, if the child has been offered ample, good teaching, then the analysis of the issue will be more complex and will need to include consideration of background features, the nature of the activities and the care taken in the teaching. It is a reasonable rule of thumb that, if a group of children have completely failed to grasp an idea, the problem lies in the teaching but if only one has difficulties then the problem is with a failure to plan for known individual needs.

If children have partially learnt the new concept, teachers usually include a brief reminder in the whole class work including another example of adult modelling and a demonstration of what is needed. They will then use some interactive work to ensure that the children now remember what to do before going on to give consolidation activities. This is never presented as 'do it again only better' as this is both boring and depressing, but as building on achievement in a new context. The difficulty in planning in this case is to ensure that the medium-term planning is not eroded by the need to consolidate for individuals. Catching up on one thing can easily mean falling behind on something else. This must not happen.

If some children have grasped the concept with surprising ease, it may be necessary to adjust planning to prevent work which is seen as pointless. Some lessons fail because the ablest children are given the drudgery of more practice work while the rest catch up. Constructive planning does not devote time to the unnecessary or take such children forward on the same linear development but asks for the learning to be focused another way. For example in Laura's 'treasure cave' lesson cited above, children who she knew found similes quite easy had to work out how to describe the cave if there was no light at all, drawing on similes from other senses. They found this difficult in an interesting way – exactly what they needed!

Planning for gradual independence

A new concept has been learnt when a child can use it effectively without prompting or support. To do this, the child needs to be able to recall key features of the learning and to make decisions. This calls for an understanding of the learning not just a repetition of well-practised actions. Graham and Harris (1997) reviewed previous research on the awareness of the learning needed to achieve independence. They noted that the quality of independent work depended on the quality of initial teaching. If a child had developed misconceptions during initial learning, they could easily become embedded in independent activities. This implies that teachers' planning must focus on both gradual withdrawal of support and the consistent self-monitoring so that errors and misconceptions are addressed.

When children are truly independent in any language skill, they will be able to identify a problem, choose knowledge which will address it and make accurate appropriate use of that knowledge. For example Laura (the treasure cave lesson student teacher) was delighted when her class teacher called her two months after the placement to tell her that, in a letter home from a Roman soldier, one of the children had written 'last night the sunset was like wine spilt on a tablecloth'. The child had identified the need to make the writing vivid, remembered the teaching and used the knowledge effectively. That is real independence of learning.

Independence usually comes through planning for systematically passing more decision-making from teacher to child, usually in this sequence:

1 *Teacher models* the new learning. This involves showing how a competent adult uses the skill or draws on the knowledge. From the earliest stages this may simply be showing the child that something is part of the repertcire of school language, so the teaching assistant in EYFS I recently heard praising a child for standing up 'straight as a soldier' was laying an essential foundation for work on imagery which might not be addressed for two or three years. The more vivid, exciting and varied the language of the adults in the school, the more effective the model that is offered. Modelling is also the starting point for active teaching. The teacher will show the children what she does, asking them to take particular note of the key aspects. Many teachers also offer a commentary in their modelling so they speak the necessary thoughts and show the decision-making. Many recruits to teaching find this deeply embarrassing so it is one of the many occasions when a glove puppet is useful. Children cannot be expected to learn something if they do not know what it is or how decisions are made. The adult model also gives them a framework for reflection on their own competence.

2 *Demonstration* is the next step to independence. This involves showing children what they will be required to do. Though it also involves commentary, the language changes to more instructional modes to link the child closely to what is being done and to offer guidance on success criteria and key decisions. This is a demonstration of the formation of lowercase letter b.

> Straight down to the line. You've got to stop and think 'now up a little bit' so up we go and stop. Now you have to remember to go to the … right … and round in a big swoop right down to the bottom and stop again. Done. Beautiful. And a pat yourself on the back if you are pleased with it.

3   *Shared work* encourages children to participate more fully in the activity by drawing on the knowledge gained from the modelling and demonstration. It is planned so that children share their thinking with each other as well as the teacher. In shared speaking and listening work and shared reading children will often be asked to act as directors, guiding the teacher how to read a particular phrase or how to make a point effectively. In writing, teachers gradually move responsibility for composition to the children while acting as both scribes and editors. As this is a whole class activity, planning takes account of the differing needs with varied levels of participation being required. The less advanced children often gain most from being participant observers for aspects which are still beyond them as they are having models of competence being reinforced.

4   *Guided work* enables the teacher to monitor and intervene in individual progress. It is a vital stage between shared class and the first independent attempts. The great thing about it is that, because the teacher is there to make sure nothing is going to go wrong, children can move forwards very quickly. The analogy of the dual-controlled car is quite useful – just as a driving instructor starts by doing a great deal with the extra pedals and aims to do less and less as the learner grows in skill and confidence so the teacher takes some control of the language work but aims to guide the learners to be ready for independence.

5   *Independent work* can usefully be sub-divided into three stages:

(a)   *Closely structured independent work* needs the teacher to plan enough instruction or support to make it an easy step forward from guided work. The planned support can take the form of frameworks, partially completed work or very detailed instructions about the decisions to be taken. This is Leila instructing a group about to undertake their first attempt at sub-headings in a report:

> We've chosen a sub-heading for the first paragraph together and on the table there's two more paragraphs. Do what we did. Read the paragraph then pick the most important phrase then take out as many words as you can so it still makes sense. Write it down. You've got time to do both paragraphs. Can the four of you work together and can Michael be scribe today?

This first step into independence can't really fail because the teacher has undertaken the difficult aspects of the decision-making. So it is not evidence of true independent understanding.

(b)   *Unstructured independent work* is the next step in planning for independence. It requires the children to instruct themselves about what they will need to do to be successful. For example, in a history lesson the following week, Leila's class were told to put sub-headings into a report but were not reminded how to do this. She was quite tough about demanding higher levels of independence because she knew they should be able to manage perfectly well without support. They did.

(c) *Unsolicited independent work* is the final step. It is exemplified by the 'spilt wine' incident above. The child made the decision to use a simile as well as reminding herself how to choose one. When a new skill is used spontaneously, it has really been learnt. To plan for this, the teacher needs to ensure that children are given freedom to make decisions and that they have created an ethos in which decision-making is celebrated.

Planning the teacher's role

Every minute of a literacy lesson involves the teacher in planned, active teaching. This does not include supervision: that is something which happens in addition to planned teaching. As well as this (as if this isn't enough) teachers also plan to observe and analyse actions and responses. This requires planning for who will be observed and what in particular the observation will include. For example, if a misconception had been addressed in a previous lesson, a teacher would probably want to know if the new learning was secure. This could be done by planning to ask a particular child to take part in a game involving the new learning and observing the success. It could also involve planned questions to elicit understanding.

Teachers also have plans for the work of teaching assistants and classroom volunteers. To make this successful, the planning needs to include time when the desired teaching method is demonstrated, usually in the shared work or the focus on the new learning. As a mutually-trusting relationship is established it is also wise to involve teaching assistants in the planning and evaluating cycle so that they share the insights into the decision-making. It is far easier for them to teach to plans developed together than ones imposed by others. When planning for the work of others it is vital that the most vulnerable learners in the literacy class do not become a satellite group taught only by assistants.

Expert reflection

Jane Weavers: Learning from your work in school

Whilst it is commonly called teaching practice, it is better not viewed as practising what you learn in university, but the opportunity to get another perspective on teaching from professionals who are on the front line putting into practice government initiatives and research. Therefore your time in school should be viewed in terms of actually doing the job (just as doctors practise their profession), learning from those on the chalk face. You are not just practising what you have learnt in university on the poor unsuspecting children.

So what will this learning involve?

- Working alongside the teacher, firstly using her planning, and then taking on the responsibility for developing lesson plans relevant to the topics the school is currently engaged in. In doing this you will draw both on what you have been learning in your university based programme and on the good practice you observe in the school.
- Your teacher will be able to give you advice about planning, drawing on their own experiences and also the specific context of the school and class.
- The opportunity to see how different schemes and materials are used by experienced teachers to enhance and develop literacy lessons and to discuss with teachers how and why they make informed choices about what is appropriate for their specific class.
- Learning from both your successes and your mistakes. Your teacher or mentor will help you to identify the learning opportunities that both yield. Remember that there is as much to be learnt from something that went well as there is from something that didn't. Both these things will help you to plan better lessons.
- Taking risks in your planning, as observation of good teachers shows that it is those who are innovative in what they plan that are the best (Ofsted, 2011).
- And finally, remember that you should go into school with your eyes and mind open. If you do this you will develop your practice and become a confident and inspiring teacher.

(Jane Weavers, Primary Programme Leader for Partnership, University of Chester)

Unplanned teaching

Some of the best moments in teaching come from the unexpected things said or done by children. When these occur, teachers need to make decisions about for how long and how far they can justify moving from the carefully planned lesson. When children bring unexpected knowledge to their work or ask questions which show that they are thinking about material in an innovative way, they are showing that they are making important connections between the immediate subject and their experiences and beliefs. It is probably reasonable to consider unplanned moments in this way: if a child offers an answer which shows a lack of understanding, teachers deviate from the plan to sort out the issue or they make a note to address it later. It therefore seems entirely justifiable to handle the unexpected brilliant or divergent answers in the same way. Sometimes the plan is there but better stuff pushes it aside: these are the memorable moments which bring the subject to life.

After the primary phase (KS3)

Planning at KS3 has to be split into planning for literacy which happens in every lesson across the curriculum as a way of ensuring that skills are used and extended, planning for literacy for those students who need additional support and the planning to ensure they succeed across the curriculums and the specific planning of furthering knowledge of literature, non-fiction genres and key language skills which all pupils gain in dedicated English lessons. These work in very much the same way as at primary school with units of study which last long enough to have some depth but not so long that they become dull. Teachers are likely to place a little more emphasis on whole class shared activity and individual and group independent work. They will plan to participate as group members when appropriate and will also lead groups to teach difficult concepts.

Chapter summary

- Teachers are decision-makers. Schemes and resources are a help in planning for a specific class
- Children learn most effectively through a combination of whole class, group and individual activities
- Planning for English and literacy usually works through the phases of speaking and listening, reading and writing
- Children need opportunities to consolidate and build upon phonics knowledge and strategies for reading and writing
- The key teaching strategies of modelling, demonstrating, sharing and guiding will probably occur in every lesson
- All planning should move children towards independence
- Children usually learn more from doing than listening

Further reading

Cliff Hodges, G. and Binney, A. (2010) *Planning for Innovation in English Teaching*. Leicester: UKLA.

Lambirth, A. (2006) *Planning Creative Literacy Lessons*. London: Routledge.

Palmer, S. and Corbett, P. (2003) *Literacy: What Works?* Cheltenham: Thornes Nelson.

References

Alexander, R. (2004) 'Still no pedagogy? Principle, pragmatism and compliance in primary education', *Cambridge Journal of Education*, 34(1): 7–33.

Goodwin, P. (2005) *The Literate Classroom* (2nd edn). London: Routledge.

Graham, S. and Harris, K. (1997) 'Self-regulation and writing: where do we go from here?', *Contemporary Educational Psychology*, 22(1): 102–114.

Moss, G. (2007) *Literacy and Gender: Researching Texts, Contexts and Readers*. London: Routledge.

Primary National Strategy (2010) *Links between APP, the Primary Framework and the National Curriculum* [Online]. Available at: http://nationalstrategies.stand-ards.dcsf.gov.uk/node/19536?uc = force_uj (accessed 8 November 2010).

Ofsted (2011) *The Evaluation Schedule for Schools January 2011*, No. 090098. London: Ofsted.

Zeichner, K. (1999) 'The new scholarship in teacher education', *Educational Researcher*, 28(9): 4–15.

CHAPTER 11

ASSESSMENT AND TARGETING IN ENGLISH

• analysis • assessment for learning • assessing pupils' performance • criterion
• formative • miscue • observation • participation • speaking and listening
• reading • spelling • summative • targeting • test • writing

This chapter aims to:

- describe the purposes of assessment
- demonstrate the importance of assessment within the teaching and learning cycle
- identify key issues in assessment in speaking and listening, reading and writing
- consider the role of assessment in improving standards of literacy
- show that assessment in English can be simple, immediate and constructive (and not at all mysterious)

Assessment is an essential part of teaching literacy. At its best it ensures that children's progress is smooth, that it is handled sensitively and that achievement is known, understood and celebrated. However, at its worst, assessment can be an ogre which distorts the curriculum, trivialises learning and induces feelings of inadequacy. Good assessment is an unobtrusive part of the flow of a lesson and the development of learning across a length of time. It is undertaken by teachers who watch, listen, question and think as part of the act of teaching and involve children in self-assessment as part of learning. Nichol (2007) identified some key features of effective assessment:

- the needs of the learner are central in the process
- it shows the child what is considered as good performance and helps her to recognise it
- it gives information which helps learners to progress
- it helps teachers to mould their work to meet the needs of individuals and classes

Assessment as part of teaching

Though 'teach' is used in Figure 11.1 to describe what happens in the classroom, it would be equally sensible to consider everything on this diagram as part of teaching. Beginner student teachers often become exasperated by the amount of recording required, believing that it detracts from focusing on teaching. This isn't true: every aspect of our work refines and focuses the processes of helping children to learn. A teacher can, for example, explain something well because she has identified the need for the explanation through observation (a form of assessment), evaluated the effectiveness of her previous explanations, targeted who needs further help (and why) and then adapted her planning to ensure that the appropriate explanation occurs. All this is informed by the National Curriculam **attainment targets** which show age related expectations.

This sort of assessment is often referred to as assessment for learning (AfL) and is essential to successful teaching. Black and Wiliam (1998) concluded that this sort of **formative** assessment (which **informs** teaching) was the most successful way of raising standards. Teachers need to:

- identify key indicators of desired learning
- plan lessons and activities based on these
- integrate teaching and observation
- create opportunities for children to reflect on their learning
- act upon the information either immediately or in subsequent lessons

Here's an example of exactly this sort of assessment from Marie's school-based training notes.

> S. concentrated when I read story today (Morpurgo: *War Horse*) even put his hand up to answer!! but took it down again. Got him on own and he told me he liked war stories. Mrs C. (teacher) very pleased. She suggested Michael Foreman's

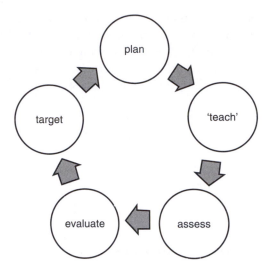

Figure 11.1 Assessment as part of a continuing cycle

> *War Game* next week. Because it's at the right level for S. She advised not to push for an answer out loud because S. hates that, but will work in a pair with DT if DT does feedback. Will make sure they are together next time.

Marie was astute, observant and sensitive: important things in good assessment. In terms of the bullet points above: Marie had identified that a key indicator of engagement as a listener *for this individual* would be stillness and a lack of disruption. She had planned an activity which would give a good opportunity for S. to show this. She managed to teach and observe at the same time and was then sensitive to the need to give S. a special opportunity to reflect on his learning. Finally she managed to modify the subsequent lessons to build upon this achievement.

Many student teachers will be expected to undertake AfL activities to a given schedule or in ways determined by the school or ITT provider. You need to be able to assess:

- learning of all the children against the main objective
- learning of the individual members of a guided group in much more detail
- any misconceptions

Additionally, it is excellent to note:

- unexpected knowledge, skills and strengths
- unexpected errors
- all brave attempts at anything beyond the objectives

To do this, you must be a self-observer so you can decide whether you taught well enough for the learning to happen and planned well enough for children to demonstrate what has been achieved. If teaching was muddled, then children can't be expected to have learnt all that was hoped.

Assessing listening

Though speaking and listening are cornerstones of all literacy lessons, they sometimes become overlooked in assessment. As they are so important to children's development, teachers need to monitor and intervene carefully to ensure progress. If speaking and listening go wrong, it is very difficult for anything else to go right.

Listening is particularly hard to assess. For example if a child is asked to listen to a poem and then discuss the meaning with another child, poor performance could be ascribed to poor listening. However, perhaps she didn't like the poem. She might have found it difficult to work with the other child or found the task too abstract. Possibly, displaying an enthusiasm would cause difficulties with peers. These factors should become evident through astute observation. To gain accurate knowledge of the child's listening, it is important to ensure that:

- the child can hear. Listening is not the same as hearing; it is about drawing meaning from the spoken word. But, without hearing well, the child cannot listen
- the child has been given a specific instruction
- there is adequate time for the child to think and to compose a response
- the child is given the opportunity to contribute to the assessment process
- the listening activity was interesting and not too long

These factors should ensure that an observation is valid but this does not mean that it will be representative of the full scope of a child's attainment. For this reason, teachers never base recorded assessments on single instances but build up a profile over time, giving the child opportunities to learn and be observed in as many contexts as possible.

 You'll need a simple screen and some Lego. (An open lever arch file will work perfectly well.) Sit one side of the screen with some Lego and ask the child to sit on the other side. She must have an identical selection of bricks. Tell her you are going to make a model and, while you are doing it, you will give her instructions to make an identical one. Then make your model giving a commentary like this: 'I've taken a green brick and now I'm fixing two yellow bricks to it so they stick out the same amount at each end. Now you do the same … ' You can vary the number of instructions and their complexity.

Compare your model to the child's. Though this activity gives valuable insights into listening, it shouldn't be used to rank children's attainment. It is simply a way of helping you to understand that assessment can occur in many contexts.

Assessing speaking

Assessment of speaking is, in its most common form, so ingrained in our ways of conversing that it is simply part of the teacher's way of using language. This can be shown from a couple of snatches of student teacher/child conversation.

Sabi: That other lady that come to our class. Who's she?
Laurie: The other lady who came to our class? The other lady who came to our class was my other tutor from university.

Laurie (the student teacher) has identified the error and corrected it unobtrusively by offering two examples of correct verb use. Later in the same lesson, Sabi is talking about planting a bean.

Sabi: In two weeks it is going to be tall. Extremely tall.
Laurie: I hope it grows extremely tall. It might take a long time. More than two weeks. I do hope it grows extremely tall.

Here she uses the same technique of repeating to emphasise good vocabulary choices. She shares his enjoyment of the word to reinforce its value. In both these examples, assessment is immediate; analysis is based on knowledge of the child's attainments and the response shows the student teacher's own knowledge and her realisation of the importance of intervention.

Hopefully, those examples have given you confidence that assessment is simple. Like so many things, it requires practice, knowledge, expertise and confidence. This example shows it going wrong!

Child: Nicholas throwed my shoes in the bin.
Teacher: Nicholas threw your shoes in the bin.
Child: I know he did! What are you going to do about it?

The child was right: this wasn't a sensible time to analyse language. Assessment of children's talk is necessary in every lesson where speaking forms a part of the desired learning. As in all forms of assessment, the purpose of the activity is the basis of what is assessed. So, if the objective was to choose vocabulary suitable for different audiences, the assessment should focus on this, not volume, duration or confidence. If you gain data on these, they are considered for future interventions.

The inclusion of **criteria** of attainment for speaking and listening in the Assessment of Pupil Performance (**APP**) materials has been a great advance for teachers. They assist in decisions about logical next steps for children and are valuable in determining whether teaching provision needs to be adjusted to ensure progress. Most constructively, they are based on the informed judgments of the teachers who know the children best as speakers. Rowe (2009) reported that science teachers thought APP materials helped curriculum development and assisted with self-evaluation and identifying next steps. It would be good if there was a similarly positive response to the speaking and listening provision. For far too long, these essential aspects of language have been underdeveloped in school.

Assessing reading

The day-to-day assessments and interventions in children's progress as readers are informal and based on the opportunities offered by the normal classroom activities. Guided work gives excellent opportunities to observe, analyse and intervene in children's reading to ensure progress. Here's a short snippet from a guided activity which shows children's understanding of a text. Kerry is the student teacher.

Kerry:	What did the 'Heavenly Ruler' do?
Mia:	Made the pig's nose short.
Kerry:	Why did He do that?
Ollie:	Because the pig hadn't been helpful.
Kerry:	This story worries me a bit. I can't decide if it was fair. Can you help me?
Isobel:	I think it was fair. The pig had been told to be helpful.
Ollie:	How can a pig be helpful? Being eaten!
Isobel:	Pull a little cart.
Kerry:	So Isobel has a reason why it was fair and Ollie has a reason why it wasn't. Anyone else?
Rosie:	It makes out that animals are only here for people to use and that's not fair.
Alex:	But it is an explaining myth from long ago and that's how people thought about animals.
Rosie:	Doesn't make it fair.

Kerry created a hierarchy of questions to discover the depth of understanding of the story. Once children reached an appreciative level she stepped back from the discussion so she didn't influence the children's thinking. She was particularly pleased that Isobel had offered a solution which showed a good understanding of the context of the story and that Rosie and Alex were bringing their knowledge from other situations to their understanding of the text.

Assessment of comprehension should:

- Focus on the knowledge needed for the type of text
- Allow for a range of responses (if a child says something unexpected, it isn't necessarily wrong)
- Explore different levels of understanding (literal, inferential, appreciative/critical)
- Consider vocabulary
- Explore the understanding of language features

Assessing errors in decoding

The technicalities of decoding text often hinder understanding, so assessment needs to ensure children move forwards with decoding. If a child fails to read a word accurately, teachers analyse what went wrong and suggest solutions which remind the child of the best strategy to use. Formative assessment of reading is still hugely indebted to the work of Goodman (1969) who suggested that it was valuable to consider the nature of errors (*miscue analysis*) as these give insight into the knowledge children bring to reading. It is also important to make a note of very long pauses and inappropriate use of punctuation as these give additional insights into reading. If a child corrects the miscue without help (marked s/c on the text) it is a very good sign because it shows she is making sense of the text and monitoring her own performance. In Chapter 3, there was a consideration of the value of analysing miscues to support and teach; the technique can also be used as an assessment device. It is usually helpful to analyse a sample of 100 words (as in this example). More than eight uncorrected miscues in 100 words suggest that the reader is not managing the text in way which would give pleasure or full meaning. However, it is often more valuable to tally the number of each type of error as this enables you to focus help more accurately.

Identify the miscues in this reading.

Charlie: 6yrs and 10 months
Reading from: *The Last Polar Bears* by Harry Horse
Context: the book was chosen by Charlie as a favourite 'because it's funny'. Charlie's reading is in italics.

Lead up to monitored passage (read aloud by adult):

'Dear Child, This morning I found some wolves in my wood-shed looking for dried fish. I told them I didn't have any and they went away, but came back later with their brothers and sisters and stole two pillow-cases off the washing line and chewed holes in my new wellingtons'.

Child reads: Repaired my boat (s/c) with the puncher repair kit and set off to Wolf Point after lunch.
Original text: Repaired my boots with the puncture repair kit and set off for Wolf Point after lunch.

The expedition was delayed because Roo refused to go past the wolves' shed.
Expedition delayed as Roo refused to go past the wolves' shed.

They were lying in there on my pillowcases, and I'm sure they had been drinking Old Sock
They were lying in there with my pillowcases, and I'm sure they had been drinking Old Sock

because they was (s/c) singing.
because they were singing.

What a rocket!
What a racket!

Roo was as bad through. [Child stops, attempts word using phonics, recognises it is 'tricky' and refuses another attempt. Word given]
Roo was as bad though,

and even if she didn't want to go past them, that didn't stop her barking at them
and even if she didn't want to go past them, that didn't stop her from barking at them

and causing a gentle fuss.
and causing a general fuss.

Some wolves came out of the shed for a fight and Roo ran away,
Several wolves came out of the shed for a fight and Roo promptly ran away,

leaving me to deal with
leaving me to deal with

Charlie read to the end of the sentence then the adult joined in. They finished the paragraph together then the adult read to the end of the chapter aloud.

N.B. s/c means self-corrected

Reading is a textbook case of a town blighted by planning decisions . ... You probably misread the first word because the context lured you into a miscue. If you feel cheated by this, it gives you some idea how easy it is for an inexperienced reader to make errors. The most constructive way to classify miscues is to group them as things which have gone wrong with the decoding (phonic and visual miscues) and things which have gone wrong with language comprehension (context and syntactic knowledge). If a child doesn't self-correct the misread word, it suggests that the two aspects aren't being used in harmony as prime approach and checking strategy. Teachers often remind children of the value of the checking strategy, as in this example.

> *Rowie*:   [reads] Merry Christmas from Mrs Brookes.
> *Teacher*:   That card tricked you! Cards often do say Merry Christmas, but look carefully at the first word.
> *Rowie*:   Oh! Happy Christmas.

The child drew on language comprehension as prime strategy so the teacher suggested checking using her phonic knowledge. This example works the other way round.

Sonney:	*[reads]* Tiger found a house with a warm [read to rhyme with 'harm'] fire
Teacher:	Something there doesn't quite make sense to me. It must be another of those tricky words. What sort of fire could it be?
Sonney:	Gas?
Teacher:	Gas! Those letters couldn't make 'gas'. Not in ten million, zillion years!
Sonney:	Warm! [pronounced correctly]
Teacher:	That makes perfect sense. Warm. Look at all the letters to double check.

This is a great example because the teacher's help moves from language comprehension to phonics as the child makes a second wrong attempt. She then goes back to language comprehension to check, followed by another phonic check to reinforce the prime approach. Both these examples show assessment being followed by analysis which is immediately followed by focused instruction.

Assessing the big picture of reading

Teachers find it valuable to make informal assessments of the child's development as a reader. This is often undertaken through observations or 'conferences' (an imposing name for what should be a relaxed, enjoyable chat). Cappellini (2005) concluded that teachers need to be flexible about the way they gather additional information. This depends greatly on what has already been discovered about the learner. This means that there has to be an opportunity for the child to surprise, which only happens in an atmosphere of open discussion. Here's an example from a student teacher's reflection on a reading conference.

> George is in the lowest group for literacy and almost never reads his reading book at home so I didn't expect he'd have much to say about enjoying reading but he told me about going away with his grandparents to their caravan and how every night they all get on his bunk and they read poems out of a red book. Then he told me his favourite starts 'Loveliest of trees the cherry now' because there's a cherry tree near to the caravan. He said this was his best reading time. It amazed me. Here he was reciting poems about trees and you could tell he was so happy about the memory. It gave me a picture of a different George.

Lucky George that his family are giving him a wonderful experience! There are two important messages from this example:

- you have to ask the right questions to discover the unexpected
- assessment and self-evaluation go hand in hand. Reading the extract above, most teachers will ask themselves what they could do to make George talk with equal affection about his experiences as a reader in school

 These ideas are a very simple starting point for observing and talking about reading with individual children. They are not a set schedule and will need to be adapted to suit both teacher and child.

Observe (in voluntary reading):

- whether the child chooses to read
- the sort of texts chosen
- the usual concentration span
- whether the child can talk with informed enthusiasm about the text

Observe (in guided or individual reading) whether the child:

- appears to be at ease
- reads at a good pace
- uses punctuation effectively
- conveys the emotions of the text
- self-corrects
- makes use of all the cues (pictures, font changes, repetition etc.)
- brings knowledge of the subject matter to the reading
- appears to like the text
- relies on an adult for reassurance or help

Talk individually (in a quiet, comfortable place) about what the child:

- likes about reading
- doesn't like so much
- thinks is most important about reading
- is her next big target
- likes most (sort of books or authors)
- does if she gets stuck on a word or a sentence doesn't seem to make sense
- does to find out information
- thinks could make reading at school better

This information, updated every half-term or so, gives real insight into the child as a reader.

Reading tests

Reading test information can be useful as tests give information about a child's performance against age-related norms or criteria. Head teachers, governing bodies and governments may need such information in order to ensure that resources are targeted to meet needs and that all children, wherever they live and learn, receive the excellent education to which they are entitled.

For class teachers the value of most test results is much less clear (Klingner et al., 2007). All are designed to give information about how a child performs in comparison to others of the same age or against set criteria. All tests have to focus on the measurable aspects of reading; these are certainly important but they are not everything. An extended metaphor might help. If a test gives a snapshot of a particular activity at a particular time, it is probably in black and white rather than colour. It could be rather blurry as tests aren't very detailed in what they cover. It may also be one of those photographs which just don't look much like the person. What is perhaps even more worrying is that, if a photo is old, it does not show how someone has changed since it was taken. This is a worst case analogy but, as the outcomes of poor use of test results can be damaging, it's wise to be cautious.

Concerns about reading tests are clustered around two identified effects: they can distort the curriculum and they can impact on children's confidence as learners. There is a danger that the test content becomes the curriculum; for example when the Schonell Reading Test (which focused on recognising decodable and irregular words in isolation) was popular, it was common for these words to be used in spelling tests and vocabulary extension work (Taverner, 1990). Teachers, being aware of the value placed on test results, worked hard to ensure children performed well, taking time from other aspects of teaching. Reedy (2010) has identified probable distortion of the curriculum as an issue with the introduction of an overly simple test of decoding at KS1.

Reading tests may also cause problems for individuals. Seifert (2004) found that learners' perception of their performance has a significant influence on their progress and motivation. Additionally, Fletcher-Campbell et al. (2009) show that general assessments are not always valuable in identifying how struggling readers can best be helped. For example some children with hyperlexia have excellent phonic decoding ability but very little understanding of text (Richman and Wood, 2002) so their needs would not be identified by a test of pronouncing phonically regular words or non-words. Though one of the arguments for screening reading ability is that it benefits vulnerable learners, there are probably other and better ways for experienced teachers to do this.

Assessing writing processes

Because writing is a long complex process, assessment derived solely from a final product will not be able to pinpoint at which point errors or misconceptions started. It is therefore valuable to assess children's performance and evaluate the effectiveness of teaching at these points:

- Task explanation
- Gathering ideas/research
- Planning
- Drafting
- Editing
- Checking for accuracy (proofreading)

Assessment of these processes is usually through observation, quick analysis of the evolving text and conversation with the child. However, many young writers dislike having to break away from the task so, as Waugh and Jolliffe (2008) suggest, guided writing offers an ideal opportunity for assessment while teaching.

This is an insight gained by a student teacher, Jo, from observing children at the beginning of a writing task.

> [*Straight after lesson*] Management – nightmare. They were all over the room. Asking questions, finding things, wanting the toilet. Looking in their trays. Couldn't make them settle to work. [*5pm*] I've realised. I don't get down to writing straight away. I need time to think. So do they. I'm going to ask Kate [*teacher*] if we can try doing Brain Gym between the introduction and the writing.

This re-enforces the point that consideration of children's work must be tightly linked to evaluation of teaching performance.

Observe whether the child:

- appears to be at ease
- writes with reasonable concentration
- self-corrects
- brings knowledge of the subject matter to the writing
- relies on an adult for reassurance or help
- uses writing position, pencil grip and angle of the paper well
- types with reasonable speed and accuracy

Observe whether the child (if there are opportunities for voluntary writing, e.g. a role play area or writing station):

- writes voluntarily
- specifies an audience
- chooses to write by hand or on the computer

Talk individually (in a quiet, comfortable place) about what the child:

- likes about writing
- doesn't like so much
- believes is important
- Identifies as her next big target
- feels proud of having written
- does if she gets stuck on a spelling
- does if she's stuck for ideas
- does to improve each piece
- thinks could be better about writing in school

Assessing right through the process

Dom et al. (1998) develop ideas about the various constructive intervention roles and their appropriateness at different times. These could include:

- Checking at the beginning – assessing the ideas
- Agreeing the plan – assessing the structure
- Monitoring progress – assessing knowledge, skills and approaches
- Reading a draft – assessing elements for extension or revision
- Proof-reading – assessing accuracy
- Reading a finished product – offering an informed, constructive review

The purpose of this sort of assessment goes further than offering the child information about attainment, praise for achievement and suggestion of next steps. It also offers a model of the aspects of critical reflection which will be needed as the writing becomes gradually more independent.

Assessing and responding to finished writing

Many teachers try to assess and respond to text while the child is present. This is particularly valuable with young or struggling writers as it makes it easier to untangle what has been written. AfL approaches often recommend that the assessment focuses closely on the stated purpose and style and involves two or three positive comments and one target. Though this can become too formulaic, it is a good way of ensuring that teachers look out for the good aspects; it is very easy to notice only the things which could do with improvement.

Here's Laura (student teacher) responding to Preston about his instructions to make a cruck barn.

> 'Lovely, you remembered to use bossy verbs at the start of every sentence. Good remembering and good listening, Preston. Now the other thing I said I was looking for was ... Let's see. Is everything in the right order? Yes it is. Great. Now, are all the stages there? Finding the right tree, splitting it, raising the cruck. Joining them. Great. But ... you forgot to instruct me to take them to the site. I'm still stuck in the forest! You're going to raise your cruck model from these instructions – got to be spot on.'

Teachers also assess the accuracy of the writing – sentence structure, spelling and presentation. The assessments give indications for future work as well as feedback to the child. There is a case for toughness here. If something which has been learnt is not being used well, it does nothing for the child's progress or self-esteem if this is not noted and made clear to her. Failing to do so suggests the learning was unimportant and that standards of performance do not matter.

Spelling

Even with well-focused phonics work, English spelling is very difficult. Due to this, it is useful to consider spelling as a hierarchy of knowledge (as in APP models). The stages of spelling are shown in Table 11.1.

Table 11.1   The usual stages of the development of spelling

Level	Expectations	Likely errors
1	*In some writing, usually with support:* Usually correct spelling of simple high frequency words. Plausible attempts at words with digraphs or double letters. Enough accurate spellings for text to be readable (including use of letter names to approximate to syllables and words *[C for sea]*).	
2	*In some forms of writing, usually correct spelling of:* High frequency grammatical function words. Common content words.	Endings for past tense, plurals, adverbs. Phonetic attempts at vowel digraphs.
3	*In most writing, correct spelling of:* Some common grammatical function words. Some words with more than one morpheme including compound words.	Some inflected endings for past tense, comparatives, adverbs. Some phonetically plausible attempts at content/lexical words.
4	*Across a range of writing, correct spelling of:* Most common grammatical function words, including adverbs with *ly* formation. Regularly formed content/lexical words. Most past and present tense inflections, plurals.	Homophones of some common grammatical function words. Occasional phonetically plausible spelling in content/lexical words.
5	*Across a range of writing, correct spelling of:* Grammatical function words. Nearly all inflected words. Most suffixes and prefixes. Most content/lexical words.	Occasional phonetic spelling of unstressed syllables in content words. Double consonants in prefixes.

Source: adapted from National Strategies APP Writing Assessment Focuses and Criteria, QCDA, 2010

Analysis of errors in spelling gives insights into the strategies being used. It is valuable to consider that children, other than those who have very severe dyslexia, can spell parts of virtually all words accurately. The misspelled parts parallel categories of miscues in reading and can be characterised as:

- additions – *hampster*
- omissions – *particully*

- substitutions – *gurl*
- reversals – *gril* (for *girl*)

If a child's spelling is causing particular concern, teachers often analyse samples so teaching can be focused appropriately.

Involving children

Assessment for learning should usually be something which is done with children rather than to them. Our aim is independence and, to be independent, children need to monitor their own performance accurately and address their own errors. This is taught through the teacher modelling constructive assessment practices and, gradually passing more of the process over to the child.

Even very young children can reflect on their performance, particularly if the reasons for the work and the key indicators of success are clear. For example, they could be asked to decide whether they are happy, unsure or unhappy about their achievements. Older children often discuss work with a trusted peer to offer each other feedback. This can then move forward to completing an assessment checklist provided by the teacher and a final stage is for the child to produce the checklist for herself. In every case, child assessments must be monitored very carefully – unrealistically positive assessments of friends' work are not unknown!

Testing writing

At present children's writing is tested formally at the end of the primary phase. The information is used to monitor schools' progress and to inform high school teachers about attainment. As with reading, the issues about testing centre on the value for the individual, the impact on the curriculum and the use made of data. It is valuable for teachers to have a clear picture of the standards which children are expected to reach but there is a concern that preparation for a test can have a very high priority (House of Commons, 2010). It is also possible that, because the test results are so significant to the school, the content of the test and the marking criteria become a curriculum not just for a revision period but for the whole school.

As it is impossible to pin down effectiveness or creativity on a mark scheme, the tests use descriptions of sentence structures, vocabulary choices and punctuation which may indicate great writing. Russell (2005) suggests that these mark schemes may be a cause of problems with the assessment of writing. Children are often taught to show these characteristics in their work without the authorial consideration of when it is appropriate to use them or, more importantly, when it isn't. This, for example, would be considered to be a level 5 sentence:

Running jubilantly, her intricately embroidered frock glistening like the outstretched wings of a swan about to soar into the air, the ecstatic bride stifled a muted cry; faltering, she held out her tiny trembling hand nervously and, pulled back her lacy veil which was as white and filmy as blossom touched by the dew.

Charlotte Brontë's *'Reader, I married him'* scores level 2. The first sentence is arrant twaddle; the second is touched with genius.

The issues raised with the SATs ways of levelling text are indicative of a much wider problem with trying to apply precise assessment criteria to the creative aspects of writing. The real difficulties are that what works well in one context could be wholly inappropriate in another so every genre would need an individual marking scheme. Equally importantly, even if a scheme were available it would probably still have to include terms such as 'well-structured', 'strong', 'appropriate', ' pace'. These require judgments on the part of the assessor and even when moderation is robust, testing cannot be completely objective.

Unsurprisingly, given the difficulty of testing of composition, testing of writing often focuses on the secretarial aspects. It is easy to make judgments about the regularity of handwriting, the range of punctuation used accurately or the accuracy of spelling. Spelling tests, in particular, have been a prominent feature of the primary English curriculum for many years. Wilde (2007) argues against the formal spelling of testing saying it does little to encourage children to make progress. Manning and Underbakke (2005) identified the prescribed list of words to learn as being counterproductive while recognising the value of assessing children's understanding of pattern and logic in spelling. It would seem that, if formal spelling testing is to be continued, the constructive focus is on strategies rather than set lists. There are a few published spelling tests which offer a standardised score or spelling age. This is useful for making comparisons of class or individual attainment against an average score providing the test is recent and is intended for children of the age being tested.

 Expert reflection

Helen Holt: The use of assessment data in primary schools

Formal curriculum testing in primary schools has been the source of much debate recently, amongst parents and practitioners alike. Some argue that end of Key Stage SATs are just devices which monitor schools' (and possibly teachers') performance and are of little benefit to the child; others consider them to be key aspects of a necessarily rigorous assessment process. It is perhaps not the actual testing itself that 'ruffles feathers', but the use to which the resulting summative assessment data is put – the formation of school league tables. However, summative assessment data is currently utilised by many primary schools to enhance children's learning by tracking and target setting.

(Continued)

(Continued)

The nationally recognised system of Assessing Pupil Progress (APP) in speaking and listening, reading and writing is now employed in most primary schools. This system provides effective benchmarking against which all children can be assessed and assigned National Curriculum (NC) levels. It helps to identify those children working significantly above or below age-related norms, ensuring that learning objectives are appropriately suited to individual needs. It is empowering to teachers. Arguably, the emphasis on externally validated assessment over the last 15 years has de-skilled primary teachers in the 'art' of assessment; APP puts assessment firmly back where it should be – in the hands of class teachers.

The data derived from regular pupil assessment enable teachers to track the progress of individuals. Assigning NC levels to a child's reading or writing provides a tangible position from which to move forward; they offer clear descriptors and are objective and unambiguous. The child's starting point is evident, as is the journey she has made, and the target for which she can realistically aim; this applies to all children of all abilities. Today every school should have clear tracking systems in place and, linked to these, manageable target setting systems – ensuring that, over time, every child makes progress. In order for these systems to be rigorous and consistent they must exploit assessment data in the form of NC levels.

Debates over end of Key Stage SATs, league tables and accountability will no doubt remain, but if the intelligent use of assessment data at school level can help to further children's learning, surely that is to be applauded.

(Helen Holt is Senior Lecturer in Primary English in Education, University of Chester and formerly responsible for data collection and handling in a large urban primary school)

Chapter summary

- Assessment is about moving children forward
- Assessment is made from several pieces of work
- Children need to participate
- Communication precedes accuracy
- Even the most advanced writers in primary schools will make occasional errors

Further reading

Keogh, B., Dabell, J. and Naylor, S. (2007) *Active Assessment for English: Thinking Learning and Assessment in English*. London: David Fulton Books.

Spendlove, D. (2009) *Putting Assessment for Learning into Practice*. London: Continuum.

Waugh, D. and Jolliffe, W. (2008) *English 3–11: A Guide for Teachers*. Abingdon: Routledge.

References

Black, P. and Wiliam, D. (1998) *Inside the Black Box: Raising Standards Through Classroom Assessment*. Windsor: NFER.

Cappellini, M. (2005) *Balancing Reading and Language Learning: A Resource for Teaching English Language Learners, K-5*. Portland: Stenhouse Publishers.

Dom, L., French, C. and Jones, T. (1998) *Apprenticeship in Literacy: Transitions Across Reading and Writing*. Portland: Stenhouse Publishers.

Fletcher-Campbell, F., Reid, G. and Soler, J. (2009) *Approaching Difficulties in Literacy Development: Assessment, Pedagogy and Programmes*. London: SAGE.

Goodman, K. (1969) 'Analysis of oral reading miscues: applied psycholinguistics', *Reading Research Quarterly*, 5: 9–30.

House of Commons Children, Schools and Families Committee (2010) *School Accountability: Responses from the Government and Ofsted to the First Report of the Committee, Session 2009–10*, 22 March.

Klingner, J., Vaughn, S. and Boardman, A. (2007) *Teaching Reading Comprehension to Students with Learning Difficulties (What Works for Special Needs Learners)*. New York: Guilford Press.

Manning, M. and Underbakke, C. (2005) 'Spelling development research necessitates replacement of weekly word list', *Childhood Education*, 81(4): 236.

Nichol, D. (2007) *Principles of Good Assessment and Feedback: Theory and Practice*. University of Strathclyde.

Reedy, D. (2010) 'Mad, bad and dangerous – the new policy on reading', *UKLA News*, Autumn.

Richman, L.C. and Wood, K.M. (2002) 'Learning disability subtypes: classification of high functioning hyperlexia', *Brain and Language*, 82(1): 10–21.

Rowe, N. (2009) *Research into the Implementation of APP in Key Stage 3 Science: Interim Report. Executive Summary: Findings from an Online Questionnaire Sent to Local Authority Science Consultants*. Slough: NFER.

Russell, J. (2005) 'Yes they get good results but by God are they bored', *Guardian*, 26 August.

Seifert, T.L. (2004) 'Understanding student motivation', *Educational Research*, 46(2): 137–149.

Taverner, D. (1990) *Reading Within and Beyond the Classroom*. London: Open University Press.

Waugh, D. and Jolliffe, W. (2008) *English 3–11: A Guide for Teachers*. Abingdon: Routledge.

Wilde, S. (2007) *Spelling Strategies and Patterns*. Portsmouth, New Hampshire: Heinemann.

GLOSSARY

Accent	The way that people pronounce words. It is usually determined by geography, class or group membership.
Analytic phonics	A way of approaching teaching in which children focus on repeated patterns across words and break these down to help with new spellings or pronunciations. Children do a lot of oral analytic work in EYFS when they begin to play with rhyme and alliteration. They return to analytic approaches once synthetic phonics has been mastered to help them to use analogies to approach new material.
APP	Assessment of Pupil Performance. This is a more formal use of Assessment for Learning techniques, used to track progress, determine current level of attainment and identify next steps.
Attainment targets	In English children are expected to meet National Curriculum Attainment targets in speaking and listening, reading and writing.
Autism	A disability characterised by difficulties in communication and interaction. As it differs greatly in severity teachers often prefer to refer to 'autistic spectrum disorders' as a better description of the range of characteristics.

Bilingual	Being able to use two languages with more or less the same level of competence. Children just starting to learn English as an additional language aren't bilingual unless they use two languages other than English. New users of English are sometimes described as 'emergent bilinguals'.
Composition	The thought processes and actions involved in creating writing.
Consonants	The letters formed by moving the tongue or lips to modify the flow of air.
Criteria	(In assessment) a hierarchy of characteristics used to describe children's attainment.
Decoding	Translating the symbols of a word into a spoken (or thought) form which is understood by the reader.
Dialect	Words and sentence structures specific to a region or a group of people.
Digraph	Two letters which make a single sound.
Dyslexia	A condition characterised by unusual difficulty in processing written language.
EAL	English as an Additional Language.
Encoding	The processes used by a writer to translate a spoken word into written symbols.
EYFS	Early Years Foundation Stage.
Genre	The classification of a text by its purpose and form and distinctive vocabulary (e.g. myth).
Grapheme	The written representation of a phoneme.
Guided work	When a teacher works with a group of children with similar needs or attainment to model and support work which they couldn't manage independently.
Jolly Phonics	A commercial scheme which gives a multi-sensory approach to learning. It is often used alongside 'Letters and Sounds'.
Letters and Sounds	A government published programme for teaching phonics in reading and spelling.
Miscue analysis	A way of working out the strategies being used by a reader by classifying and interpreting errors.
Phoneme	The smallest distinct sound in a spoken word. There are 44 phonemes in English. They can be represented by single letters or groups of letters.
Read, Write Inc.	A popular commercial programme for teaching synthetic phonics and comprehension.
Role play	The chance to explore ideas through fantasy play, often assisted by props or costumes. Role play is usually child initiated.

Secretarial aspects	The aspects of writing which focus on conventional presentation and accuracy: spelling, handwriting, punctuation and, to some extent, syntax.
Split digraph	When two graphemes which are separated by another letter are pronounced together. It used to be called 'magic e' but the terminology has been changed because it isn't magical and it isn't always e which makes the sound change (bit-bite, bit-biting). It is very useful in both reading and spelling.
Standard English	This is a high status dialect. Its written form is used for most texts. We use spoken standard English in formal situations.
Sub-lexical	A unit of language smaller than a word. For example, it could be a group of graphemes or a syllable.
Syllable	This is a part of a word which has a vowel sound which may have consonants around it. It is often represented as a single beat.
Syntax	The way sentences are constructed to convey meaning and the rules and conventions related to this.
Synthetic phonics	This is used as the prime approach to early reading in most schools. Children are taught to isolate the individual phonemes in spoken words and associate these with graphemes. In reading they translate graphemes to phonemes and then blend them together to make the word. In spelling they mentally segment the word into phonemes and then write the related graphemes.
Target setting	The short term learning goals for an individual. These are derived from analysis of performance and are, ideally, agreed in discussion with the child.
Tricky words	These are high frequency words needed by beginner readers and writers which can't be accessed through phonic approaches. They are usually taught through sight recognition for reading and by kinaesthetic methods for spelling.
Vowel	Every syllable includes a vowel or a vowel sound. They are the letters formed with a steady flow of air. Vowel sounds vary greatly with accent and have the most complex phoneme–grapheme correspondences.

INDEX